The Lamb, The Woman, and The Dragon

Studies in the Revelation of St. John

Albertus Pieters, D.D.

DEWARD
PUBLISHING COMPANY

The Lamb, The Woman, and The Dragon: Studies in the Revelation of St. John
© 2012 by DeWard Publishing Company, Ltd.
P.O. Box 6259, Chillicothe, Ohio 45601
800.300.9778
www.deward.com

This book was originally published as *The Lamb, The Woman, and the Dragon: An Exposition of the Revelation of St. John* and later reprinted as *Studies in the Revelation of St. John*. The text of this edition was reproduced from a 1946 printing of the former title.

Cover art by Jonathan Hardin.

Reasonable care has been taken to trace original sources for any excerpts and quotations appearing in this book and to document such information. For material not in the public domain, fair-use standards and practices were followed. Should any attribution be found to be incorrect or incomplete, the publisher welcomes written documentation supporting correction for subsequent printings.

Printed in the United States of America.

ISBN: 978-1-936341-35-1

CONTENTS

FOREWORD

Albertus Pieters' book on Revelation is not a verse-by-verse commentary, but is more like a set of essays which cover the book section by section. For those who are unacquainted with John's Revelation and who wish to make their first serious journey into it, it is a fine starting-place. There are some excellent recent treatments of Revelation available to those who want to trace the Old Testament backgrounds of its scenes and language in detail, or who wish to discover the many allusions to Roman culture and religion which John employed. However, while such detailed study is rewarding, it can quickly become bewildering. This is not necessarily a criticism, because Revelation is a difficult book. The fact is that it is easy to get lost in John's visions. John's simple language contains hundreds of allusions and echoes of Old Testament texts and contexts, majestically put together in an unparalleled blend of symbol, theme, history, ancient culture, and exhortation. However, for the student with the modest, yet crucial, goal of seeing the big picture and the overall point, such detailed studies quickly become like a maze, trapping the reader into an almost overwhelming set of ancient sources and scholarly theories. There are also many books currently available that attempt to do the same thing as Pieters' book, but many of these books tend to get too caught up in the latest trends of New Testament scholarship and leave the reader without a good sense of what Revelation is about.

The reader will find Pieters' approach to Revelation to be full of good sense. The value of his book is not in his treatment of details but in his emphasis on seeing the story and the overall point of John's Revelation. The interpretation is informed without being technical, and the entire book is written in a style that can be understood without having to know specialized terms. Serious students will appreciate his fair evaluations of explanations with which he disagrees and his defense of a basically preterist interpretation. The re-issue of this volume is welcome in a time when poorly-grounded interpretations of Revelation seem to be rising in popularity. While *The Lamb, The Woman, and the Dragon* may not be the last word on the subject, and is now showing its age, it still does an admirable job of removing the mystery that discourages many from studying the book, and makes it accessible.

David McClister
Florida College, October 21, 2010

PREFACE
About Myself And My Book

It seems to me reasonable that an author should introduce himself to his readers, for in estimating the value of a man's views, much depends upon our knowledge of the man himself. My father was a minister of the Reformed Church in America, and during the years of my childhood was pastor of the First Reformed Church of Holland, Michigan. My parents were old-fashioned Calvinists, knowing and loving the Bible, and believing it to be in all its parts the word of God. This faith I was taught as a child, I accepted it as a young man, I was trained in the theology of it at the Western Theological Seminary, where I am now a teacher, and I have seen no reason to depart from it.

In the year 1891 I was ordained to the ministry and went out to Japan as a missionary of the Board of Foreign Missions of the Reformed Church in America. There I labored until 1923, when family circumstances over which I had no control seemed to me and to the officers of the Board a clear providential indication that my work in that country was at an end. For three years I was College Pastor and Professor of the English Bible at Hope College, Holland, Michigan, and then I was called by the General Synod of our church to the Dosker-Hulswit Chair of English Bible and Missions at the Western Theological Seminary, my theological Alma Mater.

My position as Professor of English Bible required me to devote myself more intensely than ever before to an advanced study of Biblical questions. At the beginning I had only the very general knowledge of the book of Revelation which every minister possesses. I had never made any special study of it, or taken any great interest in it. Hence I was not prepared for the request of the Senior Class, some years ago, that I should give them a course in this book. I referred the matter to the faculty, but my colleagues thought that I should be the one to attempt it; and thus I received my providential call to become familiar with the book, its literature and its problems. It soon became a very fascinating study. As I proceeded with it, the sublimity of its conceptions, the grandeur of its doxologies, the complexity and dramatic power of its pictures, and the glory of its consummation, charmed and thrilled my mind and heart. Presently I prepared a course of eight lectures for popular audiences, and these were so well received that I have been encouraged to make the substance thereof public in book form, somewhat enlarged and re-arranged,

This is not a commentary, in the ordinary sense of the word. It is rather a discussion of some of the outstanding problems of the book of Revelation. Verse by verse exposition is not attempted. This accounts for the almost complete omission of comment upon the letters to the Seven Churches. These are better known and more frequently preached from than any other portion of the book. They are not, to be sure, free from points of difficulty, here and there, but on the whole they are comparatively easy to understand, and the ordinary principles of interpretation are applicable to them.

Neither is this book a contribution to scholarship on the Apocalypse of St. John. It is the work of a middle man, who stands between the scholars on the one hand and the general Christian public on the other; seeking to make the researches of the former available to the latter. In preparing the following chapters, I have had constantly in view two kinds of readers. First, and chiefly, intelligent Christian people without theological training, and with no theological reference library at hand. For the generality of such people, if I mistake not, the book is still pretty much a *terra incognita*. They read and love other portions of the Bible, but to read the Revelation is such blind work that they rarely open it. I can not expect to make all its mysteries plain to them—they are far from being all plain to me—but I think I may succeed in giving them some idea what kind of book it is, and how it is to be approached so that they will get some apprehension of its beauty and its teachings. Having this class of readers in mind, it will be necessary, so far as possible, to avoid the technical terms of theology and biblical criticism, or, when it is unavoidable to use them, to make necessary explanations. This may often seem tiresome to ministers and others theologically educated. I can only ask them to be patient.

The other class of readers consists of theological students, my own, and those of other seminaries, if any such do me the honor to use the book. For these it is necessary to insert references to the various commentators and other sources of information, in order that the work may be a help to further study. For the first class of readers such references may seem to clutter up the pages. I shall make them as brief as possible, putting detailed information on the works in question into an appendix or bibliography. Here, also, there will be occasion for indulgence on the part of readers to whom such references are without value.

A.P.
Holland, Michigan

I

WHO WROTE THE APOCALYPSE, AND WHEN?

Although not undisputed, it has been the prevailing belief of the Christian church, from the second century on, that this book was written by St. John, one of the twelve apostles, the son of Zebedee, and brother of the James who was martyred by Herod Agrippa I. Because this was believed to be true, the book was received as canonical and inspired.

This faith rested on very good grounds. Justin Martyr is one of the earliest of the church fathers whose writings have come down to us. He suffered martyrdom under the emperor Marcus Aurelius, about AD 166. His "Dialogue with Trypho the Jew" was written, according to Alford, between AD 139 and 161. In it he says:

> And further, there was a certain man with us, whose name was John, one of the apostles of Christ, who prophesied, by a revelation that was made to him, that those who believed in our Christ would dwell a thousand years in Jerusalem; and that thereafter the general, and, in short, the eternal resurrection and judgment of all men would likewise take place.[1]

This Justin Martyr had his home and his principal work in Asia Minor, among the very churches addressed in Revelation.

The next, and perhaps the chief, direct witness to the Johannine authorship of the Apocalypse, is Irenaeus, who was bishop of Lyons, in France, and died there about AD 190. He was born and had his education in the province of Asia, the territory of the Seven Churches. There he was a pupil of Polycarp, bishop of the church at Smyrna, one of the seven.

---

[1] "Ante Nicene Fathers," Vol. I, p. 240. Dialogue with Trypho the Jew, Chapter 81.

For the nature of this work, the "Ante Nicene Fathers," see bibliography. Hereafter, it will be referred to by initials only, thus: "A.N.F."

Irenaeus wrote a number of books, and in them frequently mentions the Revelation. He especially discusses the mysterious number, 666, the number of the Beast, which he considers identical with the Antichrist.[2] In four places he says that "John, the disciple of the Lord," wrote the book, and in another connection he identifies with "John the disciple" with the one who lay upon the breast of Jesus.

It is important to notice that only one link separates Irenaeus from the apostle John. He says also that the Apocalypse was written in the time of the emperor Domitian, who reigned, AD 81–96.[3]

Thus the time between the composition of the book and this comment by Irenaeus is about seventy or eight years, a period well within the memory of living men. The Civil War began seventy-five years ago, and there are men still among us, with unimpaired mental powers, who enlisted at the first call, my own uncle being one of them. The facts are such as Polycarp and Irenaeus would know, and there is no reason to discount their honesty in such a matter.

After Irenaeus, we meet with no one who has personal knowledge, or can be said to be in touch with one who has such knowledge; but the book of Revelation is referred to as St. John's by Clement of Alexandria[4] (c. AD 240).

Notice the geographical distribution of these witnesses. Justin Martyr traveled in Asia Minor, and Irenaeus had his home there in his youth, although bishop in France at the close of his career. Tertullian was from Carthage, in northern Africa, while Clement and Origen were resident at Alexandria, the center of learning and information in the eastern church. Thus they represent all the chief centers of Christendom at that period, except Rome. The distribution of their utterances in point of time is roughly as follows: 140—170—200—220—233—240. The longest interval is thirty years, and all fall within 150 years of the end of the apostolic era. Such testimony as this, to be rightly weighed, must be considered in view of the fact that these were all responsible men, holding high office in the Christian community, which was most deeply interested in these things. What they say stands for an immense body of conviction behind them.

The first important dissent to this general conviction is expressed by Dionysius the Great, professor at the theological seminary of Alexandria,

---

[2] "A.N.F." Vol. I, p. 558. Against Heresies, Chapter XXX.

[3] "A.N.F." Vol. I, p. 560. Against Heresies, Chapter XXXI, Sec. 3.

[4] "A.N.F.," Vol. II, p. 504. Miscellanies, Chapter XIII.

and one of the successors therein of Origen. His date is about AD 250, and he says that there have been others before (c. AD 200), Tertullian of Carthage[5] (c. AD 220), Origen of Alexandria[6] (c. AD 223) and Hippolytus[7] him who doubted the Johannine authorship of the Apocalypse. He says:[8]

> Some before us have set aside and rejected the book altogether, criticising it chapter by chapter, and pronouncing it without sense or argument and maintaining that the title is fraudulent. For they say that it is not the work of John, nor is it a revelation, because it is covered thickly and densely by a vail of obscurity. And they affirm that none of the apostles and none of the saints, nor any one in the church, is its author, but that Cerinthus, who founded the sect that was called after him the Cerinthian, desiring reputable authority for his fiction, prefixed the name.

Dionysius does not accept these criticisms as just, but quotes them as those of others. They are said to have proceeded from the Alogi, a sect of the anti-Montanists. There was also a Roman presbyter, names Caius, living AD 196–219, who *Revelation* to the heretic Cerinthus;[9] but this suggestion receives no acceptance among scholars of any school, since, as Alford[10] says, we have very full accounts of Cerinthus from Irenaeus and Epiphanius, and no intimation of such connection can be found.

The great objection that Dionysius makes is on the ground of the Greek style, which is all the more weighty because Greek was the language Dionysius himself constantly used. Comparing the Gospel of John with the Apocalypse, he finds the latter written in ungrammatical and rough Greek, and thinks it is scarcely credible that the same man should have written both.[11] This is the backbone of all subsequent, and of all present critical objection to the Johannine authorship, and has been much discussed by competent scholars. That there really is such a

---

[5] "A.N.F.," Vol. III, p. 333. Against Marcion, Book III, Chapter XV.

[6] "Post-Nicene Fathers," Second Series, Vol. I, p. 273; being a quotation from Origen by Eusebius, the church historian. Church History, Book VI, Chapter XXV. Referred to in subsequent notes as "P.N.F."

[7] "A.N.F.," Vol. V, p. 211. Treatise on Christ and Antichrist. Sec. 36.

[8] "P.N.F.," Vol. I, p. 309.

[9] "P.N.F.," Vol. I, p. 160.

[10] When an author is thus quoted only by his surname, his full name and the title of his work will be found in the bibliography.

[11] "P.N.F.," Second Series, Vol. I, p. 311.

striking difference of Greek style is generally admitted, and by us who are not Greek scholars must be accepted as established. An elaborate discussion may be found in Swete, pp. CXV–CXXV.

Conservative students, who wish to maintain the Johannine authorship are much embarrassed by this difference between the Greek of the Revelation on the one hand and of the Gospel and Epistles of John on the other. Some have sought to explain it by dating the Revelation very early, some twenty years before the writing of the Gospel, believing that St. John learned to write good Greek during that time; but, as we shall see by and by, the arguments for the late date are too strong to be set aside. Alford makes the rather curious suggestion that the Holy Spirit inspired John to write good Greek when he composed the Gospel and the Epistles, but left him unaided in that respect when he wrote the Apocalypse.[12] Not many will be inclined to accept this explanation.

Here my own experience as a missionary in Japan enables me to offer a solution, which has been hinted at by others, but has never received the attention that, it seems to me, deserves. During the last years of my residence in Japan, I was engaged in what is known as "newspaper evangelism." This consists of securing space in the ordinary secular newspapers, and publishing therein short articles on Christian doctrines. Many of these were written by Japanese Christian ministers, at my request, under their own names, but a good many others were my own, published under my name. Now I had sufficient knowledge of Japanese to speak it fluently and intelligibly, but I never ventured to send any composition to the printer without having it revised. Ordinary articles were corrected by the clerk in my office, who altered my style very little. Very important discussions were sent to a literary friend, with the request to alter them freely, re-writing any paragraph or sentence that could be more idiomatically and strikingly put, or even introducing illustrations from Japanese history, proverbs, etc., that seemed to him appropriate. Hence it came to pass that I was once or twice complimented on the excellence of my Japanese style, and upon its resemblance to that of Dr. Uemura, the foremost Christian writer in Japan at that time. This was high praise, but the credit belonged entirely to my friend, who had been one of Dr. Uemura's pupils. Yet, in spite of all such literary assistance, the articles were published under my own name, and were truly mine, inasmuch as they carried my message to the public.

---

[12] Vol. IV, Part II, p. 225.

Now if any one in the future should take the trouble to collect the articles so published, and to apply them to the accepted methods of literary criticism, he would certainly conclude that not all of them were mine. He would find some in which the Japanese is rough and unidiomatic, indicating that the writer was thinking in English and mentally translating into Japanese. Noticing also that all such articles had very few references to Japanese history or literature, he would find no difficulty in believing that an American missionary, with imperfect knowledge of Japanese, had composed them. On the other hand, he would find a group of articles, equally bearing my name, in which the Japanese style is excellent, not only grammatical but idiomatic and attractive, with quotations from Japanese authors, references to Japanese life and history, and use of Japanese proverbs such as would not naturally be expected from a foreigner. "These" he would say, "can not have been written by A. Pieters. They must be the work of a Japanese literary man who for some reason wished to hide his identity, and therefore adopted the name of the foreigner."

Have we not here an exact parallel to the situation of St. John? He was a Galilean, no doubt speaking Greek daily, in a sufficiently fluent and intelligible manner, yet without literary training in that language. While a prisoner at Patmos, he received these visions, and wrote them down, without any one to help him, in such Greek as he was master of. Later he returned to Ephesus and there, tradition tells us, was requested by the believers to put in writing his recollections of the Lord Jesus Christ. What is more natural than that they should furnish him with a competent literary assistant, who would write down these reminiscences as the apostle gave them, not altering substance, but writing freely in his own cultured Greek? This does not make it any the less the apostle's work, nor does it touch the question of inspiration, since inspiration is affirmed of the completed work, without regard to the process.

We can not, of course, prove that the Apocalypse was this written by the apostle in his own Greek, without help, and the other writings by the aid of such a scribe; but it is extremely probable, and in view of this probability the argument from the difference of Greek style must be pronounced to be of very little value in determining the authorship. On the other hand, if this suggestion be true, the phenomena are exactly what they should be, and so far confirm the testimony of Justin Martyr and Irenaeus.

Another very important confirmation arises from the fact that there is no other person in sight who might possibly have written the book.

That the author was of Jewish origin is perfectly obvious. That fact shines through all the language and symbols of the book. Equally clear it is that he must have been a man of outstanding authority in the Christian church. Hengstenberg is right when he says:[13]

> Unless the conviction had been deeply rooted in the churches that the John who held such communications with them was the organ of Jesus Christ, the authority of Christ would not have covered the author. The question was sure to be asked, whether Christ had really authorized such messages to be sent.

Where, then, shall we find such a man, at the date required? There is no possibility but the apostle John. The other apostles were by that time dead, and church history knows of no other John of Jewish antecedents, who, in any way answers to the qualifications necessary. Dionysius, to be sure, speaks of another John, a presbyter, but for this suggestion he gives only a very vague rumor, that there were in Ephesus two monuments which passed as tombs of John. Eusebius, the first church historian (AD 260–340) takes this up, and quotes from Papias (died AD 155) a reference to "John the presbyter."[14] Concerning this, much has been written, but without any general agreement, to this very day. Whether this "John the presbyter" was really distinct from John the apostle, and, if so, whether he had the qualifications necessary to be the author of the Apocalypse, remains entirely without historical proof. Dr. John T. Dean, although not accepting the Johannine authorship, says of this proposed substitute:[15]

> A phantom personage has been resuscitated in modern times to bear the burden of authorship. …Whether the dim figure of the presbyter will become clearer with the discoveries of time remains to be seen.

It seems to me that we may fairly dismiss this "phantom figure" from our minds.

Stranger still is a theory that has come forward in recent years, and that has the support of some good scholars, namely, that John the apostle suffered martyrdom early in life, not long after the death of his brother James, and that hence he never lived at Ephesus or wrote any book of the

---

[13] Vol. I, p. 81.

[14] "P.N.F.," Second Series, Vol. I, p. 171.

[15] p. 44.

Bible at all. The arguments in favor of this view may be found in Moffat: "Introduction to the Literature of the New Testament," pp. 602–619, and an adequate reply in Zahn, pp. 83–100—also in William Milligan, "Discussions on the Apocalypse," pp. 164–179. I will not trouble the reader with details of this discussion; for the theory seems to me unworthy of serious considerations. If we accept it, we must believe, not only that Irenaeus and Justin were mistaken about the apostle's having written the Apocalypse, (which is within the limits of credibility) but that there never was such a person as the apostle John in Ephesus, that he did nothing and wrote nothing there, that the Gospel of John as well as the epistle were mistakenly attributed to a man who died in early life and was unknown to the churches, and that only Justin and Irenaeus but Clement of Alexandria, Tertullian, Origen, Hippolytus and Eusebius, the best informed and most responsible men of the early Church, in speaking of the apostle's residence and work at Ephesus, were discussing an imaginary person. Much is possible, but not this. The chief ground on which the theory rests is a quotation by a writer named Georgios Harmatolos, (ninth century) from an otherwise unknown writing by Papias, "supported by an extract… from an Oxford manuscript of the 7th of 8th century, and epitome probably based upon the Chronicle of Philip of Side (fifth century)." [16]

This is believed to be confirmed by certain ancient calendars, in which the date of the martyrdom of "John and James, the apostles in Jerusalem," is to be celebrated. The first is, as Swete calls it,[17] "an unverifiable reference to a lost book," and Zahn has shown how easily, in such ancient calendars, the name of John, the son of Zebedee, could be confused with that of John the Baptist. If on such grounds we are to reject the direct testimony of trustworthy and well known witnesses, like Justin Martyr and Irenaeus, it seems to me we might as well give up the study of church history altogether.

We come back, therefore, to the conviction expressed at the beginning of this discussion, that the prevailing faith of the Christian church on this point rests on very good grounds, and in all our study we shall proceed confidently to think and speak of the Apocalypse as the work of St. John the apostle, the son of Zebedee.

---

[16] Swete, p. clxxv. (When page references are thus given in small Roman numerals, they will be found to be pages of the introduction or of the "Prolegomena" of a book, as distinct from the pages of the main treatise itself, which are given in Arabic numerals.)

[17] p. clxxvi.

Our discussion of the date can be brief, as there is now general agreement that it was written during the reign of the emperor Domitian, about the year AD 95. This also rests primarily upon the testimony of Irenaeus, who says:[18]

> For that was seen no very long time since, but almost in our day, towards the end of Domitian's reign.

Some scholars have set aside this testimony and dated the book in the time of Nero (reigned 54–68). This makes the explanation of the heads of the Beast, in 17.10, much easier, and also enables them to take the temple, in chapter eleven, as the actual temple at Jerusalem, still standing when they suppose the book to have been composed. In addition to contradicting Irenaeus, however, this date can not be made to agree either with the state of the churches in the province of Asia or with the relation between Christianity and the Roman empire that we find in the Apocalypse. As to the former, those churches were founded by the apostle Paul, shortly before his imprisonment in Caesarea, which began AD 58 or 59. There remain, therefore, at most only ten years before the death of Nero, a length of time quite insufficient for such changes as must have occurred before such letters as we find in Revelation could have been written to the said churches. Moreover, we find from the Pastoral Epistles that Timothy was in charge of the church at Ephesus after the release of Paul in AD 62, so that it is incredible that St. John should, during the reign of Nero, occupy such a position of authority there.

As to the latter consideration, one of the most prominent things in the Apocalypse is the struggle between the Christian church and the paganism of the Roman Empire. Especially in the form of emperor worship, this is the enemy to be feared and to be overcome. During the lifetime of the apostle Paul it was not so. Then the chief enemy was Judaism, dangerous to both the faith of the church and to its members. There was, to be sure, a persecution of Christians under Nero, but this was temporary, occasioned by an unusual emergency, caused by the need of finding scapegoats for the great fire. It did not indicate such a deep seated antagonism on principle between the Christian church and the Roman Empire as we find in the Apocalypse.

For these and other similar reasons, as already said, scholarly opin-

---

[18] "A.N.F.," Vol. I, p. 560.

ion has almost unanimously abandoned the Neronic date, and has settled down to the conviction that the book was written during the last decade of the first century, under the emperor Domitian.

II
OTHER APOCALYPSES

The book of Revelation is commonly called The Apocalypse, from the Greek word "apokalupsis," an uncovering, found in the first verse of the first chapter. From this word has arisen the designation of certain other books as "apocalyptic literature," or as "apocalypses." Since these expressions often occur in discussions of the Revelation of St. John, it seems well to give a brief explanation of them; particularly as it is held by some that the nature of the canonical apocalypse can not be understood except by one who has a knowledge of this entire group of writings.

There are three groups of books that bear some relation to our canonical Scriptures, but have never been accepted as part of the Bible by the Protestant churches; most of them never by any church. These are The Old Testament Apocrypha, the New Testament Apocrypha, and the Apocalyptic Books.

The Old Testament Apocrypha are books written during the period between the Old and New Testaments. They comprise two books of "Esdras" (or Ezra), Tobit, Judith, the Wisdom of Solomon, the Wisdom of Jesus the Son of Sirach, also called Ecclesiasticus, the Prophecy of Baruch, the Prayer of Manasseh, four books of the Maccabees and certain additions to the book of Daniel. These books were included in the Greek Bible, that was in circulation in the early Christian church, called the Septuagint Version, or the LXX. From this, they passed over into the current Latin Version, called the Vulgate. Most, though not all of them, are for the Roman Catholics as much a part of the inspired Scriptures as any other books. The Protestants exclude them all, since they are not found in the Hebrew canon, but many of the Protestant confessions speak of them with respect, as profitable for reading. Hence, in the old Bibles, they are usually printed between the Old and New Testament portions. The books of this group, therefore, have always been well known and most of them have been highly esteemed in the Christian church.

The New Testament Apocrypha are books written in obvious imitation of the gospels and the Acts of the Apostles. They originated in the Christian community, during the second and third centuries, and seek to supplement by imaginary tales what the writers thought were regrettable omissions in the canonical scriptures. This was especially the case with the childhood of Jesus, concerning which the accepted gospels are silent. Among the chief New Testament Apocrypha are the Gospel of the Birth of Mary, the Protevangelion of James, the Gospel of the Infancy, the Gospel of Nicodemus, also called the Acts of Pilate, and the Acts of Paul and Thecla.[1] All of these contain impossible, fantastic, and sometimes scarcely decent tales. They are of no value whatever as historical sources, and are chiefly useful as showing, by contrast with the canonical gospels, the immeasurable superiority of the latter. Some years ago an enterprising and not very scrupulous firm re-printed these books and advertised them extensively as "The Lost Books of the Bible"—a title open to objection on two counts, that they never were books of the Bible and that they never were lost. They were never books of the Bible because they never obtained recognition as canonical in any branch of the Christian church; and they never were lost, because they have remained continuously well known to students from the time they were written until the present.

From the above two groups of writings must be carefully distinguished the books now called "apocalyptic." Most of these were lost for many centuries, and have become well known only in recent years, through discovery and study. The Book of Enoch, for instance, was discovered in Abyssinia, by the traveler Bruce, in the latter part of the eighteenth century, and was first published in 1821. This book was accepted as canonical in the Abyssinian church. It is, for purposes of comparison with the Revelation, perhaps the most important of them all, and is the only one quoted in the New Testament, in Jude, verse 14. It purports to contain the very words of Enoch, the seventh antediluvian patriarch. After a brief introduction, glorifying the works of God in nature and assuring the elect of a happy and glorious future, it suddenly begins an account of the alleged union of fallen angels and human women, based upon the story in Genesis 6.1–4. There is a very complicated angelology, the names of many angels being given whose names appear nowhere in the Bible. Enoch is

---

[1] These and many other similar writings may be found in "A.N.F.," Vol. VIII.

made a messenger, to announce to these fallen angels their doom. He is then conducted through the heavens, until he reaches the very throne of God, and God speaks with him. The subject of discussion is still this affair of the fallen angels and their human wives. He thence goes on a journey much like that of Dante, seeing both beautiful and terrible things.

After that follows a section called the "Similitudes," and in this section occurs the expression. "The Son of Man." An angel accompanies him and explains things to him. In a later section Noah is introduced, and tells how the flood came about. Still further along there is a section on celestial physics, and a great vision of sheep and shepherds. It is a very much mixed-up production, and it is no wonder that the critics believe it to be a composite work, with the different sections written at very different times. There is general agreement that the earliest portions of it go back to 160 or 170 BC, while other portions are thought by some critics to be post-Christian. At any rate, there seems no good reason to doubt that most, if not all of it was in circulation during the time of Jesus and the apostles.[2]

After the Book of Enoch, perhaps the most important is the Ascension of Isaiah. This tells how Hezekiah, when he was about to die, called his son Manasseh to him, and, in the presence of the prophet Isaiah, gave him instructions. Manasseh, however, was misled by an evil spirit, called "Beliar," and finally put Isaiah to death by sawing him asunder. The reference in Hebrews 11.37 is evidently to this story, whether to this book or not is not so clear. This book, also, is analyzed by critics into three different original documents. If this is correct, some portions of the book may be early, but some sections, at least, must have been written in the latter half of the first century, because it contains a prophecy concerning an incarnation of "Beliar," who will be a "lawless king, the slayer of his mother," evidently referring to Nero.[3]

These two will be sufficient as samples of this class of literature. Among those now so classed are the Book of the Secrets of Enoch (AD 50), the Slavonic Book of Enoch (AD 50), the Book of Jubilees (60 BC – AD 70), the Assumption of Moses (AD 30), the Testaments of the Twelve Patriarchs (AD 2nd or 3rd century), the Psalms of Solomon (50 BC). The dates given are taken from the discussion by Dr. J. E. H. Thompson, in The International Standard Bible Encyclopedia. They are at best very uncertain, but if they are substantially correct, they indicate that some of these books

---

[2] Charles, R. H.: "The Book of Enoch."

[3] Charles, R. H.: "The Ascension of Isaiah."

were written and circulated during the one hundred and fifty years before the writing of the Revelation. It is conceivable, therefore, that St. John may have read them and may have been more or less influenced by them, in thought or in expression.

What links these books with those of Daniel and Revelation, and makes them a distinct class, is the use of what is called the "apocalyptic" method. The outstanding characteristics of such books are as follows:

1. That they deal largely with eschatology, that is with the end of the world, the coming to judgment, and similar ideas.

2. That their predictions are not in plain language, like that of the prophets, but are couched in visions of images, beasts, birds, cities, battles, etc., darkly symbolizing what is foretold.

3. The presence of angels as guides and interpreters.

This is the way in which much of Daniel and almost the whole of the Revelation is written. There are such elements also in Ezekiel and in Zechariah.

When comparing these "apocalypses" with Daniel and the Revelation, it is important to notice the following:

1. That in not a single case does any one know the author of one of these books, nor does any early writer name, or attempt to name, the true author. Very early in church history they called the "Pseudepigrapha," or books falsely entitled, because the names attached to them were recognized as imaginary.

2. That those which are of Jewish origin enjoyed no favor from the religious leaders of the Jewish people. They were not preserved and studied like the scriptures or the Talmud. If we had to depend exclusively on Jewish sources of information, we should know little or nothing about them.

3. That they are, compared with the biblical apocalypses of Daniel and the Revelation, very inferior, full of silly things, especially along the line of angelology. No one can read them without feeling this difference. The earlier writings are palpable imitations of Daniel, the latter, in many cases, of the Revelation. They bear much the same relation to the genuine apocalypses as the apocryphal writings of the Old and New Testaments bear on the canonical. Dr. T. W. Crafer, in Gore's New Commentary is right in saying: "Ours remains *the* Apocalypse still, because no other existing specimen, Jewish or Christian, is worthy to be compared to it."[4]

---

[4] p. 680.

4. That the writers of these books had no standing as teachers in any company of believers, either Jewish or Christian, so far as we are aware. The literature prized by the Jewish rabbis, who represent the ancient Pharisees, is preserved for us in the Talmud, but the Pharisees evidently did not care for these apocalyptic writings. The Sadducees still less, as they are full of angels and of the future life. Some conjecture that they emanated from the Essenes. It may be so, but there is no direct evidence. Contrast this with the letters to the seven churches of Asia, which at once put us into touch with historic reality.

5. That these books are not quoted or referred to in the New Testament, with the exception of the quotation from Enoch in Jude, and the possible reference to the Ascension of Isaiah in the Hebrews. The canonical Apocalypse very strongly and frankly leans on Ezekiel, Daniel, and Zechariah, but it makes no use at all of any of the visions or prophecies in any of the uncanonical apocalypses.

Dr. R. H. Charles, the foremost authority on this kind of literature, quotes many so-called parallel passages, to prove dependence of our Apocalypse upon the Book of Enoch. Some of these are real parallels: others strike one as being mere coincidences, without any force as proof. They only show that the two writers were dealing with the same general circle of ideas.

On the whole, it seems to me that we may easily over estimate the importance of these apocalypses in relation to the interpretation of the Revelation of St. John; but a study of them serves at lease this good purpose, that it shows us that the peculiar style and phraseology of that book were not so strange to the generation for whom it was written as they are to us. Dr. Swete says, with reference to the alleged resemblances between the Revelation and these books:

> While they shew the writer of the Christian Apocalypse to have been familiar with the apocalyptic ideas of his age, they afford little or no clear evidence of his dependence on Jewish sources other than the books of the Old Testament. ...The most that can safely be affirmed is that he shared with the Jewish apocalyptists the stock of apocalyptic imagery and mystical and eschatological thought which was the common property of an age nurtured in the Old Testament and hard pressed by the troubles and dangers of the times. (p. cliii)

III

GOD'S PICTURE BOOK

In this chapter we are to study the general character of the book of Revelation, and glance at the different systems of interpretation. These two subjects are closely related, for if the character of the Apocalypse were not so very peculiar, there would be no mention of systems of interpretation. There is difference of exegesis as to individual passages of the gospels, but who ever heard of distinct systems of interpretation in that connection?

There are many kinds of books in the Bible, and each kind must be understood with its own special character always distinctly in view. The Psalms, which are poetry, must not be handled like prose, or the law books like the prophecies, or the story books like this great picture book. For that is what Revelation is: it is God's great picture book at the end of the Bible.

Not only is it a picture book, but it is a picture book of a peculiar kind. Some pictures are intended to be understood just as they stand. Many of us have seen a picture of the first testing of the great Liberty Bell, in Philadelphia, in the days before the American Revolution. In it you see a bell founder's shop, with the mechanic who cast the great bell, in workman's clothes and apron, his sleeves rolled up. The bell is there, hung to the rafters of the shop. There are also a number of dignified elderly gentlemen, evidently the committee to test the tone of the bell. Finally, there is a beautiful young lady, with a hammer in her hand about to strike the bell.

In this picture, everything is exactly what it seems to be. The bell is a bell, the workman a workman, the hammer a hammer, the gentlemen gentlemen, the rafters real, honest-to-goodness rafters, and nothing else in the world. The full interpretation of the picture requires, indeed, some knowledge of history, but that is nor because of any obscurity or hidden meaning in the picture itself. So far as the objects shown are concerned, they are what they seem to be, and any child can name them correctly.

There are also well known among us pictures of another kind, which, while by no means the same thing as the pictorial representation in the book of Revelation, are sufficiently akin to them to help us in understanding them. After the political campaign of 1928, in which Herbert Hoover was elected President of the United States, there appeared in one of our papers a picture of a huge elephant, which was swinging a tiger around its head by the tail. This cartoon was entitled simply, "The End of the Tiger Hunt," without any further explanation, for nothing further was necessary. In this picture, which every one understood perfectly, nothing is what it seems to be. The elephant does not mean an elephant, but the Republican party; while the tiger represents Tammany Hall, the Democratic organization in New York City. These figures are what we might call pictures of these organizations. Properly speaking, you can not make a picture of a political party, but since some method of pictorial presentation was necessary, the problem has been solved by taking these animals as symbols and thus presenting pictorially what is in itself not capable of being so presented.

Now, as nothing is easier to understand than a good cartoon, by those to whom its symbols are familiar, so nothing is more devoid of meaning, or more liable to variety of interpretation, than such a symbolic picture, if the symbols are not familiar or imperfectly understood. For confirmation of this, you have only to look at a set of cartoons from Europe, China, or Japan. You will find them blind enough.

It is easy to see that the symbols in the book of Revelation partake somewhat of the nature of cartoons. We see there a picture of a woman, clothed with the sun, the stars for her crown, and the moon under her feet—another picture of a woman magnificently dressed sitting on a beast full of names of blasphemy—another of a city coming down from heaven, etc., etc. All of these are pictorial representations of things that can not, in themselves, be so readily presented to the thought; of the church, of evil, of terrible persecutions, of great judgments, etc.

Now, how this cartoon-like character of the book leads to distinct systems of interpretation, may be readily understood by an illusion. Suppose that our present civilization should entirely pass away, and a thousand years from now the center of learning should be in China or India. Also, that some knowledge of our times and ways, but not so very much,

should survive. Suppose, further, that under such circumstances an ex-
ploring party of Chinese archaeologists should dig up from the ruins of
New York or Chicago (perhaps preserved under the corner-stone of some
great building) a paper with the cartoon of the elephant and the tiger,
which we have described. It would be a great find, and we can imagine a
meeting of the Nanking Association of American Archaeology gathered
to discuss it. They learn the date from something printed on it, and locate
it accurately in the year 1928. Then the debate is opened by a learned
professor who says: "Mr. President: this picture compels is entirely to
alter our conception of America in the twentieth century. It has hitherto
been supposed that it was then a well settled country, without any jungles
or wild animals, but this picture of an elephant and a tiger shows clearly
that those animals were found wild in that country at that time; otherwise no such fight could have taken place. This is a jungle picture, taken
from like." This would be one interpretation, which we may perhaps call
the literal interpretation.

When the first speaker has concluded, another learned scientist gets
up and says: "Mr. President: I regret to differ with my learned colleague,
but I can not accept his interpretation of this picture. The evidence which
leads us to look upon America in the twentieth century as a civilized, well
settled country is too strong to be set aside for this one picture. There is
another interpretation which is, I am sure, the true one. These are wild
animals, to be sure, but they were not wild in America at that time. The
Americans had what they called circuses. These were shows, traveling
about from city to city, and they carried with them animals, originally
wild, brought from distant lands, that had been taught to do tricks. These
tricks were exhibited to the patrons of the circus, especially for the amusement of the children. Probably this picture is such a trick, exhibited to
show the audience the manner in which elephants in India were trained to
catch tigers when hunting." This system of interpretation might be called
the historico-literal, since to a literal understanding of the animals in the
picture, the learned Chinese added some knowledge of history.

Now a third scholar takes the floor and says: "Mr. President: both of
these explanations, to which we have listened, are perfectly natural, on the
face of the picture, and therefore sound plausible, but both are wide of the
mark. This is neither a jungle picture nor a circus picture. It is a political
cartoon, and presents to the eye the great victory won by the Republican
party in the national election of 1928, when Herbert Hoover was elected

President. The elephant is not an elephant, but stands for the Republican party, and the tiger for Tammany Hall, the Democratic organization in New York City." This we may call the symbolical interpretation of the said picture. Now, dear reader, we know perfectly well,—you and I—that the third interpretation is correct, but we can imagine how difficult, if not impossible, it would be to convince the adherents of the other two systems.

We are in a very similar situation with respect to the interpretation of the book of Revelation. Eighteen hundred years have passed away since it was written; the circumstances of that day are imperfectly known to us, and the various scenes in the book are open to divergent interpretations, without our being able in every case to decide with confidence which explanation is correct. We need not be surprised, therefore, that there are different systems of interpretation. The right thing for us to do is study these various systems, and select the one that seems to us most likely to be the right one. If this does not lead us ultimately to an entirely confident conclusion, at least the process of study can not be otherwise than exceedingly profitable.

As usually classified, there are three main systems of interpreting the Apocalypse. These are:

1. The Historicist or Continuous-Historical School. This is called, in German works, the "Kirchen-Geschichtliche" school. People who hold this system consider the book of Revelation to a symbolical panorama of all that was to happen when it was written until the end. Hence they are much interested to know at precisely what point we ourselves stand, and they look into the book eagerly to find predictions of Mohammed, the Pope, the Reformation, Napoleon Bonaparte, Mussolini, Hitler, etc., etc. I will give a more extended explanation of their positions in a later chapter.

2. The Futurist, or "End-Geschichtliche" School. These interpreters consider that almost everything in the book, from the beginning of chapter four on, lies in the future, and is to be fulfilled immediately before the Second Advent of the Lord Jesus Christ. Of these, also, I will speak more in detail later.

3. The Preterist, or "Zeit-Geschichtliche" School. Such interpreters, quite contrary to the position of the Futurists, think that almost everything in the Revelation had its fulfillment in the first two or three centuries after it was written. Of course not everything, but almost everything. They recognize that the final judgment and the perfected state are still to come. Because they look upon the fulfillment as almost all in the past they are called "Preterists," which means "the past."

Although these are the chief recognized systems not all interpreters belong to these three classes. Dr. T. W. Crafer says, in "Gore's New Commentary," p. 680:

> There is one other method of interpretation worthy of mention; it is that associated with Milligan himself.[1] He divorces that book almost completely from history, and finds in it little more than a noble expression of those great principles of the divine government whose operation we can trace in every age of the world. It is no doubt those principles which it is the great purpose of the book to make clear to us, but it is quite evident that the author is mainly concerned with his own day.

It is difficult to give a name to this school of though. Perhaps we may get nearest to a suitable name is we call it the "Philosophy of History" School, for those who belong to this group look upon the book of Revelation as containing a discussion of the forces that underlie events, not of the events themselves. Their interpretations combine readily with those of the Preterists or of the Historicists, because any symbol, understood by them to refer to a certain force or tendency may be considered fulfilled in any event in which such a force or tendency is dominant. So Alford finds in the wild beast arising out of the sea (chapter 13), "the secular powers antagonistic to the church of Christ," whenever and wherever found. In the second beast, that had horns like a lamb but spake like a dragon, he sees: "the sacerdotal persecuting power, leagued with and the instrument of the secular...in all its forms, Pagan, Papal, and in so far as the Reformed Churches have retrograded towards Papal sacerdotalism, Protestant also."[2]

Archbishop Benson is one of the representatives of this school, and states its principles in the following words:[3]

> In the mind of St. John I seem to see mirrored a comprehensive and penetrating view of the principles which maintain the self-deceiving half of human nature in its death-struggles with a Divine Wisdom which slowly vanquishes it. ...He is the giver of truth about all those most potent influences which work under the life of all society, making merchandise of virtue and vice, of truth and policy; influences which work wonders in the life of civilization as we know it, and seem bright with undying fire, influ-

[1] William Milligan, in "The Expositor's Bible."

[2] Introduction, Sec. 55–56.

[3] p. 176.

ences which have their seat not only in hostile anti-Christian religions or in old Rome, but in powerful churches, reformed or unreformed, and not less in sects which have revolted from dogmas, and which do not permit their apostles to declaim against selfishness and greed.

Hence, such expositors find no continuity in Revelation. The seals are not to be fulfilled first, then the trumpets. The seals present rather the entire course of the history from one aspect, the trumpets from another; the symbols placing before us the forces engaged in the struggles rather than the details of the conflict.

Now, one thing that it is of the highest importance that the reader shall see clearly and grasp firmly, is this: that none of these schools of interpretation can claim any monopoly on scholarship or faith. Each group numbers many fine scholars and devout Christian believers. Therefore complete certainty in regard to the interpretation of the Apocalypse is not to be had. It is our duty to do the best we can, to study the various systems and accept the view that seems to us right, but always with a certain amount of reservation and of respect for the opinions of others.

It is true, to be sure, that the Preterists have a Left Wing, in which scholarship is more evident than faith. Some of these writers have no respect whatever for the Apocalypse as an inspired writing. They class it with the other apocalypses, of which we spoke in the previous chapter. This seriously affects their exegesis. In their opinion, the writer knew nothing of the future by inspiration, and hence an interpretation that has been falsified by history does not on that account seem to them admissible. Writers of this kind are numerous among the modernistic German and English commentators. The most recent, and in many respects the best, of them is Dr. R. H. Charles, who has written a very learned work on Revelation.

We decisively reject this view, because we believe that the book was written by the apostle John, and because it is inconceivable that, if they are right, the book should have found its way into the canon of the New Testament. What Dr. James Orr says in the International Standard Bible Encyclopedia seems me eminently correct:

> On the modern Nero theory, to which most recent expositors give adherence, it is a farrago of baseless phantasies, not one of which came true. …It does not matter for this theory that none of the things predicted happened, that every anticipation was falsified. Nero did not return, Jerusalem was not saved, Rome did not perish, three and a half years did not see

the end of all things. Yet the Christian church, though the failure of every one of these predictions had been decisively demonstrated, received the book as of divine inspiration, apparently without the least idea that such things had been intended. (pp. 2582, 2584)

There is, however, also a Right Wing of the Preterists. Dr. Moses Stuart, of Andover, who published a very important commentary on Revelation in 1845, was a Preterist, but one who fully accepted the inspiration of the book and expounded it in a reverent manner; as do many today, among whom are Isbon T. Beckwith, (1919) and H. B. Swete, (1906).

Of the work of Moses Stuart, E. B. Elliott, one of the foremost of the Historicists, said, in 1846:

> There is absolutely no *locus standi* for the Praeterist system. …Professor Stewart… forced the scheme into notice; to the effect only of its final and decisive rejection both in England and elsewhere. (p. XX)

Elliott was over confident. Today scholars are prevailing in favor of this system, either unchanged, or combined with the ideas of the Philosophy of History School. Crafer says, in 1928:

> The third line of interpretation, which may be said to have ousted the other two, is the Preterist. (p. 680)

This, also, is an over confident assertion, for certainly the Futurist school is still active and influential. The two recent commentaries by Theodore Zahn and Abraham Kuyper (the latter posthumously published) are Futurist.

IV

THE HISTORICAL INTERPRETATION

The interpretation that looks upon the book of Revelation as a forecast, in symbols, of the history of the Christian church, is sometimes called, not without reason, the standard Protestant interpretation. Alford says that it was the view "held by the precursors and upholders of the Reformation, by Wicliffe and his followers in England, by Luther in Germany, Bullinger in Switzerland, Bishop Bale in Ireland, by Fox the martyrologist by Brightman, Pareus, and early Protestant expositors generally." [1]

Among those I have personally examined, of this school, the chief are E. B. Elliott: "Horae Apocalypticae," Albert Barnes: "Notes on Revelation," H. Grattan Guinness: "History Unveiling Prophecy," and "The Approaching End of the Age," David N. Lord: "An Exposition of the Apocalypse," and B. H. Carroll (1913) "The Book of Revelation." The essential idea is the same in all, with wide differences in detail.

Perhaps the fairest way to give the reader an idea of this system is to transcribe, in outline, the fulfillments traced by Barnes, as follows: (p. XXXIX)

First Seal: fulfilled in the state of the Roman Empire from the death of Domitian, AD 96 to the accession of Commodus, AD 180.

Second Seal: from the death of Commodus, AD 193, and onward.

Third Seal: the time of Caracalla, AD 211 and onward.

Fourth Seal: the time of Decius to Gallienus, AD 243–268.

Fifth Seal: fulfilled in the Roman Empire in the persecutions, particularly in the time of Diocletian, AD 284–304.

---

[1] Vol. IV, Part II, p. 247.

Sixth Seal: the invasions of the barbarians, AD 365 and onwards.

Seventh Seal: fulfilled in the Trumpets, as follows:

First Trumpet: Invasion by Alaric the Goth, AD 395–410.

Second Trumpet: Invasion by Genseric the Vandal, AD 428–468.

Third Trumpet: Invasion by Attila the Hun, AD 433–453.

Fourth Trumpet: Final conquest of the Western empire by Odoacer, king of the Heruli, AD 476–490.

Fifth Trumpet: The Mohammedans.

Sixth Trumpet: The Turks.

Chapter 10, the Great Angel—The Reformation. The Little Book open is the Bible, restored to general reading. That the angel cries with a loud voice is symbolical of the Reformation. The seven thunders heard, but not recorded are the anathemas hurled against the Reformation by the Pope.

Chapter 11—The Measuring of the Temple: the determining of what constituted the true church at the time of the Reformation. The two witnesses represent those who testified against the errors of Rome. The Seventh Trumpet: the final triumph of the church.

This is considered to be the end of the first series of visions. What follows is not a chronological continuation, but a view of the church internally. This second section, in the view of these interpreters, is concerned almost exclusively with the Roman Catholic Church. The woman in chapter 12 is the true church. Her fleeing into the desert represents the condition of the church while the Papacy was in the ascendancy. The wrath of Satan against the "remnant of her seed" represents the attempt of the Papacy to cut off individuals when open and general persecution no longer raged.

The First Beast: The Roman secular or civil power that sustained the Papacy.

The Second Beast: The Papal ecclesiastical power.

The Seven Vials: All interpreted as blows at the power of the Papacy. The first vial, the French Revolution, the second, its scenes of blood and carnage, the third, the French invasions of northern Italy, the fourth, the overturning of the governments that sustained the Papal power, the fifth, the capture of the Pope himself and the seizure of Rome by the French, the sixth, the decline of the Turkish power, the seventh, the complete and final overthrow of the Papal power (still to come). The Great Harlot—the Papacy.

The Destruction of Babylon: the fall of the Papacy.

In the development of these ideas, interpreters of this school go into great detail, in comparing the symbols of Revelation with the course of history, and this makes the reading of their books very profitable, entirely apart from any acceptance of their main position, for they bring to the task an immense amount of learning. Some have been so well convinced by the argument that it has even been said that a missionary might go out to the heathen world with a copy of Gibbon's "Decline and Fall of the Empire" in one hand and Barnes on Revelation in the other, as conclusive proofs oaf the divine inspiration of the Bible!

That some points in the interpretation, as developed by these expositors, seem excellently to fit the history, must be frankly conceded. One of the best, in my judgment, is the identification of the fifth trumpet with the rise of Mohammedanism and of the sixth trumpet with the coming of the Turks. The things there seen in the vision would surely be appropriate symbolical descriptions of those great calamities. Yet an occasional hit of this kind does not prove anything with regard to the system as a whole. It is like grading examination papers on the "true and false" system. If a pupil, in such an examination, gets half the answers right, he is graded zero, for a person who knows nothing about the subject, answering at random, may do as well. Pure guesswork is bound to be right somewhere.

A variety of the Historical Interpretation is the "Recapitulationist" view. Those who hold it accept the fundamental "Historicist" principle that the book of Revelation is intended to furnish a panorama of church history, but they do not hold that the story is in continuous chronological order from beginning to end. They think that it is presented in seven stages or pictures, each of which cover the entire period between the first and second advents of Christ. This helps them very greatly in some places, especially in chapters twelve and twenty. This view is that of the excellent works of Dr. S. L. Morris: "The Drama of Christianity" and Dr. W. Hendriksen: "More Than Conquerors." The divisions of Dr. Morris will be found in chapter VII of this book. Dr. Hendriksens's divisions are slightly different, but the essential idea is the same.

So far as the "Continuous-Historical" interpretation in general is concerned, it seems to me that it must be rejected as fundamentally unsound, for the following reasons:

1. Because the Apocalypse, so understood, is entirely out of touch with the situation of the early church, to which it was originally given. This objection will be raised again when we consider the Futurist scheme, and

seems to me fatal to both. Nothing can well be imagined more completely useless to the believers of St. John's day than this book, if the said interpretation be correct. It was not possible that they should understand it, nor would it have done them any conceivable good if they had understood it. The parallel, which such expositors draw, between the Revelation, so interpreted, and the Messianic prophecies of the Old Testament, is not to the point. Whatever the obscurities of Messianic prophecy, it was intended to direct the faith and hope of the Old Testament believers to the Coming One, and it did have that effect. Men were hoping for and expecting the Messiah when Christ came; but the book of Revelation (if the historical interpretation be correct) had no corresponding effect. For many ages it aroused no expectation at all of such events as are alleged by the Historicists to be predicted in it; and when the adherents of this system have ventured to make specific forecasts beyond their own times, they have usually been wrong.

2. The importance attached to the Roman Catholic apostasy, in this style of interpretation, seems to me quite out of proportion. Far be it from me to shut my eyes to the evils of Romanism; and yet it seems to me absurd to think that the Reformation is the only thing of prime importance that has happened since the time of Constantine the Great; that the Pope is the only enemy of true religion, or that the chief purpose of the Apocalypse is to furnish us with ammunition against the Roman Catholic Church, which is almost what one must think if he accepts the positions of Barnes and Elliott.

3. The horizon of these interpreters seem to me too narrow. They seek the fulfillment of the prophecies of Revelation only in the countries composing the ancient Roman Empire, and hence find no place in these visions for the greater part of mankind. The Abyssinian Church, the Nestorian churches of Persia, India, and China, the martyr church of Armenia, and the great Greek church, which never yielded obedience to the Pope, have no place in the prophecy. They continually speak as if the Latin Church were the Christian Church, and that alone. This manner of conceiving the situation was no doubt natural enough for the Reformers: it is out of date for us.

4. The interpretations of this school descend often into manifestly absurd detail. I will give two or three examples. Elliott seeks an interpretation of the half hour's silence in heaven (Rev 8.1) and he finds it in "the seventy years that intervened between Constantine's victory over Licinius, followed by the dissolution of the pagan heavens, AD 324, and Alaric's

revolt and the invasion of the empire, consequent on the death of Theo-dosius, AD 395." You see, he figures it out that half an hour in heaven is the precise equivalent of seventy years in Roman history and that the lack of war on earth is here spoken of as silence in heaven![2] When Barnes comes to the seven thunders, whose utterances the seer was forbidden to write (Rev 10.4), he soberly proposes as the interpretation that these are Papal anathemas hurled at the Reformation, and that they were not to be written down because in them there was nothing worth recording![3] As an example of Protestant humor this may have merit; it has none as exegesis. Carroll, one of the most recent American writers of this school (1913) explains that the three frogs that issued from the mouths of the dragon, the beast, and the false prophet, as follows: (Rev 16.13)

> Now we might fairly identify, as the three frogs, (1) The declaration of the Council of Trent, (2) the declaration of the Vatican Council, (3) the papal encyclicals and syllabuses, particularly those completing the system of Mariolatry.[4]

What Sadler says of Elliott may be fairly applied to all adherents of this school:[5]

> I have constantly referred to this work, giving specimens of its (I really must say) outrageous expositions to show the reader how little reliable a systems can be which has to resort to such expedients to maintain its continuity.

5. This method leads to calculations of times and periods, which have constantly been falsified by the event, and have wrought great harm.

These calculations are made by the "year-day" theory, namely, that a day in prophecy means a year in actual time. Hence, if the prophecy says that the Beast is to have power for forty-two months, or 1,260 days, we may be sure that the evil power represented by it (taken by this school to be the Papacy) will come to an end after the lapse of 1,260 years. According to the same criterion David N. Lord expects the millennium

[2] Vol. I, pp. 292–297.

[3] p. 289.

[4] p. 221.

[5] p. xxix.

to last 360,000 years,[6] which seems to me too long! It is extraordinary how widely this idea is held by expositors, and with what confidence it is maintained. An elaborate defense of it, accompanied by extensive astronomical calculations, will be found in H. Grattan Guinness: "History Unveiling Prophecy."[7]

Yet the scriptural basis for it is exceedingly meagre. Three passages are adduced in support of it. The first is Numbers 14.34, where, in the story of the spies, the Israelites are condemned to spend a year in the desert for every day in the journey of the spies. What possible bearing has this on the interpretation of prophecy? The second is Ezekiel 4.4–6, where the prophet is commanded to lie on his side for a certain number of days, and he is told that these correspond to years. This rule, in that passage, does not go beyond the special act of the prophet. The third passage seems at first sight more pertinent. It is in Daniel 9.25 and following verses, where we have the prophecy of the "seventy weeks." All expositors are agreed that this deals with a period of 490 years, and if the "weeks" are taken as periods of seven days each, then we do have here a prophecy in which a day stands for a year; but the word does not properly mean a "week" as we now use that term. It means a "seven," a "heptad," a group of seven units, without saying what kind of units. So understood, it has no relation to days at all. Even if in this case it is true that a day stands for a year, it does not follow that this is a general rule for prophecy. When Isaiah said that Ephraim should be broken within sixty-five years, (7.8), or that within three years the glory of Moab should be brought into contempt (16.14), or that Tyre should be forgotten seventy years, (23.15), he spoke of ordinary years. So did Jeremiah, in prophesying that Judah should be subject to Babylon for seventy years (29.10). When Daniel "understood by the books" (9.2) that the seventy years of the captivity were almost accomplished, he did not reckon a day for a year! When our Lord Jesus Christ forewarned His disciples that He should be crucified and rise again "the third day," (Matt 20.19) He did not mean that He was to lie in the grave three years. In spite of all the confidence with which this strange rule of interpretation is put forward, therefore, I feel constrained to agree with the following expressions of opinion: Dean Alford:[8]

---

[6] p. 515.

[7] pp. 392–487.

[8] Vol. IV, Part II, p. 251.

I have never seen it proved, or even made probable, that we are to take a day for a year in apocalyptic prophecy.

H. Bultema: (p. 18)

The year-day theory is thoroughly unbiblical.

Moses Stuart: (Vol. I, p. 213)

Since the days of Joseph Mede, most commentators in he English world have made each of the 1,260 days stand for a year, and striven to show when a period in each case commences, and, of course, when it terminates. ...Of all the opinions ever thrust upon the hermeneutics or prophecy, I know of none more ungrounded or more untenable than this.

This year-day calculation has done a great deal of harm in arousing expectations that were not fulfilled, and in furnishing occasion for the rise of fanatical movements. To it was due the prediction of William Miller that the world should come to an end in 1843, which caused great excitement, and ultimately led to the founding of the Seventh Day Adventist Church. Again and again the dates have had to be revised. As Alford says,[9]

One after another the years fixed on for the consummation by different authors have passed away, beginning with the 1836 of Bengel; one after another the expositors have shifted their ground into the safer future.

Thus the whole "Continuous-Historical" interpretation, with the central place it gives to the Papacy, has been shown by history to be a "will-o'-the-wisp," leading only into the bog of endless and profitless speculations.

---

[9] Vol. IV, Part II, p. 251.

V

THE FUTURIST INTERPRETATION

Quite contrary to both the Preterist and the Continuous-Historical inter-pretations is the Futurist. The Preterist says that almost everything in the book of Revelation was fulfilled long ago, the Historicist, that is has been fulfilling all the time, and some of the things foretold are happening in out own day, the Futurist that nothing of that which is prophesied from the beginning of chapter four on has yet taken place, nor can take place until just before the end.

Futurists tend to be literalists. I do not mean that they do not see any of the symbolical character of the book, but they stick as closely as they can to the literal meaning. Hence, when they read in the eleventh chapter that the temple is measured, they find here a reason for believing that the actual temple in Jerusalem will be rebuilt; just as some of the Preterists find in the same chapter evidence that when it was written the temple had not yet been destroyed. When the Futurists read in the same chapter of the two witnesses, they do not ask what these symbolize, but who they are, and they come to the conclusion, generally, that these are Enoch and Elijah, who have not yet suffered death. They take the days, also, literally, whence they find that the Beast will have power for three and a half cal-endar years. I do not agree with them, but this, at least, seems to be more reasonable than to think that three and a half years in the prophecy are 1,260 years of actual time.

A distinguishing mark of the Futurists is that they all believe in the coming of a personal Antichrist. This is a large subject which I hope to discuss in a subsequent chapter. The Preterists usually do not believe in any Antichrist at all, and the Historicists identify him with the Pope; but the Futurists believe that the Beast or the False Prophet represents a personal wicked secular or ecclesiastical ruler who will live in the very last days, and that he is the same as the Man of Sin of St. Paul (II Thess 2). As the Beast and the False Prophet are among the chief characters of the second half of the Apocalypse, you must be a Futurist, if you identify one of them with the Antichrist, and regard him as an individual.

Most Futurists are pre-millenarians, or, as I prefer to say, millenarians, that is, they believe that after the Lord Jesus Christ is revealed from heaven, at His Second Advent, the General Judgment will not take place at once, but that there will be a resurrection of the righteous, and after that a blessed reign of Christ on earth for 1,000 years, (or 360,000 years, according to some). Dr. Abraham Kuyper is an outstanding example of a Futurist who is not a millenarian. Historicists are divided on this point. Elliott, Lord, Guinness, and others, are millenarians; Barnes and Carroll are not.

Just as there are two groups of Preterists, a Left Wong and a Right Wong, so there are two sorts of Futurists. The extreme Futurists are the Darbyite dispensationalists, and a slight knowledge of their system is necessary to understand and appreciate their interpretation of the Revelation. This is the system that is set forth in the notes to the "Scofield Bible," and is taught in most of the "Bible Schools" and "Undenominational Churches" of the United States. It originated with a learned and godly man names John N. Darby, the founder of the group known as Plymouth Brethren.

The most important and distinctive doctrine of the dispensationalists is their view of the kingdom of heaven and the Christian church. They believe that Jesus came to establish a visible rule on this earth, and that this is what John the Baptist referred to when he preached that the kingdom of heaven was at hand. The Jews, however, not being willing to accept the kingdom on Christ's terms, the offer was withdrawn and the establishment of the kingdom was postponed until the Second Advent. During the interim, Christ established his church, which is not in any sense a fulfillment of the Old Testament promises, but something new, unknown to the prophets, constituting no part of the continuous development of Israel. It is a "parenthesis in history." It will come to an end in the "Rapture," whereby is meant the sudden, miraculous removal of all true believers to meet Christ in the air. This will be the first stage of the Second Advent. It will be visible to the believers but not to the world at large. The public, visible stage of the Second Advent will be seven years later and is called "The Revelation." This period of seven years, they hold, corresponds to the seventieth week of the prophecy in the ninth chapter of Daniel. The sixty-nine weeks ran out at the first coming of Christ, but with the rejection of Christ by the Jews and the postponement of the kingdom, prophetic time ceased to run. As Dr. Ironside puts it: "The prophetic clock stopped at Calvary. Not one tick has been heard since." ("The Mysteries of God," p. 54)

During the said seven years the Antichrist will rule. The Jews being then restored to Palestine, he will make a covenant with them for the restoration of their worship, for seven years. The temple will be rebuilt at Jerusalem, the Ten Tribes regathered, and the sacrificial system reinstated. In the meantime, although all true believers were taken from the earth at the "Rapture," that startling event will result in many real conversions of those left behind. These believers in Christ will eventually be saved, but they form no part of the "church," the body of Christ, properly speaking. They are called, in the literature of this group, the "tribulation saints," because they pass through the tribulation caused by the bad faith of the Antichrist, who will break his covenant with the Jews at the end of three and a half years, and will demand to be worshiped. The refusal of the true Christians and of faithful Jews, although not Christians, will bring upon them this terrible period of persecution. At the end of it, when they are almost overwhelmed, will occur the public manifestation of Christ, the second stage of the Second Advent. He will them destroy the Antichrist and establish his visible earthly kingdom, which will continue for a thousand years.

How this system influences their interpretation of the Apocalypse will be evident from one or two quotations. Dr. J. A. Seiss, in his Lectures on the Apocalypse, Vol. I, p. 106, 108, says:

> The present order, so far as respects the church on earth, must wind up and close, before one particle of this book, beyond the third chapter, in any full and proper sense, can be fulfilled. ...The true and proper fulfillment of everything beyond the third chapter is to take place only after the Church has run its course, completed its history, and received its judgment.

Thus, in this amazing interpretation, we are invited to believe that the book of Revelation, throughout the greater part of it, has nothing to do with the Christian church, its dangers, conflicts and triumphs.

The Rev. H. Bultema, another exponent of this school, says of the seventieth week of Daniel:

This year-week is the brief period during which occur all the terrible judgments of Revelation 6 to 19.[1]

It is impossible for me to accept this view. The whole Darbyite dispensational system, as taught in the Scofield Bible, seems to me unscriptural and unsound from the bottom up. To those who wish to go into the matter carefully, I recommend the books of Philip Mauro: "The Gospel of the Kingdom of God," "The Seventy Weeks and the Great Tribulation," and "The Hope of Israel, What It Is." Mr. Mauro was himself at one time an adherent of this school, but further Bible study convinced him that it was in error.

There are, however, other Futurists, who do not accept dispensationalism, or accept it only with important modifications. Among these is Dr. Henry Frost, who, in his "The Second Coming of Christ," rejects the distinction between the "Rapture" and the "Revelation," believing that the church passes through the tribulation. With regard to the interpretation of the book of Revelation, this modification is very important, for it takes away the necessity of crowding all its scenes into the short space of seven years. Dr. Frost is a Futurist, for he believes in the coming of a personal Antichrist and in the literal rebuilding of Babylon on the Euphrates. Hence he does not consider the Second Coming "imminent," in the sense that it may happen any day, but "impending," in the sense that not many years remain.

One of the most recent learned commentaries to take the Futurist position is that of Dr. Theodor Zahn, unfortunately not yet, so far as I know, translated into English. This is free from the dispensationalism of which I have spoken, but the author agrees with the fundamental Futurist idea that the events predicted in the Apocalypse belong to the "End-time," and therefore still lie in the future on our days. He believes that they are to take place shortly before the Second Coming of Christ. The same general positional is taken in the post-humously published commentary by Dr. Abraham Kuyper, who was neither a dispensationalist nor a millenarian.

Almost all Futurists begin their futurism with the fourth chapter, accepting the seven letters of chapters two and three as written to actual churches of St. John's time; but Dr. Alexander Murray of Sydney, in Australia, holds that they were not written to contemporary Christian churches but to "Jewish assemblies that will come into existence in the fu-

[1] p. 19

ture." For this he adduces as proof that an ancient heretical sect, the Alogi, denied the existence of any church in the city of Thyatira. Dr. Murray says that this denial is accepted by Tertullian and Epiphanius, but he gives no chapter and verse references to their works. I have not been able to check up these alleged confirmations of the statement made by the Alogi, although I have found a reference to it in R. H. Charles, Vol. I, p. c. No ancient writer took their objection seriously, and neither does any of the great modern commentators. I think we may as well forget it. The theory Dr. Murray lays down that the apostle wrote these messages to churches not yet in existence, but to come into existence in the time of the end is so fantastic as to deserve no refutation.

Against Futurism as such, apart from special objections to Darbyite dispensationalism, it seems to me that the following arguments have great weight:

1. It is inconsistent with the very emphatic statement of the book itself, that the events predicted would soon come to pass, or at least soon begin to come to pass. We read,

> The Revelation of Jesus Christ, which God gave unto him to show unto his servants things which must shortly come to pass. (1.1)
>
> Blessed is he that readeth and they that hear the words of this prophecy and keep those things that are written therein, for the time is at hand.

How in the world is the fundamental Futurist idea, that for eighteen hundred years nothing foretold in the Apocalypse, from the beginning of chapter 4 on, has yet happened, to be reconciled with this emphatic statement that the time of fulfillment was near? To be sure, we ought not to stretch these words to cover everything in the book, for the last judgment also finds a place in it, but certainly it is quite beyond the bounds of any reasonable interpretation to consider nothing as yet fulfilled. Approaching the shores of the United States by sea, one can say with perfect propriety: "We are getting close to America now," without forgetting or denying that the furthest limit of America is still three thousand miles away. So, if the prophecy deals with things that began to happen not long after it was written, this statement is true in its natural sense, even though the completion of the fulfillment is not attained for two millenniums more.

It is interesting to see by what curious exegetical methods the dispensationalists render void this word of scripture. The Scofield Bible, not with direct reference to this passage, but to the preaching of John the Baptist, explains the expression "at hand" to mean only that no event foretold in prophecy must take place before the event that is said to be "at hand." (Scofield Bible, Page 998)

The best answer to this is a flat denial. Neither in Greek nor in English, nor in any other language under heaven can the words "at hand" or "near," mean such a thing. No one would ever have thought that they meant any such thing, had not the demands of a highly artificial system demanded here an equally artificial interpretation.

Bultema has another way of getting around it. He falls back upon the idea that, in the Holy Scriptures, time is reckoned only with reference to Israel, and that the church age is a "parenthesis." He says:[2]

> Both the reader and the interpreter of this book should bear in mind that in it not our ordinary human method of reckoning time, but God's, is used. It is frequently said in the Revelation that the Lord will come quickly—1.1, 3; 3.11; 22.7; 10.30. But since that time nineteen centuries have passed, and the Lord has not yet come on the clouds of heaven. …The solution of this difficulty lies simply herein, the prophecy is based not on our reckoning of time but the Lord's. God's method of reckoning has this peculiarity, that the Church of the New Covenant and the absence of Christ lie entirely outside of this reckoning; and further, that time is reckoned according to Israel only. During the rejection of Israel in this dispensation it stands sill, absolutely.

This idea that prophetic time is reckoned only in relation to Israel seems to me quite as unfounded as the "year-day" systems, which Mr. Bultema emphatically and rightly rejects. Isaiah certainly reckoned time with relation to Moab and Tyre, (16.14; 23.15) and Ezekiel did the same in relation to Egypt, (29.11). What right has any one, then, to lat down the above rule? It is only the "parenthesis theory" that leads men to such a notion, but that theory itself is, in my judgment, wholly unscriptural. I see nothing for it but to accept as it stands the statement that the time was at hand when the book of Revelation was written. If so accepted, it is fatal to the Futurist interpretation in all its forms.

2. This system leaves the Apocalypse quite out of relation to the needs of the church to which it was addressed.

---

[2]pp. 13–14.

This objection has already been raised against the "Continuous-Historical" view. It applies with added force to the "Futurist." It is one of the great basic principles of prophecy that it takes its start with the generation to which it is addressed, and has primarily its origin in the need of that generation for comfort, warning, instruction, etc. The more we come to know of the historical circumstances under which the prophets of the Old Testament delivered their messages, the more clearly do we perceive this to be the case. This is one of the great gains that have come from the Bible study of the last fifty years. Isaiah, Jeremiah, Ezekiel, Daniel, and as many as we have spoken, have proceeded in this way. We may lay it down as a rule to which no exceptions are to be allowed, or, if any, then only on the clearest evidence: *Prophecy begins with its own generation.*

This is not the same thing as saying that it stops there! Far from it. Beginning with the needs of the people before and during the Babylonian captivity, the vision of the prophets stretched out for centuries to come, until the time of Christ and the establishment of his kingdom on earth. So, in the Revelation also, we must be prepared to find predictions that were fulfilled long after the time of John, or that have not yet been fulfilled. Nevertheless, unless this is a sort of magical performance, quite out of line with the rest of prophecy, it must have been to some degree intelligible to, and of value for, the church of the second century. Hence Dr. H. B. Swete seems to me correct when he says: (p. ccxiv)

> No one who realizes that the prophecy is an answer to the crying needs of the seven churches will dream of treating it as a detailed forecast of the course of mediaeval and modern history in Western Europe.

Still less, of course, will such an interpreter dream of treating it along Futurist lines.

3. In addition to the two general considerations given above, much in the visions seems to me utterly incompatible with Futurism. This will appear later, in the discussion of the various scenes, particularly the twelfth chapter. That seems to me most clearly to speak of the birth of Christ and the immediately succeeding events, but the Futurists are obliged by their principle to explain it of the Israel of the end-time, thus making the Revelation, at its very center, a Jewish rather than a Christian book. Dr. H. Grattan Guinness, a prominent pre-millenarian, presents a strong argument against the Futurist and dispensationalist view in his "Approaching End of the Age," p. 132–138. He concludes by saying:

We claim that without all contradiction, the church is on earth during the action of the Apocalypse, and that therefore the Apocalypse is a Christian prophecy, fulfilled in the events of the Christian Era.

VI

PRINCIPLES OF INTERPRETATION

We have seem what the chief systems of interpretation are, and have reminded ourselves that each of them is represented by scholarly and believing advocates; but they are mutually inconsistent, and we can not follow
them all. Which shall we adopt as our guide in this study?

My own decision is to side with the *Preterists*, for the most part, but
mixing in, to a considerable degree, the views of what I have called the
"Philosophy of History" school. These two are not incompatible with one another, for any symbol, understood by the latter to refer to a certain force or
tendency may find an appropriate application to some great even in early
church history. In such a case, both the older schools and the Philosophy
of History school will point to that event as a fulfillment of the prophecy,
but to the Preterist or the Historicist it is the event itself to which the
prophecy referred, while to the others it is the force or agency, which may
be found in other events as well. Hence, to this last school, any prophecy
in the book of Revelation may have repeated fulfillments.

My decision, as above, results in my adopting the following principles
of interpretation.

1. The writer must be supposed to have written primarily for the encouragement and edification of the church of his own time. Therefore the
circumstances of the early church must be carefully studied, and, as far as
possible, the symbols must be explained in terms of persons, events, trials,
dangers, and triumphs related to them. This is the fundamental Preterist
principle, and it seems to me sound. If you take the Historicist position,
you must believe that the Holy Spirit supplied to the distressed and persecuted sub-apostolic church a to them utterly unintelligible program of
church history, having only a very little to do with them, occupied chiefly

with the events of mediaeval and modern Europe; if the Futurist, that he informed them of what was to take place at so remote a period that after eighteen hundred years nothing of it has yet to begun to happen. "He that is able to receive it, let him receive it"—I cannot.

H. B. Swete, in what seems to me the very best extant commentary on the Apocalypse, states the view to which I have myself come as follows: (p. ccxiii)

> Another important landmark for the guidance of the interpreter is to be found in the purpose of the book and the historical surroundings of its origin. The Apocalypse is cast in the form of a letter to certain Christian societies, and it opens with a detailed account of their conditions and circumstances. Only the most perverse ingenuity can treat the messages to the seven churches as directly prophetical. The book starts with a well defined historical situation, to which reference is made again at the end, and the intermediate visions, which form the body of the work, can not on any reasonable theory be disassociated from their historical setting. The prophecy arises out of local and temporary circumstances; it is, in the first instance at least, the answer of the Spirit to the fears and perils of the Asian Christians toward the end of the first century. Hence all that can throw light on the Asia of AD 70–100, and upon Christian life in Asia during that period, is of primary importance to the student of the Apocalypse, not only in view of the local allusions in (chapters 2–3), but as helping to determine the aim and drift of the entire work. No one who realizes that the prophecy is an answer to the crying needs of the seven churches will dream of treating it as a detailed forecast of the course of mediaeval and modern history in Western Europe. So far as the Apocalyptist reveals the future, he reveals it not with the view of exercising the ingenuity of remote generations, but for the practical purpose of inculcating those great lessons of trust in God, loyalty to the Christ, king, confidence in the ultimate triumph of righteousness, patience under adversity, and hope in the prospect of death, which were urgently needed by the Asian churches, and will never be without meaning and importance so long as the world lasts.
>
> It will all be seen that an interpretation conducted upon these lines will have points of contact with each of the chief systems of Apocalyptic exegesis, without identifying itself with any one of them as a whole. With the 'preterists' it will take its stand on the circumstances of the age and locality to which the book belongs, and will connect the greater part of the prophecy with the destinies of the Empire under which the prophet lived; with the 'futurists' it will look for fulfillment of St. John's pregnant

words in times yet to come. With the school of Auberien and Benson it will find in the Apocalypse a Christian philosophy of history; with the 'continuous-historical' school it can see in the progress of events ever new illustrations of the working of the great principles which are revealed.

2. When we have found an event to which, or a person to whom, the prophecy is fairly applicable, we may consider it fulfilled in such an event or person, but not therefore exhausted; for it is intended more for the purpose of showing us the forces, for good and "evil, that make history, than for the prediction of particular events. This is the chief principle of the "Philosophy of History" school, and this also seems to me sound. There is not necessarily any inconsistency between this and the Preterist position: therefore, it seems to me that we can hold the two together.

3. The Book of Revelation (after the first three chapters) is a divine picture book, a book of spiritual cartoons, a pictorial presentation, through symbols, of certain forces which underlie the historical development of the Christian church and its unceasing conflict. Therefore, the ordinary rule of interpretation must be reversed in our study of it. Ordinarily, the words of any passage of scripture must be understood in their plain and natural sense, unless there is reason to take them figuratively. The presumption is always in favor of the literal sense: if any man takes it otherwise, he must show his cause. This is not so in the Revelation. Here, the entire book being in the realm of pictorial, i.e. symbolical presentation, we are to assume that any picture shown to us has a symbolic meaning; unless it is clear that the expression must be taken literally. Here the symbolical, not the literal, interpretation has the right of way. If two interpretations are possible, one being the literal meaning of the words and one a symbolical sense in harmony with the general nature of the book, the latter is to be preferred.

We have therefore, with regard to any complete scene in the Apocalypse, two duties instead of only one, as in the ordinary books of the Bible. To illustrate, when we read of the fight of David with Goliath, we seek to see the picture set before us, the giant, the youth, the sling, the fall and death of Goliath, etc. When we have seen this, we have seen all there is to see. We may then proceed to use the story to teach courage, faith in God, the duty of slaying giants of sin in our own day, etc., etc., but this is to use the story, not to interpret it. When we see, in the twelfth chapter of Revelation, on the other hand, the scene of the fight between Michael and his angels on the one hand and the Dragon with his angels on the other, we must equally seek to understand the passage just as it lies before us; but having done that, we must ask: "What does this symbolize?" We must take it, not as information concerning heavenly battles, but as symbolizing some fact or truth in the spiritual life or the experience of the church. It will be seen how fundamentally I disagree with such a writer as H. Bultema, who says (p. 20) "Revelation must, as far as possible, be understood literally." In my judgment, such a writer starts off in the wrong direction and the further he goes along that line the less he will understand the meaning of the book. In that canon of interpretation he shows that he has not grasped the "apocalyptic" character of the composition. He is applying to it the exegetical principle that is appropriate in other books, not here.

No one, of course, understands the Revelation literally in all its parts. Even Bultema recognizes much that is symbolical, but many writers pass from the symbolical to the literal interpretation in an arbitrary manner. Every one, for instance, sees that the woman in chapter 12 must be a symbol although there is difference of opinion as to what she symbolizes. Yet the immediately following account of the war among the angels is accepted as literal information. If the Apocalypse is really such a book, passing from symbolism to literal information without notice and without any apparent reason, then certainly the task of the interpreter is a hopeless one. Hence it seems to me that we must try resolutely to apply the symbolical interpretation everywhere. We must always ask two questions: first, "What is the picture?," and then, "What does the picture mean?" Thus, when we read in the eleventh chapter of the two witnesses, we must not ask who they are but what they and their witness symbolize; so also with the war in heaven, so with the battle of chapter nineteen, so especially with the first resurrection and the thousand years of chapter 20. We must not take it as information that there will be such a resurrection and such a period of imprisonment for the devil, but we must ask what is symbolized by such things.

4. The meaning of the symbols is to be sought in the "usus loquendi," that is, the manner of speaking, of the prophetic portions of the Old Testament, especially the "apocalyptic" portions of Ezekiel, Daniel, and Zechariah. There is no other book of the New Testament so thoroughly permeated with Old Testament expressions and imagery as the Revelation. The writer was certainly a man "mighty in the scriptures." To a much less extent, but yet really to come extent, it is useful to compare the characteristic "usus loquendi" of the uncanonical apocalyptic books discussed in a former chapter.

5. In interpreting the visions, we must seek to grasp the significance of any one vision or any series of visions as a whole without entering much into details. I have no doubt that sometimes the details also have significance, but I feel sure that often they merely belong to the "scenery" of the vision, without having themselves any distinct meaning. This is often so in poetry, and the Apocalypse, while not in form a poem, is essentially poetic. Read, for instance, the Ninety-first psalm, in the following verses:

Thou shalt not be afraid for the terror by night,
Nor for the arrow that flieth by day;
For the pestilence that walketh in darkness;
Nor for the destruction that wasteth at noonday.

Taken in connection with the whole purpose of the psalm, as building up by concrete details the idea that the believer is always under the protecting care of God, this is fine, and true. Take any of the details buy itself, and it is not true. Believers fall in battle, are ill with contagious diseases, etc., as well as others. The details are not intended to be so taken. They are intended, by their cumulative effect, to assure men that God cares for those who trust in Him, and that all things work together for good to them. So also, I believe, it is with some of the scenes of the Revelation. Take, for instance, chapter 6.12–17. Taken as a while, it makes an overwhelming impression of approaching doom and of human terror, but it is worse than useless to ask what is meant by the falling stars, the removal of the heavens, and the moving of the mountains.

6. Finally, it is important to bear in mind that the Revelation addresses itself chiefly to the imagination. God who made man, and knows what is in him, in preparing the Book, took care to attune different portions of it to different keys. The Epistle to the Romans appeals to the reasoning faculty, the Psalms to the emotions, the commandments to the will. This book appeals to the imagination, one of the noblest of all the faculties with which the human mind is endowed. As you read it, you must deliberately seek to see in your mind's eye the various dramatic episodes, as if you were standing with St. John when he saw the visions. You must yield yourself to the majesty of the scenery and to the sublimity of the music. Unless you can do this, you will not get much good out of the book. If a man has no imagination, or is afraid to use it in his Bible study, he will do well to let this book alone. This is, if I may so call it, an "impressionist" book, one intended far more to create a certain impression than to give

information. Many years ago I heard a lecture by Dr. V. Hepp, of Amsterdam. Speaking of the great hail, every hailstone the weight of a talent, (more than a hundred pounds) he said: "Naturally, you do not take this literally, but you get the impression." That is the point. The great thing in reading the Revelation is to get the impression. I will not discourage any one from careful study, and do not dent that he does well who seeks to know the meaning of every detail, so far as it can be ascertained; but this I do say, that he who uses the book to get an overwhelming *impression* of majesty, and reverence, and awe, and assurance of victory, and certainty that, come what may, Christ is supreme, that man makes the right use of the book, even though he be wrong in almost every point of interpretation.

VII

A BIRD'S-EYE VIEW OF REVELATION

In seeking to become acquainted with an unfamiliar country, it is often helpful to ascend a slight elevation, and to get a bird's-eye view, locating, in their respective relations, the forest, the river, the meadows, the hills, and the other features of the landscape, before making a closer examination of any of them.

If we undertake this task with respect to the Apocalypse, we immediately perceive that the actual message begins with the fourth verse of the first chapter. The first three verses are a title, and read as if they were added by those to whom the book was addressed; perhaps written on the outside of the manuscript roll, contained in a box with others belonging to the church, to distinguish it from them.

Similarly, we recognized in 1.4–8 the salutation of the apostle, and in the ninth verse the beginning of his communication, which is an account of his vision of the glorified Christ and how he was commanded by Him to write to the churches. This is introductory, and the message to the churches, strictly speaking, begins with the second chapter.

It ends with the seventh verse of chapter 22. From 22.8 on we see at once that the "Revelation" is over. John now begins to speak about his book. Strictly speaking, he is no longer writing it. This may be called the "Epilogue."

The main body of the book, therefore, is from the beginning of the second chapter to the seventh verse of the twenty-second, and in this main body the letters to the seven churches individually are easily recognized as a separate section. I say expressly, the messages to the seven individually, for the whole nook is a message to the churches, collectively.

What sections shall we recognize on what remains, namely, from 4.1–

22.8? Here it is more difficult to make a satisfactory analysis, and the schemes offered by commentators differ. Any one can see that the seven seals, the seven trumpets, and the seven vials, or bowls, form distinct sections, but how is the intervening material to be distributed, and what is the larger plan of the work?

Zahn divides the whole into ten divisions, as follows: I—1.9–3.33; II—4.1–8.1; III—8.2–11.19; IV—12.1–15.4; V—15.5–16.21; VI—17.1–18; VII—18.1–24; VIII—19/1–21; IX—20.1–21.8; X—21.9–22.7; Epilogue: 22.8–21.

Dr. S. L. Morris, in "The Drama of Christianity," divides the material into "Cycles," as follows: First Cycle: The "Seven Churches," Types of Spiritual Life; Second Cycle: "Seals"—Agencies Employed; Third Cycle: "Trumpets"—Judgments upon the World; Fourth Cycle: "Dragon" and "Beasts,"—Trinity of Evil; Fifth Cycle: "Vials"—Judgment of Apostasy; Sixth Cycle: "Babylon"—Judgment of "Beast" and "False Prophet"; Seventh Cycle: "Thousand Years"—Judgment of Satan and the Dead; Finally. Not classed as a "Cycle," "The New Jerusalem"—Eternity—Epilogue.

In this interpretation, each "Cycle" is, in general, considered to cover the entire Christian dispensation, between the First and Second Advents of Christ.

Joseph Mede, (died 1638) one of the earliest Protestant interpreters, takes the contrast between the Great Book, Sealed, (5.1) and the Little Book, Open, (10.2) as significant for the divisions of the Apocalypse, and is seems to me that he is right. If so, we have in this the writer's own indication that from 4.1–11.19 must be regarded as in some sense a whole, contrasted with 12.1–22.7. Although the eleventh chapter stands after the gift of the Little Book, Open, to the seer, yet it must be regarded as belonging to the former section, since it is in the latter part of that chapter that the seventh angel sounds his trumpet and the final end of the world is reached in the Judgment Day. Whether 11.19 belongs to the same section or ought to have been made the first verse of the next chapter, is a disputed point, not to be confidently determined. I prefer the division into chapters as it stands, making 12.1 a new beginning.

If we are right in considering the Great Book section and the Little Book section thus contrasted with one another, what is the point of the contrast? It will appear in full, of course, only in the interpretation, but it may be briefly stated as follows: The Great Book is God's secret counsel with regard to judging a sinful world; the Little Book His revealed counsel with regard to the Christian church and her conflict with her foes. The Great Book has a larger scope; therefore it is the Great Book. It involves the fortunes of all mankind. It is also "sealed," that is secret, known to no one, read by no one, revealed to no one, but to Jesus Christ, who is the Administrator of Judgment, the Executive Officer of the Universe, the Prime Minister of God. On this section men do not fight God, they are helpless in His hands. The church as church is not found here, although provision is made for the safety of all those who belong to God in the midst of the storms of judgment which He brings upon the world because of the sins of men, especially because of the innocent martyr-blood shed upon the earth.

The center of gravity of the second section is entirely different. The action is no longer so "transcendent," that is, the thing in the foreground is no longer what is determined in heaven and sent down from heaven upon the earth: everything is viewed from the standpoint of the church militant, her glory, her foes, her sufferings, her conflicts, and her eventual triumph. God intervenes on her behalf, to be sure, by pouring out His wrath upon her foes, and by sending in chapter nineteen, a heavenly army to fight for her, but nevertheless the great subject of the section remains what the church is, does, and suffers, rather than what God is and does, as it was before. That the church is to have such experiences must not be kept secret from God's people, lest they faint in the midst of the trial; therefore the book is not only open, but the seer is expressly told to eat it, that is, thoroughly to familiarize himself with it, that he may tell is to his brethren.

Thus we have here two great panoramas, dramas, or pageants,—choose the word that suits you best—namely: THE SOLEMN PAGEANT OF THE DIVINE JUDGMENTS and THE DRAMA OF THE WOMAN AND THE DRAGON.

These two constitute the main body of Revelation. The reader will see that this conception of the book has given rise to the title of this discussion: "THE LAMB, THE WOMAN, AND THE DRAGON." In the Great Book section, the Lamb is the dominant figure: in the Little Book section, the chief characters are the Woman and the Dragon, and the two sections are finally seen to be two parts of one whole when, the Dragon and his allies being overcome, the Lamb marries the Woman and lives with her in a beautiful home for evermore.

VIII

THE INTRODUCTION

We are now ready to begin a study of the text. As already remarked, it is not my purpose in this book to write a commentary, in the ordinary sense of that word, expounding the book verse by verse, but rather to discuss the outstanding problems of interpretation, with special attention to some of the more important verses, as may seem most profitable.

The title calls it (1.1) the "unveiling" of Jesus Christ, which must be understood to mean, not something that unveils Him, but an unveiling wrought by Him and belonging to Him; an unveiling peculiarly His own, to which he, and He alone, has a right. It comes to us from Him and through Him.

We read again that it is something "which God gave him to show unto his servants." Its origin lies, therefore, even further back than Jesus Christ. It comes as a gift from the Triune God, handed on to us by Jesus Christ as the Mediator between God and man. The Lord Jesus Christ has the three offices of Prophet, Priest, and King. In this first verse, it is in the capacity of prophet that He presents himself. This book is therefore a step in advance in Christ's revelation of God and the truth of God. We may expect it to contain something additional, something not previously sufficiently and clearly set forth. It is also the final utterance of the greatest of all prophets, in His exalted and heavenly state. It is no wonder that the church, receiving such a book, placed it at the end of the inspired volume, as the capstone of all inspiration; and has ever since steadfastly refused to believe that anything further can be added.

We read further, in the same verse, that the things revealed in this book *"must shortly come to pass,"* an assurance repeated in the third verse in these words: *"the time is at hand."* These words seem to me consistent either with the Preterist or the Historicist system of interpretation, but, as already said in a previous chapter, they seem to me decisive against the fundamental idea of the Futurist interpretation, according to which nothing of the prophetic portion has yet begun to be fulfilled.

The third verse pronounces a special blessing upon him who reads and those that hear the words of the prophecy. Notice the singular number in the case of the reader and the plural number in the case of the hearers. "He that readeth and they that hear." Evidently, our book was intended for public reading, in the assemblies of the church. That was the only way in which most of the members could become familiar with it, for the ordinary Christian could not read, and books were far too expensive to be found in any homes but those of the wealthy. Zahn (p.1–3) supplies interesting evidence that the Apocalypse really was so read in the churches, and that the Christians of the second and third centuries were familiar with it. He says:[1]

> From no other Biblical book did the Christians of that day, (referring to about AD 200) laymen as well as clergy, women as well as men, draw an equal degree of comfort amid the sufferings of the persecution and of courage for the confession of their faith by word and blood.

This importance of reading in the public assemblies has been greatly lessened by the invention of printing and the general ability of people to read. At present there is but little public reading for the sake of making people acquainted with the contents of a book or document. It is simpler and better to hand it out in printed form. Yet we do still read from the Holy Scriptures in public worship. How seldom are such portions taken from the book of Revelation! Alford, commenting on this verse, complains that, with one or two exceptions, none of the designated readings of the Church of England are taken from this prophecy. Non-episcopal churches have usually no such fixed list of required readings, but the practice of such churches is not at all different from that of which Dr. Alford complains in his own church. If our ministers continue in this manner to ignore the book of Revelation, they incur a just retribution of earnest but ill informed men outside the regular pulpits undertake to expound it, and if the Lord's people run after such men to receive what they can not get from their own pastors.

---

[1] Vol. I, p.1.

Verses four and five are the salutation, and it opens with familiar words: *"Grace to you and peace."* This is the characteristic Pauline salutation. It does not occur in the three epistles of John, in the Hebrews, or in James and Jude; although we find it in the two of Peter. It is as if John desires here to link himself with St. Paul, since the churches to which his Revelation is primarily addressed were largely, if not all, founded by Paul or by Paul's assistants.

But if the words "Grace to you and peace" here reminds us of Paul, the rest of the salutation is very different. This grace must come "from him who is, and who was, and who is to come; and from the seven spirits that are before his throne, and from Jesus Christ." Here we have the Trinitarian formula of blessing, but in a new form. For "God the Father" we have "He who is and who was and who is coming." At this point we have an interesting divergence from the rules of Greek grammar. The preposition "from" is, in Greek, "apo," and it requires the noun or pronoun following to be in the genitive case, but the word following is in the nominative. This grammatical irregularity does not appear in the English, either in the Authorized or in the Revised Versions; but it is preserved in Dr. Moffatt's translation. He renders it: "Grace be to you and peace from HE WHO IS AND WAS AND IS COMING."[2] This is, no doubt, because the whole phrase is to be regarded as an indeclinable title. There is an interesting parallel to this usage in Rider Haggard's "She," where we find the title of the queen to be "She Who Must Be Obeyed," and when this title is preceded by a preposition, the pronoun "She" is not put into the objective case. Thus we have expressions like this, taken from chapter six, but common throughout the book: "Four suns since was the word brought to me from She Who Must Be Obeyed. ...Let them be brought to the land of She Who Must Be Obeyed." The very roughness of such an ungrammatical structure adds to its effectiveness. So it is with this expression in Revelation 1.4.

This title, literally, "The Being, the Was, the Coming," is an amplification of the name given by God to Moses, in Exodus 3.14: "Thus shalt thou say to the children of Israel, I AM hath sent me unto you." This is, in Greek, "Ho Ohn," THE BEING hath sent me. So St. John takes this word but puts it also in the past and in the future: THE BEING, THE WAS, THE COMING."

The appearance of the name of Jesus Christ as also a source of grace and peace, is what we are accustomed to in other places, but who or what

---

[2] James Moffatt: "The New Testament, A New Translation," p. 371.

is this: "The seven Spirits that are before the throne"? Dr. Moses Stuart, the great Andover expositor, understands this of the seven great angels, which, in Jewish apocalyptic books are said to stand always before the throne of God, and are called "The seven angels of the presence." The objection that at once occurs, and that is considered fatal to this interpretation by most commentators, is that grace and peace can not come to the soul from any created being, but are constantly said to come to us from God the Father and Jesus Christ our Lord, through the operation of the Holy Spirit. We have obviously here to do with a modification of the ordinary Trinitarian formula, and therefore must understand here the Holy Spirit. So almost all interpreters take it.

If this is correct, we get here our first lessons in the symbolism of numbers, as used in the book of Revelation, for the word "seven" here then does not mean seven *numerically*, but symbolically. It stands for one Holy Spirit in the sevenfold plentitude of his grace and power. It is well to remember this, for we shall find many cases in the book where numbers are used, not arithmetically, but spiritually. When we find the 42 months and the 1,260 days, and the thousand years, we shall not take it for granted thoughtlessly that these are to be understood in terms of ordinary arithmetic.

Following this greeting, we have a doxology, the first of many doxologies in the book, but this one from the heart of John himself:

> Unto him that loveth us, and loosed us from our sins by his blood; and he made us to be a kingdom, to be priests unto his God and Father; to him be the glory and the dominion for ever and ever. Amen.

This is from the Revised Version, and has two or three very interesting points of difference from the King James Version. Instead of "washed us from our sins" we have "loosed us." The difference rests upon a variation in the Greek manuscripts, some have the verb "luein" to loose, and others the verb "louein" to wash. The pronunciation being exactly the same, it is easy to see that as one person was dictating and several others were writing (a common method of preparing books in those days) some of the scribes wrote it one way and some the other. Either is true and makes good sense, but the rendering "to loose" may come to some of us with new force, and much needed force. It is, alas, only too evident that many Christians who believe they have been "washed" from their sins in the blood of Christ, have not been "loosed" from them. Christ's redemption is not only a washing, it is also a loosing.

Another difference is much more important. The new version, (also on the basis of better manuscripts) says: "He made is to be a kingdom," instead of "He made us kings" as the old version has it. There are some Bible students who are not willing to admit that Jesus is king of the church, or, indeed, a king at all, as yet.

Such students should reckon with the new reading of this sentence. "He made us to be a kingdom," sings John in his doxology. "I am your brother in the kingdom," he says to his fellow believers in the ninth verse of the same chapter. "Thou madest them to be unto our God a kingdom," sing the cherubim and the elders in 5.10. God "translated us into the kingdom," says Paul in Colossians 1.13. If we have been brought over into the kingdom of Christ, as Paul says; and if He has made us a kingdom, as John says; then "how say some among you" that there is as yet no kingdom? That Christ is on the throne of a kingdom may be learned also from 1 Corinthians 15.25: "For he must reign, till he hath put all his enemies under his feet." Some strangely turn this around, and tell us that Christ will begin to reign *when* all his enemies have been put under him. That is not what it says: He must reign *till* that takes place. He is reigning now—he has a kingdom, and we are it, says John, if we belong to Him. It is no wonder that those who have such views are Futurists in their interpretation of Revelation. They can not well be anything else, but in being Futurists, for such a reason, they seem to me to condemn their own system; for if there is anything that rings with triumphant confidence throughout this book it is that Christ is on the throne and therefore his people need have no fear.

This expression: "He hath made us to be a kingdom, and priests," is all the more interesting and important when we realize that it is taken from Exodus 19.6. Jehovah is there speaking to the people of Israel, and says to them: "Ye shall be unto me a kingdom of priests, and a holy nation." This was the high calling of Israel, announced as the purpose of that great organization covenant entered into at Sinai. It was not realized in them, but it is realized in us who believe in the Lord Jesus Christ. Here we find it stated as an accomplished fact: "He made us to be a kingdom, priests unto his God and Father." Who can fail to see that the destiny of Israel is continued and accomplished in the church of Jesus Christ?

The next verse at which we desire to pause is verse 10: "I was in the Spirit on the Lord's day." The expression, "In the Spirit" need not detain us. It is found also in Ezekiel 37.1, and plainly means a state of supernatural inspiration through ecstatic vision. The expression "on the Lord's day" is commonly, and I think rightly, understood of the first day of the week, our Sunday; but by some interpreters it is taken as an equivalent for another very common Scriptural expression, "The day of the Lord"; which means, in general, "God's time," the time when the Lord will carry out His purposes, usually purposes of judgment. Thus in the New Testament it usually means the day of the Lord's second coming, as in 2 Thessalonians 2.1–2: "Now we beseech you, brethren, …be not troubled… as that the day of the Lord is just at hand."

If this interpretation is adopted, the passage means that John was transported, through inspiration, to that future day of the Second Advent, and was shown what must then take place. This view is, of course, in the interests of the Futurist interpretation. Although some good scholars, such as Wetstein, Todd, Maitland, and others, are said to have adopted it, I think we may, without hesitation, in company with the great majority of interpreters, reject it. The two expressions, "The Lord's Day" and "The Day of the Lord" are, in the English, precise verbal equivalents, the one to the other; but they are not so in Greek, where the former is "kuriake hemera," and the latter, "hemera tou kuriou." It is the latter that is the Greek translation of the Old Testament, "Day of Jehovah." The former is the feminine form of the adjective found also in 1 Corinthians 11.20. "kuriakon deipnon," the Lord's supper; the supper especially instituted by the Lord Jesus, to be observed in remembrance of Him. So when the same adjective is applied to a day, and that day is called "kuriake hemera," it means the day observed in remembrance of the Lord Jesus, namely, of His resurrection; which is, Sunday, the first day of the week. In this sense the word is used frequently in the earliest Christian writings, in the Didache, or Teaching of the Twelve Apostles, in Ignatius, in the Gospel of Peter, and in Melito of Sardis. (Swete, p. 13) Alford puts it strongly: "It really is astonishing how any even moderate Greeks scholars can persuade themselves that the words can mean that which these commentators maintain."[3]

We now come to the command to John that he shall write to the seven churches, and to the vision that met his eyes when he turned to see from whom the voice came. We have already said that the book of Revelation must be looked upon as a great picture book, a gallery of symbolic scenes through which certain great impressions are made upon the soul of the

---

[3] Vol. IV, Part II, p. 554.

reverent reader. With this thought in mind, let us read the description of the Lord Jesus, as John saw Him in the vision:

> Having turned, I saw seven golden candlesticks; and in the midst of the candlesticks one like unto a son of man, clothed with a garment down to the foot, and girt about at the breasts with a golden girdle. And his head and his hair were white as white wool, white as snow; and his eyes were as a flame of fire; and his feet like unto burnished brass, as if it had been refined in a furnace; and his voice as the voice of many waters. And he had in his right hand seven stars; and out of his mouth proceeded a sharp two-edged sword: and his countenance was as the sun shineth in his strength. (RV)

Dr. J.A. Seiss, in his "Lectures on Revelation," well says:

> If a sublimer conception of Divine and glorified humanity, so true to the Saviour's offices and work, ever entered into the imagination of man, I have never seen it, and never heard of it. (p. 86)

We agree heartily; but we are shocked to read, in the same lecture, that Dr. Seiss considers this to be an exact and literal description of the Lord Jesus, in His present form of existence. He says:[4]

> For my own part, I believe that our blessed Lord is at this moment arrayed just as he is here described, and that is the dress in which He will deal with the churches, and be seen of the saints, when the judgment begins.

By such literalism he spoil it all. How a man can think such things is beyond my understanding. Does he then suppose that there is an actual and literal sword, a piece of cutting steel, coming out of the mouth of our Lord? This description is "for inspiration, not for information," as one of my colleagues on the seminary faculty has well put it. We are not to try, even to get from it any information as to the way the Lord Jesus now looks or is dressed. No such questions must be allowed to interfere with the impression, the inspiration, of the passage. We are intended to yield ourselves completely to the glorious majesty and sublimity of the scene, and to fall down, as John did, before the regnant and triumphant Christ.

In verse 17 Zahn has a beautiful and very attractive translation, which

---

[4] Vol. I, p. 78.

I have not found elsewhere. Instead of "Fear not, I am the first and the last, and the Living one," he has "Fear not, It is I, the first and the last, and the Living One."[5] This he brings into connection with Matthew 14.27 and Mark 6.50. He thinks John's memory must at once have gone back to that wild night on the sea, when the same words came across the waves: "It is I, fear not." The Greek can bear this rendering, and it adds a touch of tenderness that is welcome in so overwhelmingly grand a scene.

---

[5] Vol. I, p. 204.

IX

THE LETTERS TO THE SEVEN CHURCHES

In his very first vision, St. John sees Christ in the midst of seven golden candlesticks, and these are explained as meaning the seven churches of the Roman province of Asia, in the western section of what we now call Asia Minor. Thus, as we got our first lesson in the symbolism of numbers when the one Holy Spirit was spoken of as the "seven Spirits that are before His throne," so now we get an elementary lesson on the symbolism of things. "The seven candlesticks are seven churches." It is an easy lesson, for we can readily see why a candlestick, or, rather, a lampstand, is an appropriate symbol of the church, or of any local church. The Lord Jesus made us familiar with the basic idea when He said: "Ye are the light of the world... neither do men light a lamp and put it under the bushel, but on the stand. ...Even so let your light shine before men." St. Paul probably heard of this teaching. At any rate he was in line with it when he said to the faithful Philippians: "Ye are seen as lights in the world." (Phil 2.15) It is basically the same idea when he speaks of the church of the living God as "the pillar and ground of the truth." The church is the trustee of the gospel, and holds it up to enlighten the world, as a lighthouse, firmly based on a rock, holds up the light. There is no inconsistency in taking the light as sometimes the gospel and sometimes the believer, for the gospel of Christ accomplishes nothing in the world but through those who accept it, and make its light manifest in word and deed.

The words "golden candlesticks," are no doubt intended to carry our thoughts back to the tabernacle and temple worship, where there were seven lamps, although all upon one golden candlestick. It is common for the Revelation to take an Old Testament figure in this way, and freely to adapt it to the New Testament conditions. So long as worship was centered, by divine appointment, in one sanctuary, it was appropriate that there should be one lampstand only, but the days had come of which the Lord Jesus spoke to the woman at the well of Sychar: "The hour cometh, when neither in this mountain nor in Jerusalem, shall ye worship the Father." That being the case, it was right that each lamp should have its own stand, and that there should be seven instead of one. To use the symbol of the lampstand for the visible and organized local church is most appropriate also in this, that as the golden lampstand, precious though it can be, can not itself give light but only holds up the light, so with the church. It has no light of its own, but it holds up the light. This is the chief duty of any local church, its reason and excuse for existence in the world.

So far the interpretation is easy; but what of the seven stars? "The seven stars are the angels of the seven churches." Here is an explanation that needs itself to be explained. Who are these "angels?" Four interpretations claim our attention.

1. That they are messengers of the churches, sent to visit John in his exile at Patmos.

So, among others, the Scofield Bible. This is very unsatisfactory. The only point in its favor is that the Greek word "aggelos" does, in its primary significance, denote a messenger. It is so used in some places of the New Testament, although the prevailing sense is that of our English word "angel."

Against it is the obvious consideration that, in times of persecution, when the purpose of the authorities was to suppress the Christian movement, the visit of such a delegation to John would scarcely have been permitted. It is no answer to say that St. Paul received such visitors in prison, for the charge against him was a personal one, and his imprisonment was no part of any governmental policy. If messengers from the churches had undertaken to visit John secretly in disguise, there would hardly have been more than one or two, whereas here we have seven. Further, the letters contain no reference whatever to such messengers, or any acknowledgement of the courtesy of the churches in sending them. Compare with this St. Paul's hearty thanks for such a kindness on the part of the church of Philippi. (Phil 4.10–18) Thirdly, the language used: "to the angel of the church at _____ write, " is not in accordance with this interpretation, for one does not write to a messenger who is present in person: one speaks to him, or gives him a written message to carry back to the church. Finally, a mere messenger could not be held responsible for the spiritual state of the church from which he came, as the "angel" is constantly held responsible in the various letters.

2. That these "angels" are real angels, heavenly beings, the guardian angels of the churches, and that the communications were actually addressed to them.

This is Alford's idea, and it has in its favor that it agrees with the common New Testament meaning of the word "angel," but this is all that can be said for it. We do find reason to think of guardian angels as appointed to watch over, help, guide, and protect, individual believers, especially children (Matt 18.10), but nowhere else is there any suggestion that churches have such guardian angels. If there be such guardian angels, they must be unfallen, holy angels. If so, how can such severe words of rebuke be addressed to them as we find here and there in these letters? Also, how could such letters, written by St. John, ever have been delivered to the angels concerned, or what occasion was there for the glorified Redeemer, in case He had need to communicate with such heavenly beings, to use as intermediary the apostle John? From every standpoint, except only that of the literal meaning of the word, this interpretation is unacceptable.

3. That these "angels" are the officers of the churches, their bishops or pastors.

If we take this interpretation, which is by far the most common one, we get a good meaning, in view of the praise and blame accorded the "angel," for the pastor is, in the first place, personally responsible for the state of the church, to a great degree, and, in the second place, he may be properly considered, in his official capacity, as representing the entire church. In chapter 2.20, some manuscripts read: "thy wife" instead of "the woman." It is a very small difference in the original, for "wife" and "woman" are the same word in Greek, as in Dutch. If this reading were undisputed, it would settle the matter, for then we have here mention not only of the minister, but also of the minister's wife. The Revisers, however, in company with the prevailing sense of scholars, have retained "the woman." (King James Version, "that woman.") If so read, it furnishes no clue to the meaning of "angel."

Against this interpretation it may be said that we are left without any reason why the word "angel" should be used of officers who had other well recognized official titles. The church at Ephesus is the first church on the list, and in Acts 20.17, 28, we find that their responsible officers were called "elders" and "bishops." The same thing appears in the letters to Timothy, who was himself bishop of the church at Ephesus. Sub-apostolic church history finds the designation "bishop" well established. Such being the case, why should St. John have disregarded the regular official title of the men to whom he wrote and have used another, not readily intelligible, of which not a trace remains in early church usage?

Zahn argues very strongly for this meaning, and adduces proof that in the ancient Jewish synagogue the presiding officer, who led the worship, was called by a Hebrew word meaning messenger, because in prayer he carried the messages of the congregation to God.[1] This is interesting, but not very convincing, for the Christian churches from the beginning had their own terminology, quite distinct from that of the synagogue, and the churches addressed were composed of Greeks, who would not be familiar with synagogue terms.

Some have adduced Malachi 2.7, as the origin of his term, "angel," but this also does not fit, for the priest there is a messenger of Jehovah, sent *to* the people, whereas the messenger *of* the church would have to be sent *by* the church.

On the whole, it remains possible that this is the true interpretation. I am not very confident that it is not, and yet it does not satisfy me so well as the next. In any case, I can not agree with Zahn, who makes the messages exclusively personal to the bishop of each church. According to this scholar, it is the bishop whose love has grown cold, who hates the Nicolaitans, who is lukewarm, etc. It seems to me obvious, as it does to almost all commentators, that whatever is said in praise or blame reveals the state of the church in question, not personally and exclusively the spiritual state of the pastor.

4. The "angels" addressed are the churches themselves personified.

This is the interpretation of William Milligan, in "The Expositor's Bible." He says:

> The true idea seems to be that the "angels" of the churches are a symbolical representation in which the *active*, as distinguished from the passive, life of the church finds expression. To St. John, every person, every thing, has its angel. God proclaims and executes His will by angels. He addresses even the Son by an angel. The Son acts and reveals His truth by an angel. The waters have an angel. (16.5) Fire has an angel. (14.18) The

---

[1] Vol. I, p. 214.

winds have an angel. (7.1) The abyss has an angel. (9.11) On all these occasions the 'angel' is interposed when the persons or things spoken of are
represented as coming out of themselves and taking their part in inter-
course or action. In like manner the 'angels' of the churches are the church
themselves, with this mark of distinction only—that, when they are thus
spoken of, they are viewed not merely as in possession of inward vigor, but
as exercising it towards things without.

This is the only interpretation that supplies a reason why the word
"angel" should here be used, namely, that it is required by the symbolical
and dramatic nature of the book. We have something like this in our pageants. From time to time, in such presentations, there appears some one,
generally a young woman with a torch, who is addressed as "The Spirit
of Education," The Spirit of Courage," "The Spirit of Hope," etc,. etc. In
a pageant setting forth the history of Chicago, one might well have "The
Spirit of Chicago" sitting downcast in the ashes, after the fire of 1871, with
the "Spirit of Courage" urging her to rebuild. As Swete puts it: (p. 22)

In this symbolical book the angel of the church may be simply an expression for the prevailing spirit, and thus be identified with the church itself.

Although I choose with some hesitation, the third interpretation also
having a good case, this final view seems to me the best. We have then,
for each church, two symbols; the lampstand, as standing for its outward
form, as an organization, entrusted with the light of the gospel: and the
star in the hand of Christ, representing the "angel," namely, the church
itself, in its inward spiritual state and its active influence upon the world.

It does not fall within the purpose of this book to consider in detail
the seven letters to the seven churches of Asia. Happily, this is the less
necessary, because they are the best known and best understood portion
of the Revelation; indeed, almost the only portion that receives treatment
in our pulpits. They are admirably adapted to such homiletic use, for the
rebuke, praise, warning, and exhortation they contain are all as applicable
to our church life today as in the time when they were first written. In
this very fact we find the most obvious, and, no doubt, the correct view
of these letters, considered as a whole. They were intended primarily, of
course, for the particular churches addressed, and were based upon an
accurate knowledge of the conditions and needs of each; but at the same

time they were intended by the Spirit of God to be a message to the Christian body as a whole, throughout the entire course of its history.

This is indicated by the number—seven. There were more churches in Asia at that time. We need only to think of the one at Colosse, to which Paul wrote; but only seven are selected, to indicate by that symbolic number that the entire church at large should receive the instruction. It is interesting to recall here that St. Paul's letters to seven separate churches, and no more, have been preserved to us in the canonical scriptures, although he must have written many more. These only are preserved, no doubt, "the Holy Spirit this signifying," that together they constitute a message for the entire visible church of God, without distinction of time or place.

It is most important to notice that when Christ is said to walk among the golden candlesticks (2.1) the reference is to the churches, not as purely spiritual groups of those whom He has redeemed, but as organizations existing visibly in the world, composed of regenerate and unregenerate members, full of faults, meriting in many respects the most severe rebuke; and yet acknowledged by the heavenly and exalted Christ as His own. He walks among them, there He is to be found, and they form the object of his constant solicitude. There is a tendency among some, in the supposed interests of a purer and deeper spiritual life, to think lightly and speak disparagingly of the visible church organization, to care nothing for its discipline, to point eagerly to its faults, and to separate from it on very light and insufficient grounds. Not so our exalted Lord. He makes its condition His unceasing care, and clasps in His right hand the stars that are the symbol of its inward life.

There is a view of these letters that we must briefly consider, namely, that they represent, in prophetic forecast, periods in the history of the church; and thus stand, not only for the church as a whole, in all phases of its life (which we also believe) but separately for successive stages in its development, from the first coming of Christ until the second. The Scofield Bible teaches this with the utmost confidence. (p. 1331)

Archbishop Trench[2] tells us that this view was not found in the ancient church, but was first suggested about the year 1200, by Joachim of Floris, and found, among Protestants, its first serious exposition in Holland, in the commentary of Vitringa, who died in 1722. His system is as follows:

---

[2] pp. 296–312.

Ephesus: From John to the Decian Persecution—AD 100–250.

Smyrna: From the Decian Persecution to that of Diocletian—AD 250–311.

Pergamos: From the end of Diocletian Persecution to about AD 800.

Thyatira: From AD 800 to AD 1200.

Sardis: From AD 1200 to AD 1500 and the Reformation.

Philadelphia: The earlier time of the Reformation.

Laodicea: The Rationalistic Age, and later.

Vitringa therefore believed himself to be living in the age of Laodicea. Other schemes are similar, in general, yet with wide variations in the method of dividing the periods—variations so wide as at once to undermine our confidence that there is here "a precise foreview of the spiritual history of the church, and in this precise order"; as Scofield affirms. He, for instance, makes Sardis to represent the period of the Reformation, and Vitringa considers it to stand for the state of the church from AD 1200 to AD 1500. Some difference!

Although in some circles this interpretation is accepted as fully established, and as indisputably confirmed by history (albeit no two interpreters see the same confirmations!) I find it impossible to accept it, for the following reasons

1. Because there is not the slightest hint of any such meaning in the wording of the epistles or in the connection.

If the golden candlesticks appeared in the vision successively, this would be such a hint, but the whole impression is that of a simultaneous condition. While one church was in persecution, another church was in prosperity; while one was faithful, the other was cold, etc.

2. Because it is opposed to the sharp division noted in the first part of Chapter 4, combined with 1.19.

We read in 1.19 that John was to write three things: (a) What he had seen, i.e. the glorious Christ walking among the golden candlesticks; (b) "the things which are," i.e. the present condition of the churches, and (c) "the things which shall come to pass hereafter." Then, in 4.1, he is called upon to view the things of the third division.

This is not arbitrary, but necessitated by the whole structure of the Apocalypse. The book deals with Christ and His church. It has three main divisions: Preparation—Action—Conclusion. In the Preparation the two parties are placed before us. The glorified Christ is made known; and so is the church, in its weaknesses, sins, faithfulness, coldness, distresses, and dangers, as well as in the watchful care which Christ exercises over it. After we are thus made thoroughly acquainted with the parties concerned, the scroll of the future is unrolled. To introduce the idea of prophecy in this first part is, in my judgment, quite to mistake its character.

3. Because the reason given by Dr. Scofield rests upon a view of the book, the futuristic view, which must be rejected. His view is: that the church is not found in the book of Revelation after chapter 3.22. Hence he naturally seeks to find a reference to the church in the first three chapters, as otherwise it would not appear at all. (Scofield Bible, page 1331)

I have already considered this idea. A crushing argument against it may be found in H. Grattan Guinness: "The Approaching End of the Age," pp. 132–138.

4. Because all such division of church history into periods, and such application of the characteristics of the Seven Churches to such periods, would require such a complete and accurate knowledge of the internal spiritual condition of the church in those periods as no one possesses.

Only He who "searches the reins and hearts" (2.23) would be competent for such a task. I deny emphatically the right of any man now living to pass such a judgment upon our own generation as would be involved in calling it the Laodicean era: for no man has the wide and intimate knowledge of the whole church that would be required. If this is true of our own age, how much more it must be true of other ages, with which we are acquainted only through historical study?

5. Because all such schemes are confined to the Latin church, the church of southern and western Europe.

The people who make up these divisions seem to think that this Latin church is "The church." That is comprehensible in a Roman Catholic, but not in a Protestant. What of the Armenian and Nestorian churches, that did such great missionary work in the early ages, reaching even India and China? What of the Coptic church of Egypt, the Abyssinian church, the Russian Greek Orthodox church, and the churches now arising in India, China, Japan and Africa? Are they not a part of the church as a whole? No arrangement into periods that ignores all these can possibly be the right interpretation of the Apocalypse. Yet in no scheme that I have seen are they so much as alluded to.

6. Because all such schemes rest on the assumption that the book of church history is well nigh closed.

Almost of necessity every writer who attempts to draw up such a scheme places himself at the very end, in the period of Laodicea. This, to be sure, is not true of Holzhauer, a Roman Catholic theologian (1613–1658) who put himself in the Period of Sardis. Yet a man certainly must rank his own age well on towards the end, otherwise he cannot attempt to make such a division.

Yet how do we know that we are near the end? It is easy to point to many things that seem to be "signs of the times" and to predict an early return of Christ, but believers have done the same thing in every age since the ascension, and usually with quite as good reason as can be assigned to-day. They were wrong—how can we be sure that we are right? If the world stands for another thousand years, or two, or three, will not our division into periods seem foolish?

Vitringa, dying in 1722, was discouraged, not without cause, at the increasing spiritual deadness of his day, throughout Protestantism, and thought that the age of Laodicea was upon him. He could not foresee the wonderful work of John Wesley, who was nineteen years old when Vitringa died. That work revolutionized the spiritual life of Protestantism. Nor did Vitringa know of the great revival of Calvinism in his own country in the nineteenth century. He had no vision of the modern missionary movement, beginning seventy years after his death, whereby the Christian church began again to put forth her strength, with the result that there are now churches in the South Seas, Madagascar, Uganda, South Africa, India, China, and Japan—churches with a martyr history; of all of which Vitringa never dreamed. If he had had eyes to see these things, he would not have placed his own age "and forward" in the period of Laodicea. As it was with him, so it certainly may be with the prophets of despair in our own day. We can not know, and where we do not know, let us be silent.

For these reasons, I am constrained to agree emphatically with the following verdicts:

E. B. Elliott: "Horae Apocalypticae," Vol. I, p. 78–79:

> To myself, the view seems quite untenable. For not a word is said by Christ to indicate any such prospective meaning in the descriptions. On the contrary, in the twofold division of the Revelation given to St. John—a division noted by Christ himself—'the things that are' and 'the things that are to happen after them,' it seems to me clear that the Epistles to the Seven

Churches were meant to constitute the first division, being a description of the state of things in the church as they then were; and that the visions that followed—visions separated with the utmost precision from the former—alike by a new summons by a trumpet voice, and a scene and scenic accompaniment altogether new also, constituted, alone and distinctively, the visions of the future. ...The hypothesis of the Seven Epistles depicting seven successive phases of the Christian church, appears to me an inference altogether rude and unwarranted.

Archbishop Trench:[3]

The multitude of dissertations, essays, books, which have been written and are still being written, in support of this scheme of interpretation, remain a singular monument of wasted ingenuity.

H. B. Swete:[4]

Only the most perverse ingenuity can treat the messages to the seven churches as directly prophetical.

Theodore Zahn:[5]

Completely excluded is the interpretation—which even today has not yet died out—of the falsely so-called Seven Letters as successive stages of the development of the church.

---

[3] p. 312.

[4] p. ccxiii.

[5] Vol. I, p. 207.

X

A SOLEMN PAGEANT OF THE DIVINE JUDGMENTS

The section we are to consider in this and the following chapters, presents itself to us as a dramatization, in successive acts, of God's judgments, as seen in human life and history. As a key text, we might take Psalm 46.8: "Come, behold the works of the Lord, what desolations he hath made in the earth." The Greek drama was in its flower in Ephesus in the days of the apostle John, and it is not unreasonable to believe that the form and order of the visions which he saw and records indicate that he appreciated the power and beauty of dramatic art.

In saying that this section dramatizes the divine judgments, I do not mean to intimate that it was ever acted or intended to be acted in a theater. In that sense it is not a drama, but it is one in the sense that the dramatic method is employed, and that some things in it can not be appreciated without taking this fact into consideration. As instances, I may name the delay in finding some one to open the sealed book, the terror stricken state of mankind under the sixth seal, and the silence in heaven when the seventh seal is opened. These things, I believe, are due purely to the need of dramatic effect, as will appear in the discussion.

A form of drama not so unfamiliar to church people as the theater is the pageant, often presented out of doors, in which great historical scenes are enacted. In such a pageant, if given at night, the stage only will be lighted. The audience sit in the darkness and watch scene after scene brought before them. Sometimes the chief characters simply march across the stage, apparently on their way to do some great thing. We see them for a moment and they are gone, but we know that what they went to do will presently appear. Sometimes, also certain "spirits" come forward, representing a group of men or a period, such as "The spirit of '76" or "The spirit of Abraham Lincoln." In the book of Revelation the angels from time to time take some such part as this. One of the characteristic things about such a pageant is the choir, which, at appropriate moments, will break the dramatic presentation and rest the eye by raising a song of praise, of triumph, or of lamentation. Sometimes there will be interludes, not strictly necessary to the progress of the story, but reiterating and emphasizing something already seen.

All of these things are found in the book of Revelation, and attention to this will aid very greatly in making it intelligible. At critical moments, the story stops, and we hear the heavenly hosts sing a doxology, or a triumph-song. If such a drama is well written and well played, it produces an impression upon the audience far deeper and more vivid than can be produced in any other way. A number of years ago, a student of mine went to see Drinkwater's play: "Abraham Lincoln." He came back full of enthusiasm, and I said to him: "What pleased you so much? Did you learn anything new about Abraham Lincoln?" "No," he said, "nothing at all. I knew it all before, but I was never so deeply impressed with it. You remember what Tennyson says: 'Things seen are mightier than things heard.' So it was with me." That is exactly the point to be remembered in reading the Revelation. There is very little information in the book that may not be learned from the rest of the Bible; but in the doctrinal books it is presented to the mind, here to the eye, and by this means it gains a vividness far beyond anything that can otherwise be attained.

If we look at the matter from this standpoint, we shall find it profitable to divide the Apocalypse, from the beginning of chapter four to the end, into two plays, or dramas, with chapter 10 as the announcements of the second play, and chapter 11 as a kind of interlude, preparing the mind for what is coming. The first of these plays we shall entitle: "A SOLEMN PAGEANT OF THE DIVINE JUDGEMENTS UPON A WICKED WORLD."

The acts and scenes may be arranged as follows:

Act I. The Hall of Judgment

Scene 1—Throne of Judgment. 4.1–11.

Scene 2—The Book of Judgment. 5.1–4.

Scene 3—The Administrator of Judgment. 5.5–14.

Act II. The Seals—Preparation

Scene 1—The instruments of Judgment—First Four Seals. 6.1–8.

Scene 2—The Demand for Judgment—Fifth Seal. 6.9–11.

Scene 3—The Terror of the Approaching Judgment—Sixth Seal. 6.12–17.

Scene 4—The Church Militant Safe in the Midst of the Judgments. 7.1–8.

Scene 5—The Church Triumphant Safe Above the Judgments. 7.9–17.

Scene 6—Breathless Expectation—Seventh Seal.

Act III. The Triumphs—Action

Scene 1—The Announcers Make Ready. 8.2–6.

Scene 2—The Prayers of God's Suffering People Ascend. 8.3–5.

Scene 3—First Trumpet: Judgment Upon Vegetation. 8.7.

Scene 4—Second Trumpet: Judgment Upon the Sea. 8.8–9.

Scene 5—Third Trumpet: Judgment Upon Fresh Waters. 8.10, 12.

Scene 6—Fourth Trumpet: Judgment Upon Sources of Light. 8.12.

Scene 7—Fifth Trumpet: Judgment by Hellish Locusts. 9.1–11.

Scene 8—Sixth Trumpet: Judgment by Hellish Cavalry. 9.13–14.

Scene 9—Announcement of Approaching End: Programme for a New Pageant in the Little Book, Open. Chapter 10.

Scene 10—Interlude of the Measured Temple and the Two Witnesses. 11.1–14.

Scene 11—Seventh Trumpet: Triumphant Consummation. 11.15–19.

Let us now try to imagine ourselves seated in the audience with the above program in our hands. The curtain rises, and we have before us Act I, Scene 1, "The Hall of Judgment." In a passage of great sublimity the prophet tells us what he saw, as in a vision he stepped within the open door, and what we see, as in imagination we are seated in the audience at the pageant.

Behold, there was a throne set in heaven, and one sitting upon the throne: and he that sat was to look upon as a jasper stone and a sardius; and there was a rainbow about the throne, like an emerald to look upon. And round about the throne were four and twenty thrones, and upon the thrones I saw four and twenty elders sitting, arrayed in white garments, and on their heads crowns of gold.

Commonly, and I think rightly, these four and twenty elders are taken as symbolizing the whole church of God, the number being taken from that of the twelve patriarchs and the twelve apostles. It is not a valid objection to this that not all the sons of Jacob were good men, and that, since John was still living, only eleven apostles could be in heaven. Nor is it at all in place to fuss about the question whether the place of Judas Iscariot was, in this company, taken by Matthias or Paul. All this arises from confusing symbolism and reality. John did not see these four and twenty elders because they were really there! They exist only in the visions, as symbols, representing the church of God, of which the twelve patriarchs and the twelve apostles were the historic founders.

These representatives of God's people are here sharing with God in His sovereignty, joint rulers, assessors of the heavenly court, for they sit on *thrones* (not seats as in the AV) and they wear *crowns*, both indicating sovereignty. This is the Supreme Court of the Universe; God and His people sitting together to judge and rule the world. Let us not think it strange that the church should thus be associated with God in discussing and making plans for the judgment of the world; for such is the condescension of God that, once He has entered into covenant with His people, He will not act without their concurrence. To Abraham He said "Shall I hide from Abraham that which I do… seeing all nations of the world shall be blessed in Him." Abraham was God's partner, and God was not willing to bring judgment upon Sodom without consulting him. (Gen 18.18) What we see before us in this pageant is an embodiment of the same truth.

These are guards about the throne—of course there are. What great king is ever without them?

> And in the midst of the throne and round about the throne, four living creatures, full of eyes before and behind. And the first creature was like a lion, and the second creature like a calf, and the third creature had a face as of a man, and the fourth creature was like a flying eagle." (RV)

These are the cherubim of Ezekiel, chapter one and ten, in a somewhat modified form. That they are both "in the midst of the throne" and "round about the throne," may be best understood, I think, by conceiving the throne as semi-circular, placed against the further wall, and reached by steps. The cherubim then stand where the body guards of the monarch would naturally stand, half way up the steps, barring any unauthorized approach, and facing in all directions. That they are "full of eyes" indicates their intense vigilance as such guards.

> And I saw in the right hand of Him that sat on the throne a book, written within and on the back, close sealed with seven seals."

What is this book? Evidently, the curtain rose immediately after the business of the Supreme Court was concluded. We are not privileged to be present at the conference of the Supreme Judge and his Associate Judges. Of all that we hear not a word, but we see in the hand of Him that sitteth upon the throne a sealed book, or document, in the form of a roll, in which the decisions of the court have been recorded. We may call this book by different names, all in the end coming to the same thing: "The Book of Judgment"—"The Book of Destiny"—"The Book of the Secret Counsel of God"—"The Plan of Campaign"—"The Sealed Orders." It is the book in which the purposes of God with reference to a sinful world are written.

The book is "sealed with seven seals," all plainly in sight, on the outside of the roll, in a row; not some hidden within, as if part of the roll could be unrolled after the first seal is broken, another part after the second seal, etc. So it is often taken, but I think, erroneously. Such sealing would be most unnatural, and it is difficult to imagine any method by which it could be accomplished and still the seals be visible. In my understanding of it, at this point, I am following Alford, who quotes an ancient Roman Catholic writer, Cornelius a Lapide, as follows:[1]

> For nothing in the book would be read except after the opening of all seven seals; for when all were opened, then at length the book could be opened and read, not before.

This point is of considerable importance in the interpretation, for if it is true that there can be no opening of the book until after the seventh seal is broken, what happens as the successive seals are opened must be understood as preparation only, not as something that had been written in the book.

The book was written "within and on the back"—indicating that nothing more can be written in it later. All is on record, everything is determined, nothing is left uncertain, as if God's plans were in some sense

---

[1] Vol. IV, Part II, p. 603.

contingent on unforeseen developments. This is the usual, and probably the correct explanation; but Zahn has a different translation here, which, if accepted, modifies the meaning: "Written within, and sealed on the back with seven seals."[2] In this form the sentence emphasizes the secrecy, for evidently if there were writing on the outside, a little, at least, could have been known by one who could not or dared not break the seals. So the book of the divine judgments is ready, but now there is no need of some one wise enough, good enough, great enough, to undertake the task of carrying these purposes into effect. Therefore there ensues here a most impressive scene. "A strong angel," not just an ordinary angel, but one of outstanding rank, is sent to find some one of that kind. He goes out and makes the announcement to all the world, not only in heaven but in earth and hell: "Proclaiming with a great voice, Who is worthy to open the book and to loose the seals thereof?" As the sound of the great voice dies away, we look with eagerness to see who will respond, but in vain. Michael, Gabriel, all the archangels and angels stand in serried ranks, but no one steps forth to volunteer. Why not? Why is it so great a thing to take the book and open the seals thereof? Because that would be to accept the commission to bring to pass what is written therein. It is not merely to break the seals and read out the contents. It is much more than that. This roll is like the "sealed orders" received by the admiral of a great fleet, to be opened out at sea. The fleet sets sail, no one knows whither. The admiral himself does not know where it is to go and what is to be done until he breaks the seal and reads his orders. Then it is his responsibility to carry them out. What the secret purposes of God may be the angels do not know, and not one of them is so bold as to think that he can carry them into effect.

The seer waits in the oppressive silence until he can bear it no longer. Then he breaks down in bitter weeping. "I wept much, because no one was found worthy to open the book or to look thereon," He weeps, not from disappointment because he can not know what is in the book, but from dismay lest the great purposes of God may not come to pass. Now this is all pure pageantry. It is perfectly clear, is it not, that no such thing ever took place or ever could take place, in actual reality. God did not need to search through heaven and earth to find the Lord Jesus Christ. Neither have this unsuccessful search, this oppressive waiting, and this bitter weeping of the prophet any prophetic or doctrinal significance. These

---

[2] Vol. I, p. 327.

things are presented in the vision purely for dramatic effect. All this is intended greatly to deepen our appreciation of how great a thing it is to which Christ here is called. It does deepen it, if in imagination we sit in the audience and yield ourselves to the influence of the drama.

> And one of the elders saith unto me, Weep not, behold, the Lion that is of the tribe of Judah, the Root of David, hath overcome to open the book and the seven seals thereof. And I saw in the midst of the throne of the elders, a Lamb standing, as though it had been slain, having seven horns and seven eyes, which are the seven Spirits of God, sent forth unto all the earth. (RV)

It is one of the characteristics of the book of Revelation that it is so gloriously independent of ordinary human logic and of any natural limitations. Here is one and the same heavenly being described as a Lion and as a Lamb. The seer is told to look up and see a Lion: he looks and, behold a Lamb! The Lamb, again, is a slaughtered Lamb, yet he lives, and takes the Book of Destiny from the hand of God. Do not ask how a Lamb can take a book. Little things like that do not trouble the writer of this Apocalypse—they do not even seem to him to call for explanation. Whatever suits him as an expression of thought is immediately made use of, no matter how impossible it may be from the natural point of view, or how inconsistent with some thing else he has just said. We shall find many cases of this kind—a star that is handed a key—a flying woman whom the Dragon seeks to overwhelm with a flood—a mortal wound that is healed, etc., etc. Hence it must be remembered that we can not reason about this book quite the same way as about other books. There is no rigid consistency about its symbols: they are extremely flexible and adjustable. The only thing the writer demands is that they shall be vivid expressions— word pictures—of his ideas. That they always are.

The Lamb whom he saw had seven eyes—fullness of knowledge: and seven horns—fullness of power: symbols of omnipotence, omniscience, and omnipresence. No sooner has he received the book, and thus accepted the office of Lord High Commissioner of Judgment, than there is a great burst of praise and joy in three doxologies. First those nearest the throne lead off, the cherubim and the redeemed, "and they sing a new song, saying:

> Worthy art thou to take the book, and to open the seals thereof; for thou

wast slain, and didst purchase unto God with thy blood men of every tribe, and tongue and people, and nation, and madest them to be unto our God a kingdom, and priests; and they reign upon the earth.

Then the angels join in, to the number of "ten thousand times ten thousand, and thousands of thousands," saying with a great voice,

Worthy is the Lamb that hath been slain to receive the power and riches and wisdom and might and honor and glory and blessing.

And finally "every created thing which is in the heaven and on the earth, and under the earth, and on the sea, and all things that are in them," sing,

Unto him that sitteth on the throne and unto the Lamb, be the blessing and the honor and the glory and the dominion, for ever and ever.

The doxologies close with a grand "Amen" and a solemn act of adoring worship.

We can not help asking: "Why so great a joy?" If we think here merely of taking a book and opening the seals thereof, it is quite out of proportion, but the scene means much more than that. Jesus Christ is here taking his place at the right hand of God, to be God's "right hand man," the Prime Minister of the Divine Moral Government, ready to "rule the nations with a rod of iron." The church has always believed and confessed that Christ is so seated. Here is the same truth dramatized. This is his inaugural, his coronation, his enthronement ceremony, his induction into office. Henceforth it is certain that the things written in the sealed book will be carried out, with wisdom and might. It is an occasion for heaven and earth greatly to rejoice.

In reading the first doxology it is important to note the differences between the Authorized, or King James Version and the Revised Version, the latter based upon the better Greek manuscripts. The AV has it: "Thou has redeemed *us* and... Thou hast made *us* kings and priests," but the Revised: "Thou didst purchase unto God with thy blood *men of every tribe*, and madest *them* to be unto out God *a kingdom*." If the reading of the AV were right, the Four Living Creatures, the Cherubim, must also have been redeemed men, to join in such a song; which would be quite out of harmony with their real nature. They are the guards of the divine majesty, symbolic, not actual, creatures, representing, probably, all the forces of nature.

On the reading "Thou hast made them a *kingdom*, not *kings*, we commented when we found a similar change in 1.6. Notice now also the change in 5.10, not *"We shall reign on the earth,"* as if believers are speaking, and are expecting to reign with Christ at some future time, but *"they reign on the earth."* The heavenly beings praise God that their brethren on earth have already entered upon a position of royal authority and freedom in a spiritual sense. All true believers are kings, incognito.

These grand doxologies have brought us to the end of Act 1, Scene 3, the inauguration of the Administrator of Judgment.

XI

OPENING THE SEALS

We have now before us Act II of this heavenly pageant—The Seals—Preparation.

> And I saw when the Lamb opened one of the seven seals, and I heard one of the four living creatures saying as with a voice of thunder, Come. (RV)

Not, as in the old version: "Come and see," as if the words were addressed to St. John, but simply "Come," a summons to begin, to appear upon the stage. This must not be considered here to be a prayer for the coming of the Lord, but a call to the stage characters, the actors of the pageant, now to come forward and take their parts. Zahn has here the translation "Go!"[1] and considers it a command to each of the four horsemen to go forth upon his mission. This also is not impossible, for, curiously enough, the Greek word may have either meaning. All the standard versions, however, have "Come."

The response comes promptly. One by one, as successively called by the four living creatures, four horsemen appear. They say nothing, and they do nothing, except silently to ride across the stage and disappear. Who are these wondrous riders, and what go they to do?

There are many divergent explanations, which we have not space to mention and discuss. The explanation that seems to me the right one is also the most common, that the White Horse symbolizes the gospel; the Red Horse, war; the Black Horse, scarcity, hard times, the bitter struggle for bread; and the Pale Horse, death. I think they are not to be thought of as operating successively in time, although they appear in order here. They

---

[1] Vol. II, p. 348.

are exhibited here as the Instruments of Judgment, or, perhaps better, the Instruments of the Divine Moral Government, the four chief forces which Christ employs in directing the course of human affairs.

We find another white horse and conquering rider in chapter 19, and there the horseman is undeniably Christ himself. This tempts one to explain the white horse and rider here in the same way, but that would be against the analogy of the other riders, who are not persons but historical forces. Yet we can hardly separate the white horse here altogether from the one in the nineteenth chapter. We preserve, therefore, on the one hand the connection, and on the other hand, the difference, if we understand this one of the gospel of Christ, preached in the world, going forth conquering and to conquer.

That the Red Horse means war, hardly requires any explanation. The Black Horse does not mean famine, in the full sense of the word, but scarcity, the high cost of living. "A measure of wheat for a shilling." The Roman denarius, here translated "shilling," in the old version, "penny," was the ordinary day's wage of a laboring man, and a measure of wheat was a day's rations. He thus merely makes a living, if he is to eat wheat. "Three measures of barley for a shilling"—if he has a wife and child, they can still eat enough, but of the coarser grain. If he is out of work, or has more than one child, they go hungry much of the time. Yet some of the good things of life are left: "And the oil and wine hurt thou not." Bleek tells us that the price of wheat here given is twelve times the normal price of that day, and barley eight times.[2] The Pale (or Livid) Horse represents death, as, indeed, is plainly enough said: "His name was Death, and Hades followed after him." Hades means here the grave, and as personified, acts the part of a servant to the horseman. As Death cuts men down on every hand, the grave gathers them in. Zahn has here the curious remark that Hades must have sat on the same horse with Death, since no mention is made of any other horse, and it is unthinkable that a footman should keep up with a horseman, and serve him![3] He should visit Japan, where it is not uncommon to see a military officer trotting along on his horse, and his servant on foot behind him.

These, then, are the chief things the Administrator of Judgment is to use, when he has opened all the seals, and has read his orders. We all know them, and all generations before us have known them. The genera-

---

[2] p. 211.

[3] Vol. II, p. 356.

tions to come will know them too. They have ridden silently across the stage, and off into the darkness, but we shall not forget them. Four great permanent elements of life have been recognized: The Gospel of Christ; War and Bloodshed; The Hard Struggle for Bread; Disease and Death.

As the next thing on the program of our pageant, we hear a stern demand for judgment:

> I saw underneath the altar the souls of them that had been slain for the word of God, and for the testimony which they held, and they cried with a great voice, saying: How long, O Master, the holy and true, dost thou not judge and avenge our blood on them that dwell on the earth? (RV)

Difficulty has been felt by some to reconcile this demand for vengeance with the Christian spirit. Jesus did not so speak when he was being crucified, but prayed: "Father, forgive them"; and Stephen said: "Lord, lay not this sin to their charge." Shall then the souls of those that have been redeemed, and have passed beyond all suffering and imperfection, into the glory and holiness of heaven, be so eager for revenge as to importune God for it? Influenced by such thoughts, some have thought that these must be Old Testament martyrs; but this can hardly be true, for the expression St. John uses to describe them is a distinctly Christian one, the same as he used of his own sufferings in exile: He was in Patmos, "for the word of God and the testimony of Jesus" and these were slain "for the word of God and the testimony which they held." It may be that the Old Testament martyrs should be included, but I think it can not be confined to them.

The difficulty disappears if we adopt the interpretation of William Milligan, and notice that these souls were "under the altar," which was the place where the blood of the slain victims was poured out. To speak of martyrdom as a sacrifice, and of martyrs as victims, whose blood is poured out, is a natural figure, and is used by St. Paul of his own impending death (2 Tim 4.6). As for such blood crying out and demanding divine vengeance upon the murderers, we have it as early as Genesis 4.10: "The voice of thy brother's blood crieth unto me from the ground."

Thus we can see that this demand from under the altar symbolizes the moral necessity of judgment. The death of God's own witnesses, who had been cruelly and foully murdered, must be avenged. The demand is not really from the spirits of just men made perfect, as a conscious personal desire. It arises from the blood itself, from the fact of their murder. Such a thing can not be allowed to go unpunished. In a moral universe this demand for retribution must arise, and it must be conceded. So this scene finely lays the necessary moral foundation for all the terrible things that are to follow. They are not arbitrary. They come because they must. Milton voiced the same demand when he said:

> Avenge, O Lord, thy slaughtered saints, whose bones
> Lie whitening on the Alpine mountains cold.

With such a demand God can not but comply.

In Scene 3 of this Act (see program) men begin to be aware of the gathering storm. The evidences of it appear:

> There was a great earthquake, and the sun became black as sackcloth of hair, and the whole moon became as blood: and the stars of heaven fell unto the earth, as a fig tree casteth her unripe figs when she is shaken of a great wind. And the heaven was removed as a scroll when it is rolled up, and every mountain and island were moved out of their places." (Rev Vers)

These are familiar expressions for great and terrible events. St. Peter said that the prophecy of Joel 2.28–32, from which the forms are partly taken, was fulfilled on the day of Pentecost, (Acts 2.17–21) although on that occasion there was no blood or fire, or vapor or smoke, neither was the sun turned into darkness, nor the moon into blood. So we see that they are not to be taken literally, but as symbolizing the overturning of all that hitherto has been considered most firm and unshakable. It is not unusual for commentators to see here the final day of judgment. Alford says: "We are thus brought to the very threshold itself of the great day of the Lord's coming";[4] and Morris bases partly on such an interpretation his idea that each vision or cycle (he considers the Seals to constitute such a cycle) "ends with the coming of Christ or the Judgment Scene." (p. 29)

Is seems to me that this is untenable, especially because this is not under the seventh seal, but under the sixth. Also because the nature of the agencies to be employed, as we have just seen, and the protection afforded to the saints, which we shall see immediately, do not seem to me to harmonize with the final judgment day, but rather to point to earthly calamities brought upon men by God as judgments; such things as are

---

[4] Vol. IV, Part II, p. 622.

presented under the trumpet series. I take it, therefore, that we have here the terror of men who see calamity approaching.

> And they say to the mountains and to the rocks, Fall on us and hide us from the face of him that sitteth on the throne, and from the wrath of the Lamb, for the great day of their wrath is come, and who is able to stand? (RV)

It is important to notice that, in all this, we do not yet see any man hurt. No judgment has yet fallen, but a terrible fear grips men's hearts as they begin to realize that God's patience is exhausted, and that His judgments are about to go forth in the earth. If you insist that "The great day of their wrath" can mean only the final Judgment Day, you may be right, but notice that this cry comes from men, not from any authoritative source. It shows only, at most, that they think the Judgment Day is near, and men have often been mistaken about that. As Swete says: (p. 93)

> Fear anticipates the actual event. ...There have been epochs in history when the conscience of mankind has antedated the judgment, and believed it imminent.

Yet the storm does not at once break, for there is an important question to be answered before the drama can proceed, and to answer this there is a comforting episode, which somewhat breaks the work of judgment. The question is this: "What of God's people? If such terrible things are to take place in the earth, will they not be overwhelmed with the rest?" The next scene in this Pageant of Judgment shows that God has not forgotten them.

> After this I saw four angels standing at the four corners of the earth, holding the four winds of the earth, that no wind should blow on the earth or on the sea, or upon any tree. (RV)

Here the impending judgments to be let loose upon the earth are likened to a storm, in which fierce winds rush forth upon sea and land. These winds are ready, but they are held back, each by an angel, as dogs are held in leash until the moment of command.

> And I saw another angel ascend from the sunrising, having the seal of the living God; and he cried with a great voice to the four angels to whom it was given to hurt the earth and the sea, saying, Hurt not the earth, nei-

ther the sea, nor the trees, till we have sealed the servants of our God on their foreheads. (RV)

Sealing is for a variety of purposes. Sometimes the seal is used as a signature, to certify a document, sometimes to close a letter or a receptacle, that no unauthorized person may open it, sometimes as a stamp, or brand, to indicate ownership. The last sense is the one in which it is used here. The seal put upon the forehead of the believer marks him as God's, just as the brand upon cattle indicates to whom the said cattle belong.

This scene is borrowed from Ezekiel 9.1–11. There, also, destroyers are ready to bring God's judgment upon a sinful city, but they are told to wait until a writer with an inkhorn has put a mark upon all the faithful. After that is done, the judgment proceeds, but the destroyers may not come near any man upon whom is the mark. So here: the sealing is for the purpose of preservation in the midst of the judgments that God is about to bring upon the world. The righteous are not removed from the world before those judgments take place. They suffer together with the rest, so far as earthly things are concerned. Yet they are spiritually kept, as in the hollow of God's hand, and for them all things work together for good. For them "tribulation worketh steadfastness, and steadfastness approvedness, and approvedness, hope, and hope putteth not to shame." (Rom 5.3) Thus we have here a dramatization of what the apostle says: "Nevertheless, the foundation of God standeth sure, having this seal: The Lord knoweth them that are His. (2 Tim 2.19)

The record of the sealed is under Old Testament names. There are twelve thousand sealed from every tribe of the children of Israel. In this enumeration, Levi, usually omitted, because it has no separate territorial allotment, is counted, and, to keep the number twelve, Dan is omitted. The name of Joseph is substituted for that of Ephraim, his younger son. No doubt these variations from the ordinary naming of the tribes have meaning, but I have not found any explanation worth passing on to my readers.

After the sealing is finished, we see another company:

A great multitude, which no man could number, out of every nation, and of all tribes and peoples and tongues, standing before the throne and before the Lamb, arrayed in white robes, and palms in their hands. (RV)

It has given commentators no end of trouble to decide who these two companies are, and why they should be so distinguished. One very plausible view is that the first are Jewish Christians, the "elect remnant" of which St. Paul speaks (Rom 11.1, 5) and to which he himself belonged. These accepted Christ in the early apostolic days, in the face of His rejection by the mass of their fellow countrymen. They were a noble company, and history tells us that they were signally protected in the destruction of Jerusalem. The others, then, are, by antithesis to the first group, the innumerable Gentile Christians. This beautifully fits the contrast drawn so clearly in the vision, between those "from every tribe of the children of Israel" on the one hand, and the multitude "out of every nation, and of all tribes, and peoples and tongues" on the other. It may be the true explanation.

Yet there is another view which is more generally adopted, and which seems to me still better. It is that the first group represents the true believers on earth, while they are still subject to the storms of divine judgment that break over the world; while the second group symbolizes the believers who are already in heaven; not in heaven after the final judgment, as if we have here a view of the end of the world, but the company of those, who, one by one, have departed to be with the Lord. The two groups, then, are respectively, "The Church Militant" and "The Church Triumphant." This agrees strikingly with the fact that the members of the first group are sealed, the others not. If we understand the first company to be Jewish Christians and the second company Gentile Christians, we get no explanation of this feature, for in this world all have the same need of protection. It agrees also with the fact that all the members of the first group are counted, while the second group are uncounted. God needs, so to speak, to keep count of His own here below, to make sure that not one is without His loving and gracious care, which the great multitude above no longer needs in the same way. The number of those sealed is 144,000, the number of the utmost completeness, one thousand, multiplied by the square of the number of the church. We meet the same company again in 14.1, not there, as here, a distressed flock needing the shepherd's care, but a mighty company of warriors, ready for battle, under a victorious leader. "They follow the Lamb, whithersoever He goeth." It is the same "Church Militant," seen under another aspect of its life.

So we are assured that, whatever happens upon the earth, not a hair shall fall from the head of God's own people. He knows each one, He seals and counts each one, and He will keep them, every one, until they stand with palms in their hands, singing the great song:

Salvation to our God, which sitteth upon the throne, and to the Lamb.

This vision was, no doubt, a great encouragement to the early church, made aware of terrible events soon to burst in dark clouds of divine wrath upon the Roman Empire. It was to them, in the fine metaphor of the Dutch language: "Een riem onder 't hart," a band passed under the heart, to keep it from sinking in despair and fear. The comfort of it is for us, as well as for them.

Now we are ready. We have seen the instruments of judgment, have heard the demand for judgment, have seen the terror of the approaching judgment, and we have seen the people of God provided for. Surely there need be no more delay. The next scene must be one of tremendous action. So we sit and wait, in awed and breathless silence. This seems to be the very state of mind that St. John wishes to indicate, when he says:

When he opened the seventh seal, there followed a silence in heaven, about the space of half an hour.

The seventh and last seal is broken, the sealed book is fully open, what must not the next thing be? So the hosts of heaven stand silent, in breathless expectancy, waiting for the solemn pageant to proceed. Notice that this silence is, again, a purely dramatic touch, having no prophetic or doctrinal significance in itself, but placed here because the principles of dramatic art require it.

Thus silently and breathlessly watching, we are not disappointed. To the seven chief angels, "the angels of the presence," there are given trumpets, and every one knows what that means. Seals are to hide things that must not yet be made known: trumpets, on the contrary, to summon armies and to give the signal for the charge. No more delay, then, the hour has come. When the trumpets sound, the avenging forces will go into action.

While the trumpeters make ready to sound, there is another scene, similar in its meaning to the cry of blood from under the altar, but more personal. An angel takes his stand at the altar of incense, and offers to God the prayers of the saints—not of the saints in heaven, but of the saints on earth, the laboring, struggling, and suffering saints. It is their cry for deliverance and help, and it shall not go unheard. Those prayers have an echo upon earth, for the angel throws of the fire of the altar upon the earth, and immediately we hear ominous rumblings of what is to come:

There followed thunders, and voices, and lightnings, and an earthquake.

Now the angels sound, one after another, and there follow six sore judgments, patterned after the plagues of Egypt, but worse. By the first, one-third of the vegetation is destroyed, by the second, sea-going commerce and fish, by the third, drinking water is spoiled, and by the fourth the sources of light are darkened. These four are judgments upon nature, not yet directly upon human life, and they are limited to "one-third." Life is still tolerable. This is different in the series of the bowls of wrath, in chapter 16. This gradually increased severity may be observed in the Egyptian plagues also. Then follow two other calamities, in which men suffer: first armies of hellish locusts, and then an army of 200,000,000 hellish cavalry.

If you ask me what all this means, and expect that I shall be able to point to something in history that corresponds to the burning mountain cast into the sea, to the falling star called "Wormwood," to the locusts from the pit, or to the terrible cavalry rushing up from beyond the Euphrates, I can not answer. I am sorry to disappoint my readers, and sorry to appear so ignorant, but really, I do not know what these things mean.

I can refer you to some books in which you will find it all explained: E. B. Elliott: "Horae Apocalypticae"; Albert Barnes: "Notes on Revelation"; David N. Lord: "An Exposition of the Apocalypse," and similar works. These writers have found, to their own satisfaction, some explanation for every detail; for the tails of the locusts, the dying of the fish, the long hair, like woman's hair, which the locusts had, and for the fire and brimstone that proceeded out of the mouths of the terrible horsemen. You can find it all there, and in your study of these authors you have my best wishes; but as for me, I must frankly confess that I see no sense in most of their interpretations, and that I suspect they are on the wrong track in seeking any concrete interpretations at all.

I do not say that these details have no meaning. They may have, and possibly the early church understood them better than we, although of this there is no proof in the extant early literature. For me they have no meaning, and I am comforted to find myself, in this respect, in the excellent company of men like Alford, Swete, and others, who either openly confess that they can not interpret them, or silently pass them by. Alford says:[5]

I have never seen... an interpretation of these details at all approaching

---

[5] Vol. IV, Part II, p. 635.

to versimilitude: never any which is not obliged to force the plain sense of words, or the certain course of history, to make them fit the requisite theory.

To a man who thus despairs of reaching an interpretation of the separate figures, does this portion of the book become useless? Not at all. As I read these chapters, I sit in imagination at the great panorama of the moral government of God in history thus unrolled before me, and yield myself to the impression the successive scenes make upon me. I watch in wondering awe those mysterious horsemen riding silently across the stage, bound on some tremendous mission. With the opening of each seal I watch eagerly for what is to come. I feel a surge of indignation when the cry of the martyr's blood reaches my ears. I hear with a sort of stern delight the rumbling of the oncoming storm, and rejoice with joy unspeakable at the consolation of the sealing. When the great throng stand, with white garments on, and palms in their hands, singing the song of salvation, I am like John Bunyan, who, when he caught a glimpse of the heavenly hosts, through the entering in of his pilgrim, "wished himself among them."

As for the great happening of the trumpet series, I do not take much interest in locating them here or there in history, for it seems to me I know them. Have we not ourselves twice, in 1914–1918 and again in 1939–1945 seen the bottomless pit opened, and the heavens darkened by swarms of evil things that issued from it? Has not the thunder of the two hundred million hellish horsemen shaken the earth in our own day, so that we can never forget it? So it seems to me, as I see the pageant unroll, act after act; and finally I turn away with profound confidence in the plans of Him that sitteth on the throne, written in the unsealed orders that are in the hands of the Lamb.

XII
THE GREAT ANGEL AND THE LITTLE BOOK

The woe of the Sixth Trumpet has appeared; yet the Seventh Trumpet does not immediately sound. Before we hear it, there appear two separate sections, that of the Great Angel with the Little Book, of chapter 10, and that of the Measured Temple and the Two Witnesses, of chapter 11. Such passages are by most commentators called "episodes," or "interludes"; by the Scofield Bible, "parenthetical," because they do not carry forward the main action of the drama.

The chief purpose of the first one, in this case, seems to be to assure the audience at the pageant, (or the reader) that although the pageant is drawing near its close, and will end with the Seventh Trumpet, there is another drama to follow.

"And I saw another strong angel." The expression at once refers us back to the only "Strong angel" previously mentioned, the one sent out to find a person worthy to open the Sealed Book. It has no other meaning than to indicate that the work to be done is of unusual importance. That work is two fold, to assure the waiting universe that God's plans will suffer no undue delay, but will promptly come to fulfillment, and to qualify St. John, the seer, for further revelations.

The things said of this angel, the cloud with which he is arrayed, the rainbow upon his head, his face being like the sun, and his feet as pillars of fire, are taken from the description of the glorified Redeemer, and of the one sitting upon the throne. This has, not unreasonably, given rise to the idea that this is Christ himself, and so it is taken by some of the best commentators. Yet it seems to me that the others, who deny this, are right. Throughout this book the angels are the servants of God and Christ, sent out to do the work assigned to them, and it is incongruous to think of

Christ as such an angel. Especially is this true in the present drama, where the first scenes show Him as Commander-in-Chief. That he should leave his position as such and appear here as an "angel," that is, as a messenger, seems out of harmony with the whole conception.

In every conceivable way the vision surrounds this angel and his message with majesty and solemnity. He takes possession of all the earth by planting one foot upon the sea and the other upon the land, and, lifting up his hand, swears

> by him that liveth for ever and ever, who created the heaven and the things that are therein, and the earth and the things that are therein, and the sea and the things that are therein, that there shall be delay no longer, but in the days of the voice of the seventh angel, when he is about to sound, then is finished the mystery of God, according to the good tidings which he declared to his servants the prophets." (RV)

Before he does this, however, "the seven thunders"—which seven thunders we know not—uttered something understood by the seer, which he was about to write, but was forbidden to write. Since it is to be kept so secret, it would be not only useless but improper for us to seek to know it. We might properly, however, explain why such a thing is inserted here, what it means that by the voice of seven thunders something is made known to St. John that he may not tell; if we could explain it! So far as I have learned the views of expositors, most of them do not attempt any explanation, and those who do attempt it produce nothing worth repeating. This must, therefore, remain among the unexplained, and unexplainable passages of the book.

Besides announcing that the end was at hand, the Great Angel had another office, to give the apostle a further revelation. This is in accordance with 1.1, where we are told that "he (i.e. God) sent and signified it (the Revelation) by his angel unto his servant John." That an angel also was instrumental in causing him to see the earlier visions, is not expressly said, but is to be understood. Here the angelic agency appears clearly, and with majesty. The angel had in his hand a "little book, open," that is, not sealed, the contents accessible to any one who received it. This fact, that it is "open" contrasts it at once with the sealed book that was in the hand of the one who sat upon the throne, in the early part of this drama. This can scarcely be without meaning for the exposition. That other book was not expressly called a "great book," but that this one is so emphatically called a "little book,"—literally a "booklet," for it is one word in the Greek—seems to be an intended contrast, and justifies our thinking of the first one as "great." Upon the basis of this contrast, it seems reasonable to think that this book was like the other in containing the purposes of God, but unlike it in being a record only of such purposes as may be known to the people of God: purposes, therefore, that especially concern them, as a group distinct from the mass of mankind.

It is a very common, and, I think, a correct interpretation, to regard the little book as containing everything in the Apocalypse after the sounding of the seventh trumpet. This constitutes a new drama, one concerned not with the judgments of God upon a sinful world, as was the first, but one dealing with the Christian church, its foes, and its fortunes. It is not "little" in the sense of having a less number of words than the first pageant,—in fact, it is larger—but it is "little" in that it deals with only one section of the wide range of the divine purposes in the first book. This whole majestic vision of the mighty angel and his oath, then, is intended to make use feel how great a thing it is that God communicates to us His purposes in relation to the Christian church, and to prepare our minds for the most reverent and thoughtful reception of what is disclosed with regard to her future. It has, so far as I can see, no other meaning. That is to say, this vision is neither literal information about something that once took place, or will in the future take place; nor is it symbolical of any such event. The Historicists, Elliott, Barnes, and others of that school, consider the descent of the great angel to symbolize the Protestant Reformation, and the little book to be the Bible, restored to the common people at that time. This is because they are completely obsessed with the idea that the Roman Catholic apostasy is the chief thing in the book of Revelation. If one can accept their system, this is as good an interpretation as any; but to one who can not so regard the book it carries no weight.

That the apostle is commanded to take and eat the book indicates that he must thoroughly master its message. That it was sweet to his taste but bitter in digestion, is because, as Beckwith says: (p. 576)

> Sweet as it was to be the messenger of God, to feel in his heart that closeness with God enjoyed by one whom he makes his prophet, the execution of his office was fraught with bitterness in the announcement of the awful oracles which form so large a portion of these prophecies.

In connection with the seer's taking the little book, certain voices—

we are not told whose—say to him: "Thou must prophecy again over many nations and tongues and kings." The word *again* shows that he had been doing this very thing and was now about to start on a new commission of a similar nature. When had he "prophesied over many nations and tongues and kings?" No occasion can be pointed to unless the section from the beginning of chapter four is such activity. This confirms our conviction that the main body of the Revelation must be divided into two portions, corresponding to the Great Book Sealed and the Little Book Opened.

Before we leave this vision, it is well to notice how the visions of the Apocalypse rest upon those of the Old Testament; without slavishly or precisely reproducing them. The vision of the great angel is very much like that in Daniel 10.5–6 and 12.6–7. That of the little book to be eaten is like the vision in Ezekiel 2.8–3.3. When we find such similarities, we are not to think that the two passages prophesy the same things, but only that his intimate acquaintance with the Old Testament supplied the seer with materials that are worked into the form of the visions of his own book.

XIII

THE MEASURED TEMPLE AND
THE TWO WITNESSES

The eleventh, seventeenth, and twentieth chapters of the book of Revelation are the hardest to understand; as is shown by the great number of different interpretations and the very wide divergence between them. This is not caused primarily by obscurities in the text of these chapters, but by the fact that what is in them is related to other portions of the same book or of the Bible elsewhere, in such a manner that the view one takes of such other passages must influence one's exposition of these chapters. For instance, a man who believes that the return of the Jews to Palestine is prophesied elsewhere, will be led thereby to interpret the "temple" here spoken of as a future edifice to be erected in Jerusalem, and one who considers the "Beast" of chapters thirteen and seventeen to be a personal Antichrist, is bound to understand also the eleventh chapter differently from one who believes that the said Beast is the Roman Catholic church. Add to this the fundamental difference between the four chief schools of interpretation, and we have plenty of reason for the complete inability of interpreters to reach common ground in the eleventh chapter.

As for myself, I take for my own here the words of Dean Alford in regard to 5.1.[1]

> One who distrusts his own as well as all other explanations, and believes that much of this mysterious book is as yet unfathomed, is no match for one who hesitates not on every occasion to show his confidence that he is in the right, and all who differ from him are wrong.

---

[1] "New Testament for English Readers," Vol. II, Part II, p. 983. This is a popular English work on the lines of his learned "Greek Testament." This passage does not appear in the latter.

Yet among all the interpretations offered, there is one that seems to me more probably right than the others, and my endeavor in this chapter will be to inform the reader of the chief divergent views, and then to point out why I prefer the one of my choice. In doing so, let us first seek to see clearly the picture, that we may then the better seek to understand what the picture means.

> Rise and measure the temple of God, and the altar, and them that worship therein. And the court which is without the temple leave without, and measure it not, for it hath been given unto the nations, and the holy city shall they tread under foot forty and two months. (RV)

To "measure" evidently here is a symbol for God's acknowledging it to be His own, and taking it under His protection. This is agreed upon by all, and is evident enough from the contrast between the portion "measured," and the rest, which was to be left out in order that it should be trodden under foot. In fact "leave out" is too mild a translation of the original. It means properly "cast out," "reject," thus showing, by contrast, that the "measured" portion was not rejected, but continued to be holy and under the protecting care of God.

There are two words in the Greek for "temple." They are "naos," meaning the inner temple, the Holy and Most Holy Places, and "hieron," meaning the entire structure, including the courts. The former is the word here, and the use of the singular "court," instead of "courts," seems to indicate that the prophecy refers to the Old Testament temple, not to that of Zerubbabel or to the later one of Herod the Great, which was the one familiar to John from personal knowledge. That temple had several courts, not merely one. This is further indicated by verse nineteen of this chapter, where the ark of the covenant is seen in the heavenly temple. There was no such ark in the two post-exilic temples.

Taking the "naos" to be the inner shrine, comprising the Holy of Holies and the Holy Place, we are led to think of the "altar" here not as the brazen altar of burnt-sacrifice, for that stood in the court, but as the golden altar of incense, within the Holy Place. "Those who worship therein" (referring it to the temple) or "thereat," (referring it to the altar) are then the true worshipers, who are all priests (1.6; 5.10) for only the priests might enter the Holy Place.

"It hath been given to the nations"—better, here, Gentiles, for the Greek word can be translated either way. This carries back our thoughts at once to Luke 21.24, where our Lord says that "Jerusalem shall be trodden down of the Gentiles, until the times of the Gentiles be fulfilled."

During this period, while the Gentiles are "treading under foot" the holy city, Jerusalem, two witnesses preach in the city, clothed in sack-cloth, evidently, therefore, with a message of repentance. They are called "the two olive trees and the two candlesticks standing before the Lord of the whole earth," therefore in some sense parallel, in office and work, to Zerubbabel and Joshua, in Zechariah 4.11–14. They are immortal until their work is done, then they are slain, and their dead bodies suffer extreme indignity. Their death is the cause of great rejoicing, but they are raised up and ascend to heaven in the sight of their foes. The enemy that slays them is the "Beast" out of the abyss, evidently the same as the one of chapters thirteen to nineteen. The time, also, during which they prophesy is the same period as that during which the Beast has power, for forty-two months, or 1260 days. During their preaching they exercise the miraculous powers of Moses and Elijah. Finally, when they rise from the dead and ascend to heaven, there is a great earthquake, with seven thousand deaths, and with the unusual and happy result that the rest of the people are converted, which seems to be what is meant by the expression "gave glory to God." This is in striking contrast with the result of all the plagues inflicted under the trumpet series, where it is emphatically said (9.20) that no repentance took place.

Such is the picture. What does the picture mean? Two schools of interpretation regard it as a literal statement of what the seer expected would some day take place. These are the extreme Preterists and the extreme Futurists; for here the old saying is verified, that extremes meet. The extreme Preterists think that this section was written before the destruction of Jerusalem in AD 70, and that it is intended to predict that in the impending siege only the outer city would be captured, the inner temple remaining an impregnable fortress. The witnesses, then, were to be two men, exactly as here related, and would have such fortunes as are here depicted. The interpreters of this school know, of course, that nothing of the kind took place. The Romans took and destroyed the temple as well as the rest of the city, and history knows nothing at all of such remarkable men and miraculous events in that connection. This does not trouble the said scholars, however, for they have no respect for the book as an inspired production. We need not consider their view any further.

The extreme Futurists also take everything here literally, but, as there is not now any temple in Jerusalem, they think that one is to be built, and that the prophecy refers to such a new temple, to be erected by the Jews, under covenant with the Antichrist. After three and a half years the Antichrist, however, will break faith with them and begin a persecution, in the course of which Jerusalem will be taken by his army, with the exception of the temple. This they relate to Zechariah 14.1–8. This view may be found in J. A. Seiss: "Lectures on the Apocalypse," who devotes to this chapter nearly a hundred pages, from p. 150 to p. 246. For him the temple is the rebuilt temple in the geographical Jerusalem; the two witnesses are Enoch and Elijah, in person, returned to this earth; the time is the last three and a half years before the coming of Christ; the Beast is a personal Antichrist; the two witnesses are slain, lie unburied, ascend to heaven, etc., exactly as here foretold.

Of course, all this presupposes the return of the Jews to Palestine and the re-establishment of their national government there. This they consider to be clearly predicted in many passages of the prophetic scriptures. In the book entitled "Jesus Is Coming," the writer, Mr. W. E. Blackstone, devotes a whole chapter to this subject, and quotes a very large number of texts which, he thinks, indicate such a restoration. It will be well for the reader to make a study of this subject for himself. All I can do here is record my own very strong conviction, after careful examination of all the passages submitted by him and others, that not a single prophecy in the whole Bible gives any ground for the expectation that the Jews will be re-established in Palestine as an independent nation, and will rebuild their temple in Jerusalem. The prophecies of a return from exile are abundant enough, but they all refer to the return from Babylon. If I am confronted with those in the Post-exilic prophets, I reply that the return was a long process, like the exile, and that those promises refer to them as yet uncompleted portions of the return. The strongest text on that side is Amos 9.15, where it is said that Israel will be planted in their own land, *not again to be plucked up*. Since they certainly were plucked up after the return from Babylon, it looks, at first sight, as if nothing remains but to acknowledge that this event must be still future. All this confidence in this prediction disappears, however, when we, as sound exegetes, compare scripture with scripture, and take into consideration Jeremiah 18.9–10; where the people of Israel are expressly warned that no promise of God will be fulfilled to a disobedient and rebellious people. New sins demand new punishments, and the crowning sin of rejecting and crucifying the Savior brought the nation into a position where, as St. Paul solemnly affirms: "wrath is come upon them to the uttermost."

In all this, I beg the reader to note very carefully what I say. It is only that, so far as I can see, there is no prophecy that ought to lead us to expect a national restoration for the Jews in Palestine. If any one thinks he has a reason to expect such a thing on the ground of recent political developments, that is quite a different matter. I do not say they never will succeed in regaining control of Palestine and re-establishing their national existence there; but only that I do not find any such thing foretold. There are, no doubt, unrevealed purposes of God, as we are taught in the utterances of the seven thunders, which St. John was forbidden to write. If God has such a thing in mind, he will bring it to pass, and we shall see it when it happens, but even if I should see it tomorrow, that would not alter my conviction that it is not predicted in the prophetic scriptures.

Holding such views in regard to the national restoration of the Jews, I also, of course, expect no rebuilding of the temple, at least no such rebuilding with divine approval, and in accordance with prophecy. The exposition of Ezekiel's temple is exceedingly difficult, and not required here. Only I wish to say very earnestly that any such view as that of the Scofield Bible, which looks for the building of such a temple in the last days and for the re-institution of bloody sacrifices in the millennium, seems to be utterly out of harmony with the New Testament, particularly with the book of Hebrews and with the teaching of St. Paul. It is a return to "the weak and beggarly elements" of Judaism, and is unworthy of Christian interpreters.

To accept a restoration of the Jews and a rebuilt temple as contemplated in this eleventh chapter of the Apocalypse is impossible for me also because it requires a literal interpretation. As already argued, this is a symbolic book, and all the important scenes in it must, I am very sure, be symbolically interpreted. If we do not do that, everything becomes arbitrary. There are, to be sure, some few expressions, not belonging to the principal vision, that must be understood literally. When St. John says: "I was in the Isle called Patmos," that is literal, of course; but the visions must be consistently interpreted as symbols, or we shall be all at sea.

Setting aside, then, the two literal interpretations, as above, there are three symbolical interpretations to be considered, first, that of the Historicists, second, that which finds here a vision of the Christian church, third, that which considers it in relation to the Israel of the early Christian centuries.

The Historicists consider the Beast to represent the Roman Catholic church, and this obliges them to explain the vision in harmony therewith.

According to Barnes,[2] to "measure" the inner temple is to draw clearly the line between the true church and the false, which was done at the Reformation; the treading under foot the outer court means that the outward and visible church was polluted by the evils of Romanism; the two witnesses symbolize all who protested against the errors of Rome, including the Waldenses, the Albigenses, Wickliffe, Huss, and others. The war of the beast against them is their persecution by Rome; the three days and a half during which the dead bodies lie in the street unburied is the period from May 5, 1514, when it was announced in the Lateran Council that all opposition to Rome had ceased, to October 31, 1517, when Luther nailed his ninety-five theses to the church door in Wittenberg. The resurrection of the two witnesses symbolizes the sudden, mighty, and triumphant resuscitation of the church in the protesting voice of Luther and the glorious Reformation. The earthquake then naturally means the political convulsions that followed the Reformation, and the repentance of the citizens the general acceptance of the Reformed doctrines.

Of course, one has to be a convinced Historicist, on general principles, to believe so involved and strange an explanation. I have perhaps said enough already about this system, which I utterly repudiate as an interpretation of the Apocalypse.

That view that regards this chapter as symbolizing the fortunes of the Christian church, I shall take from Dr. S. Greijdanus,[3] the foremost contemporary Dutch expositor of the Revelation. He agrees, in substance, with many of the recent English and American commentators.

According to this interpretation, the temple represents the Christian church, the measured inner portion, those in the church who are true believers; the outer court, cast out, those who are merely nominal adherents of the gospel. That these are trodden under foot of the Gentiles, means both the outward persecution and the prevalence in the church of the views and practices of the sinful world. The forty-two weeks are the entire duration of this dispensation, from the first coming of Christ to the second. The two witnesses symbolize the preachers of the gospel during that period, whoever and wherever they may be. As Zerubbabel and Joshua were the leaders of God's people in their day, so the ministry of the word is set to mediate the grace of God in the church.

[2] pp. 303–316.

[3] pp. 168–184. The reference is to his "De Openbaring des Heeren aan Johannes," one of the volumes of the set entitled: "Korte Verklaring der Heilige Schrift," published in 1930. There is a similar independent commentary by Dr. Greijdanus dated 1908, with the same title.

Dr. Greijdanus accepts the idea of a personal Antichrist, to appear immediately before the Second Advent. He will apparently destroy the church, and this destruction is symbolized by the death of the two witnesses. "The great city," in the streets of which they lie, is Jerusalem, not in a geographical sense, but as a symbol of the antichristian world power. The resurrection of the two witnesses is the resurrection of believers at the return of Christ, spoken of in 1 Thessalonians 4.17.

There is much to be said in favor of this interpretation. As H. Grattan Guinness very cogently argues in "The Approaching End of the Age," p.116 sq., the Apocalypse is a Christian book, dealing with the fortunes of the Christian church. Except for very good reasons, no portion of it should be understood of any other group. Further, it is an established New Testament symbol to speak of the church as the "temple" of God. This is probably the meaning of 2 Thessalonians 2.4, and certainly so in 1 Corinthians 3.16–17; 2 Corinthians 6.16; Ephesians 2.21; 1 Peter 2.5.

Against this view, as presented by Dr. Greijdanus and others, is that it furnishes no explanation of the conversion of those remaining after the resurrection and ascension of the two witnesses. He makes this identical with the resurrection and rapture foretold by the apostle Paul in 1 Thessalonians 4.17. If he is correct, this is a strong argument against the "secret rapture," unseen and unheard except by believers, which the dispensationalists believe in. The two witnesses ascend: "and their enemies beheld them." But is he right? In the Pauline conception, the second coming of Christ coincides with the events of 1 Thessalonians 4.17, and at the same time all unbelievers perish. He says, in 2 Thessalonians 1.7–9 that those "that know not God and obey not the gospel of our Lord Jesus... shall suffer punishment, even eternal destruction." If, then, all believers are taken up to glory, and all the others are destroyed, who remains to "give glory to God?"

In Beckwith's interpretation, the temple is not the Christian church as such, but refers to the people of Israel, and the problem here symbolically set forth is the problem of their rejection and future restoration. He says:[4]

It appears reasonably certain that in the thought of our author Jerusalem here represents Israel as a whole. ...The church must often have asked with perplexity, What is to become of God's ancient people in the future of the new covenant? Are they to continue alienated to the end and to be

---

[4]pp. 588–589.

excluded from a share in the Messiah's kingdom?...St. Paul had discussed the subject with fullness and intense earnestness (Rom 9–11) and while finding as yet only a remnant preserved (the temple and its worshipers of our passage) he had foreseen the incoming of Israel as a whole at the last.

This fits the first part of the chapter very well. The temple is then a symbol for the people of Israel, the inner portion, acknowledged and preserved, represents those Israelites who had accepted Christ, the outer court those who did not believe and were rejected. These are "trodden under foot of the Gentiles," as Christ had foretold in Luke 21.24. It is no small merit of this interpretation that it thus leaves this expression to bear its normal sense. It is another great advantage that "the holy city," and "the great city," obviously referring to Jerusalem, can then be applied to the Jewish people; instead of the former referring to the church and the latter to the antichristian world in general, or to Rome. For the use of Jerusalem as a symbol of unbelieving Israel we have the warrant of Galatians 4.25: "Jerusalem that now is… in bondage."

When Beckwith goes on to identify the Beast with a personal Antichrist, to appear in the last days, and to explain the conversion of verse thirteen of the final restoration of Israel, as foretold by the apostle Paul in Romans 11.26, I find it more difficult to follow him, because of my view of the Beast. As will appear in the discussion of chapter thirteen and later, this, to me, symbolizes the persecuting pagan Roman empire, and not at all a personal Antichrist of the time of the end. Hence it is incumbent on me to explain the eleventh chapter also in harmony with that conception of the Beast.

Taking Beckwith's view for the beginning of the chapter, and modifying it at the close, I get the following interpretation, which is offered to the reader with diffidence:

The temple symbolizes Israel, the chosen people of God; the measured portion, the true Christian believers from among the Jews, the "elect remnant" of Romans 11.4. The outer court and the holy city represent the unbelieving Jewish community, in the condition in which they were at the time of writing this book. That condition was marked by two characteristics. On the one hand they were "trodden under foot," so far as Palestine and Jerusalem were concerned. On the other hand they were still, in many portions of the Roman empire, very numerous and influential. As such, they were among the bitterest enemies of the Christian church and of their own believing countrymen, continually inciting the pagans to persecution and rejoicing at the sufferings and death of Christians. All this is well symbolized by Jerusalem in a state of occupation by conquering Gentiles. In such a city the original inhabitants (here believing Jews) and the conquerors dwell side by side, but on comparatively friendly terms as compared with the attitude of both to the impregnable inner citadel and its garrison (believing Jews).

In this situation appear the preaching witnesses, whether issuing from the inner temple or not is not stated. These symbolize the whole preaching activity of the church of that period, both to the Jews and to Gentiles. Their death at the hands of the Beast signifies not any one great historical event (such as the complete overthrow of Christianity) but stands for martyrdom in general. Each Christian preacher was invulnerable until his work was done: until "they finished their testimony." Similarly, their lying dead in the city for three days signifies no special event, but, in general, the shameful indignities offered even to the dead bodies of the martyrs and the joy of their enemies, both Jews and pagans, but particularly the former, at their destruction. Their rising from the dead and ascending to heaven, symbolize the victory of the Christian cause at the rise of Constantine the Great. The earthquake appropriately stands for the political revolution accompanying that event, and the conversion of "the rest" is the turning of the population *en masse* to the winning faith.

It will be seen that this is a thorough-going Preterist interpretation. Nothing that is here foretold is referred to the time of the end and there is no personal Antichrist. Everything was fulfilled long ago. The reason why such an interpretation seems to me better is my adherence to the fundamental Preterist principle, which may be thus stated:

> Whenever two interpretations of any passage are possible, so far as the wording itself is concerned, one of which fits the situation in the early church at the time of the book, while the other does not, the former is to be preferred.

The problem here discussed, if Beckwith is right, was certainly an important problem for the early church, as we see from Romans 9–11. The very strong language used with regard to Jerusalem is also characteristic of that period. It is called "spiritually Sodom and Egypt." It was then too early to apply such terms to the outward organization of the Christian church, appropriate and common as it became in later centuries. On the other hand, the feeling of Christians against unbelieving Jews was already very strong, as we see from 1 Thessalonians 2.14–16, and Revelation 2.9.

After the parenthetical episode of the measured temple and the two witnesses, the pageant resumes its course, in the sounding of the seventh trumpet. This is spoken of as "the third woe," which turns out to be the end of the world. No details are given, but certain great voices in heaven declare that God's judgments have taken effect, not, indeed, in the conversion of men, but in the crushing of all opposition and in establishing the rule of God in the earth. Then the four and twenty elders give God thanks that the time has come for the dead to be judged and the saints to be rewarded. This is therefore the triumphant consummation of the divine enterprise, to the leadership of which the Lamb was commissioned by his receiving the sealed book. The work that was then begun is now finished.

There are some students who think that verse 19 should be the beginning of the next chapter, introducing a new vision, but it seems to me that the chapter division is correct as it stands. This is a most worthy "finale" to the entire pageant of the Seals and the Trumpets. As the last scene closes, the audience catches a glimpse of the heavenly temple, and of the ark of the divine covenant, which underlies all God's dealings with men; and a postlude of indefinite but solemn grandeur brings the presentation to a close.

Swete has, it seems to me, correctly stated the nature of this finale and the break that occurs here between the eleventh and twelfth chapters, as follows: (p.142)

> The second great section of the Book (4.1–11.19) ends, as it began, with a vision of the heavenly order. ...With the seventh trumpet-blast the Kingdom of God has come, and the general judgment is at hand. Thus the second section of the Apocalypse brings the course of history down to the verge of the Parousia. If the Book had ended here, it would have been within these limits complete. But the Seer pauses for a moment only to take up his role again with a fresh presentation of the future, in which the vision is to be carried to its issue. A new prophecy begins in chapter 12, the contents of the open little book which the Seer had been directed to take from the hand of the Angel and consume. ...This second message occupies the remainder of the Book.

XIV

THE RADIANT WOMAN AND THE RED DRAGON

As already stated, with the beginning of the twelfth chapter we enter upon a section of the book of Revelation quite different, in structure and design, from the two sections we have already considered. From this point until the end of the book, or at least, until the tenth verse of the twentieth chapter, we seem to have a sort of continued story, which may be appropriately called The Drama of the Woman and the Dragon. It is a dramatization of the fortunes of the people of God in conflict with the great enemy, the devil.

The basic passage of the Old Testament seems to me to be Genesis 3.15, where the Lord, after the temptation and fall of man, says to the serpent:

> I will put enmity between thee and the woman, and between thy seed and her seed: he will bruise (or crush) thy head, and thou shalt bruise his heel.

This is truly one of the most wonderful passages in the Old Testament. Dr. Delitszch quotes the fine utterance of Drechsler in regard to it:[1]

> General, indefinite, and obscure as the primeval age to which it belongs, it lies marvelously and sacredly on the threshold of the lost Paradise, like an awe-inspiring sphinx before the ruins of a mysterious temple.

It has been generally regarded as a Messianic prophecy, the very first promise of victory and salvation. Therefore it is called in English theology the "Prot-evangelium," or first proclamation of the gospel; and in Dutch theology by the still more beautiful name of "Moeder-belofte," or "Mother Promise," as if it carried in its womb all other promises of God.

---

[1] New Commentary on Genesis, Vol. I, p. 164.

Yet it is a striking fact that this text is nowhere in the New Testament expressly quoted as Messianic. Many other passages are adduced as foretelling the coming of the Redeemer, some of them having much less clearly any reference to Christ than this one, but this is not cited by any apostle or evangelist. Perhaps it was expressly so reserved by the Holy Spirit, that it might be made the basis of this chapter. Here we do certainly find again the two parties that are set over against each other in the Prot-evangelium: the Woman and the Serpent, and here, as there, these two parties are in mortal conflict. Here, also, it is through the Seed of the Woman that the triumph is wrought, and, it is "the rest of the seed," enlisting under the banner of the great Seed, against whom the unceasing enmity of the Serpent is directed. (v.17)

Here we need not speak hesitatingly, or express merely an opinion, for the key is given us in v. 9. The Dragon is "the old Serpent, he that is called the Devil, and Satan, the deceiver of the whole world." The description of the conflict goes on through the following chapters, until the Dragon is finally disposed of in 20.10. After that, we hear of him no more. Thus this twelfth chapter is a dramatic device similar to that of a moving picture show, in which, before the action starts, we are given a "close-up" of the chief characters. Let us now look at some of the details.

A great sign was seen in heaven.

That is, as I understand it, those who saw this sign were in heaven. Many take it that "heaven" or, "the heaven," as the Greek has it, means here "the sky," as if this scene were a constellation, or a picture thrown against the sky as a background. However, most of the things described certainly take place on the earth, and nothing is said about the Woman's being transferred from heaven to earth; so that it seems to me simpler to think of this phrase, "was seen in heaven" as meaning that it was seen from the heavenly point of view.

A woman, arrayed with the sun, and the moon under her feet, and upon her head a crown of twelve stars.

See how glorious this Woman is: the sun, moon, and stars—all the sources of light—are clustered about her. The writer here again shows us how independent his symbolism is of all natural possibility. Who ever heard of a dress being made of the sun, and how could you make a dress of it? Never mind, that is not the point. The psalmist already had said of God, "Who coverest thyself with light as with a garment" (Psalm 104.2) and here God's own glory is given to the Woman, and she becomes the great light-bearer. The light of God is upon her, and around her, and beneath her: all that heaven can contribute, of glory and beauty, is lavished upon her.

Who is this Radiant Woman? We find that she is in a state of expectancy for a time, that from her the Seed is born, after which she is persecuted, and yet preserved. From this description, and by comparison with Genesis 3.15, we can not hesitate to see in her a symbol of the church of God, considered in the broadest possible manner, as the body of the redeemed people of God, whether under the Old Covenant or the New. This meaning is more generally agreed upon than the meaning of almost any other of the chief figures of the book of Revelation. We can see now what is meant by the statement that this glorious Woman is seen in heaven, i.e., from the heavenly point of view; for the church does not seem to be so glorious, when viewed from the earth, and measured by human standards. On earth she appears as a company of people not very important, with many faults, divisions, and blemishes. It is only when we think of her as she appears to heavenly eyes that she is clothed with the sun, has the stars for her crown, and the moon under her feet.

> She was with child, and she crieth out, travailing in birth and in pain to be delivered.

This is the state of waiting, hoping, and suffering in which the people of God were for so long a time before the birth of Christ; fitly symbolized here by the state of an expectant mother. The Radiant Woman therefore does not symbolize the New Testament church alone, or the Old Testament church alone; not the visible church, to the exclusion of the invisible church, nor the invisible to the exclusion of the visible church of history. She represents the church in the broadest possible sense. This includes, on the one hand, the visible church that began to exist with the Abrahamic covenant and on the other the much older invisible church of which the Heidelberg Catechism speaks, in the Twenty-first Lord's day:

> What believest thou concerning the 'Holy Catholic Church' of Christ?
>
> That the Son of God, from the beginning to the end of the world, gathers, defends, and preserves to Himself, by His Spirit and word, out of the

whole human race, a church chosen to everlasting life, agreeing in true faith, and that I am, and ever shall remain, a living member thereof.

It is impossible to understand this chapter, as well as some other important portions of God's word, if we refuse to recognize the unity and continuity of the people of God, in both Old and New Testament times. Granted that there is a sense in which the Christian church began with Jesus Christ, and did not exist before: it is a complementary and also very important truth that it was continuous, in its inward life, and in its relation to the promises of God, with the people of Israel, considered as God's group, the group through which and within which he was working out his redemptive purposes. This is emphasized with a singular approach to unanimity by commentators on this passage. Even J. A. Seiss, Premillenarian and Futurist as he is, with whom I so frequently feel obliged to differ, says on this point: (Vol. II, p. 277)

> It does not refer to the Jewish Church exclusively...It is not the Christian Church exclusively. ...The Church of the Old Testament and that of the New are, after all, not so alien to each other. ...There has really been but one church on earth, existing through all times and under all economies. And so we have here, as the symbol of it, this one glorious Woman.

The point is one of such prime importance for the interpretation, not of this one chapter only, but of the entire Apocalypse, that it will be well to insert here a number of similar statements from famous expositors.

Auberlen: (p. 247)

> It is equally impossible to understand by the woman only the Old Testament church, or Israel, as it is to refer the expression merely to the New Testament church. For we know that Israel ceased, soon after the ascension of Christ, to be the congregation of God. ...And yet, in Revelation 12.6, 13, the woman is spoken of subsequently to that event. Thus, the text referring both to the past and future, our former view is confirmed, that the expression "woman" relates to the congregation of God in this world, generally and universally, and can not be limited to any particular period or epoch.

Moses Stuart: (Vol. II, p. 252)

> It must, then, be the church; the church not simply as Jewish, but in a more generic and theocratic sense,—the people of God.

Lange: (p. 245)

The Woman is the Old and New Testament Church of God in undivided unity.

Gebhardt:[2]

What, then, are we to understand by the Woman? Simply the Church of God, which already existed in the prophetic fact of the old covenant, and which now exists in the time of its fulfillment in Christendom, and will exist in its eternal completion in the new heaven and the new earth.

Beckwith: (p. 621)

She is the heavenly representative of the people of God… represented alike by the people of the old and new covenants. …With our writer there is only one true Israel, embracing alike the Jewish and the Christian church.

Swete: (p. 146)

Doubtless the Church of the Old Testament was the Mother of whom Christ came after the flesh. But here, as everywhere in the book, no sharp dividing line is drawn between the church of the Old Testament and the Christian Society; the latter is viewed as the Jewish church come to its maturity. Thus the woman who gave birth to the Christ is identical with her who after His departure suffered for her faith in Him, and who is the mother of believers.

The next portrait drawn for us by the inspired artist is that of the devil, or Satan, and this is the way he looks, when seen from the heavenly standpoint. (From the human and earthly point of view he often looks like a very fascinating lady or an eminently respectable gentleman.)

And there was seen another sign in heaven: and behold, a great red dragon having seven heads and ten horns, and upon his heads seven diadems.

Red, no doubt, to indicate his fierce and bloody nature: having seven heads, perhaps, to show how clever he is. An English poet, satirizing the village schoolmaster, says of him:

---

[2] Quoted in Meyer's Commentary on Revelation, p. 358.

And still the wonder grew—
That one small head could carry all he knew!

There was too much wisdom in this serpent to be contained in one head, he needed seven. Possibly, however, this does not mean that he was so clever, but only that he was so hard to kill. Some of the mythical monsters had this advantage; it was no great loss to them to have a head cut off, there were plenty more. He had ten horns, therefore abundance of power, especially power for destruction; and upon his heads were seven diadems.

> And his tail draweth the third part of the stars of heaven, and did cast them to the earth.

Some seek a special meaning in the stars and in their being cast down, such as that they represent the fall of the angels, or kings and nobles deposed, or Christian bishops corrupted; but having regard to the pictorial and dramatic character of the passage, I doubt whether any such meaning is intended here. Rather it seems to be like a not uncommon poetical and dramatic device, to draw attention to some comparatively trifling thing about a character, in order thereby indirectly to give an impression of his importance. Thus Milton, seeking to convey an overwhelming impression of the greatness of Satan, accomplishes that purpose by describing his walking-stick!

> His staff, to which the tallest pine
> Hewn on Norwegian hills to be the mast
> Of some great admiral, were but a wand,
> He walked with, to support unsteady steps,
> Over the burning marl.

Without saying a word about Satan himself, he thus causes us to stand in awe of his size, for if this was his cane, how great was he?

So here: this dragon was so big that there was not room enough for him under the sky. As he stood there before the Woman, lashing his tail, the stars came tumbling down!

> And the dragon stood before the woman which was about to be delivered that when she was delivered he might devour her child.

So not only the Woman is expectant, the Dragon knows of the coming

Child and recognizes in him the great enemy to be overcome. The Messianic prophecies were evidently read and understood in hell. Alas, poor woman, and poor baby: what chance have they against a read dragon, with seven heads, and ten horns, and a tail lashing about in fury, so as to tear down the stars from their appointed places? At last the time comes;

> And she was delivered of a son, a man child, who is to rule all nations with a rod of iron.

The expression "a son, a man child," is very peculiar. Is not every son a man child? Of course, but in the Greek this is a very unusual and very rough phrase, which we might render, a little more literally, "a son—a male!" Perhaps we shall still better get into the spirit of it if we borrow a slang phrase, almost a coarse phrase, from the language of the street, and translate it: "a son, a he-man!" It is vehement, almost a fierce, assertion of the virility of the Christ, as if the writer means to say that here comes a regular two-fisted fighter, with whom his enemies will have their hands full.

Here, again, St. John gives us a hint as to the interpretation. He is so eager that we shall make no mistake about this baby that he gives us a quotation from the second psalm, to identify him: "Who is to rule all nations with a rod of iron." This is so plain that I am astonished to find other interpretations. As Alford says: "Here, at least, all ought to have been plain." Yet there are other interpretations, and of necessity there must be, if the Historicists and Futurists are to save their systems. Let us see what they make of it.

The Historicist view is that the book of Revelation presents to us in symbols a continuous view of the fortunes of the Christian church. Therefore, having already expounded the seals and the trumpets in terms of church history to the time of Gregory the Great and later, they cannot very well go back and interpret this chapter of the birth of Christ and the immediately succeeding persecution of the church. In spite of the very clear terms in which the case is presented, they must find something after the fourth and fifth centuries to which it may be applied. But what that is, they are not agreed. Carroll (p. 170) says: "The man-child represents the martyrs that were put to death in this coming persecution." Barnes (p. 337) believes the entire presentation to refer to the time of the rise of the papacy, and that the bringing forth of the man-child represents the church in its increase and prosperity. Lord thinks the man-child means Constantine the Great, and that the Woman cries out to be delivered denotes "the importunate desire and endeavor of those whom she symbol-izes, to present to the empire one who should as their son, rise to supreme power."[3] It seems to me hardly necessary to refute such interpretations as these. No one would have thought of them unless the system to which he was already committed had forbidden his accepting the obvious meaning.

Some of the Futurists do regard the man-child as the Lord Jesus Christ. Bultema says: (p. 192) "Who this man-child is, requires no special discus-sion. He is none other than the Lord Jesus Christ." The same view is found in Ford C. Ottman, "The Unfolding of the Ages," p. 288. These interpret-ers separate this first episode of chapter twelve from all the rest, and thus save their Futurism. This they do by the familiar device of the "parenthe-sis." It is Israel that brings forth the Man-child, and although He is recog-nized to be the Lord Jesus, the Woman who flees into the wilderness and is persecuted is not the Church of Christ but the Israel of the end-time. Hence nearly two thousand unnoticed years lie between verse five and verse six. As Ottman puts it: "With Christ born and definitely rejected, time for Israel is not counted until after the Church has been removed from the earth and Israel's prophetic history is again taken up." So also S. D. Gordon. (p. 189) This line of interpretation seems to me untenable. No principles of exegesis that I know of can justify this "parenthesis" theory. Other Futurists go to the length of denying that the man-child refers to Christ. Seiss, as we have already seen, denies absolutely that anything in the book of Revelation beyond the third chapter, can be fulfilled before the time of the end. He therefore cannot admit that the opening verses of chapter twelve look back to the birth of Jesus. For him, the birth of the man-child symbolizes the rapture of the living saints and the resurrection of those already fallen asleep, as foretold in 1 Thessalonians 4.16–17.[4] Ste-vens takes the same view; the Woman is the church of the last days, the man-child symbolizes those who have part in the first rapture.[5] Since Dr. Abraham Kuyper is also committed to the Futurist exposition, one looks with eagerness to see what he makes of this chapter, to find, with surprise, that he omits all reference to it! One admires his discretion, but this omis-sion is practically a confession that on Futurist principles no reasonable exegesis of this chapter is possible.

Thus, it seems to me, both Historicist and Futurist systems suffer ship-

---

[3] p. 313.

[4] Vol. II, p. 332, sq.

[5] Vol. II, p. 198.

wreck on the rock of the twelfth chapter. I am constrained to agree with the judgment of Dean Alford, when he says:

> All Scripture analogy, and that of this book itself, requires that these words should be understood of our incarnate Lord, and of no other. Any system seems to me convicted of error, which is compelled to interpret the words otherwise.[6]

While this judgment of Dean Alford applies only to the interpretation of the man-child, I feel ready to add that any interpretation that finds itself compelled to separate verses five and six by a period of nearly two thousand years, is as clearly out of the question.

Let us return, now, from this controversial digression, to direct exposition of this chapter. The Radiant Woman, as already seen, is a symbol for the people of God, compromising all true believers before the coming of Christ, and the Christian Church from that time on. The period of expectancy is the time of the Messianic hope, the birth of the Man-child the birth of Jesus Christ, the attempt of the Dragon to destroy the child sums up all the attempts to get rid of him during his earthly life, beginning with the attempt of Herod the Great until the crucifixion. That the man-child is nevertheless rescued and is taken up to heaven sets before us the resurrection and ascension of Christ. We need only ask ourselves how the believers of the Seven Churches, first receiving this letter, would understand it. Would not their thoughts turn, and were they not intended to turn, to the story so familiar to them?

Let us not fail to notice the additional words "to His throne." The man-child was not only taken up to God to be protected, He was taken up to *His throne*, that is, to be enthroned, to share in the divine sovereignty and government. Here we have the truth confessed in the Apostles' Creed and symbolized by the great enthronement scene in chapter five of this book. Let us never think that Christ is sitting idle at the right hand of the Father. "He must reign, till He hath put all His enemies under His feet." (1 Cor 15.25)

Two things follow: war in heaven and persecution on earth. The significance of the former we hope to treat in the following chapter of our exposition. Laying it aside for the present, we follow the fortunes of the Radiant Woman, now bereft of her child, but still the object of the Dragon's hate. She is given "the two wings of the great eagle" wherewith she flies into the

---

[6] Vol. IV, Part II, p. 249, Sec. V, paragraph 23 of Prolegomena.

wilderness, to a place prepared for her by God. There she is in safety, and receives nourishment, for a period of 1260 days, evidently the same period as is referred to by the expression "a time, and times, and half a time." Everything here leads our thought back to the Old Testament history and prophecy. The "two wings of the great eagle," remind us of Deuteronomy 32.11 and Exodus 19.4. The great eagle is God Himself, and the two wings are a symbol of his protecting care. The nourishment given the Woman in the wilderness corresponds to the manna received by Israel in the wilderness, perpetual symbol of the inward grace by which God nourishes the spiritual life of all who trust in Him. The wilderness is an outward state of affliction, a state also of separation from the visible presence of the Lord, a state intermediate between redemption and the full enjoyment of salvation. When the Israelites had crossed the Red Sea, they were fully delivered from the Egyptians, but the wilderness period intervened between them and the enjoyment of the Promised Land. So the Christian individual and the Christian church. Having believed on Christ, we are fully redeemed, and justified, but we are not yet glorified. The stage between is the wilderness of this life, for the individual, and is the state of outward affliction for the church. It is tempting to refer the 1260 days, therefore as some do, to the whole period between the first coming of Christ and His Second Advent; but this I hesitate to do, in view of the other passages in which the same period is referred to. Some of these passages are so joined to the history of the Beast, that we can not come to a satisfactory exposition of the days without first having an interpretation of the Beast and his activities. We shall therefore take up this point later.

Seeing that the Woman was about to make good her escape, the Dragon "cast out of his mouth after the woman water as a river, that he might cause her to be carried away by the stream." It is a curious instance of the very free—not to say careless—manner in which symbols are used in this book, that the Serpent is here represented as trying to destroy a flying woman with a rushing flood, evidently an absurd procedure. The fact is, the author passes from figure to figure with such extreme freedom that he seems one moment to forget what he said the moment before. Wings with which to fly away are a good figure for God's help and protection. Therefore the wings are there. A rushing flood is a fine figure for an irresistible onslaught, therefore the river is there. That the two figures do not agree, gives our author no concern. This peculiarity of the book must be remembered by us in the exposition, and we should be careful not to reason confidently from one symbol to another. Each symbol stands upon its own merits in the place where it is used. This attempt also comes to nothing. The earth helps the woman and swallows up the stream. Probably the apostle was thinking of the rivers of Damascus, well known to him, that comes down with a rushing flood from the eastern slope of Lebanon, and seem like mighty streams, but find their way into the desert and presently are swallowed up in the sand, without ever joining any other stream or emptying into any sea, or coming to anything at all.

That this attempt comes from the mouth of the dragon, seems to indicate some attack upon the church by word of mouth, such as calumny or false doctrine: most likely, it seems to me, the latter. The river then means the flood of heretical doctrine that ever and again threatens to engulf the church. In the early church Ebionitism, Gnosticism, Manichaeism, Montanism, Arianism and Pelagianism endangered the life of the church. They are remembered now only by church historians. The earth helped the woman and swallowed up the flood. Later it was Romanism and Socinianism. In modern life it is Unitarianism, Modernism, Mormonism, Russellism, Christian Science, Spiritualism, etc., etc.—a long list of movements of Satanic origin that come on like a flood, and for a time make timid believers afraid that the church will be overwhelmed and the gospel permanently lost to the world—but it never comes to pass. The present heresies will disappear as did those of the past.

"And the dragon waxed wroth with the woman and went away to make war with the rest of her seed." "Went away" seems to indicate that he gave up the attempt to destroy the woman, having found it true, as the Savior had foretold, that "the gates of hell shall not prevail" against the church. "To make war upon the rest of her seed," introduces a collective meaning into the word "seed," indicating that it includes more than the person of the single Man-child. This should not be difficult for Bible readers to understand, when they remember Galatians 3.16 and 29. There, as here, Jesus Christ is the Seed, and yet believers, because of their union with Him, are also called the "seed." It is possible that those who, in the conflict, have followed their Lord through death to glory, are included in the conception of the seed that was snatched up to heaven, but this we can not say with confidence. In any case, we are warned that the devil, finding it impossible to destroy the church of Christ as such, continues his bitter enmity against the members of the church as individuals, and departs, not to cease from the conflict, but to seek allies who will help him carry it on.

XV

THE WAR IN HEAVEN

In studying the twelfth chapter, we did not take verses 7–12 in the order of the text; because they somewhat break the continuity of the story of the Radiant Woman and her fortunes. Logically and spiritually, however, they are in exactly the right place. Three things are presented in all of the "Little Book" section of the Revelation, namely, the Woman, the Dragon, and the Conflict. As the writer gave us first a "close-up" of the two chief actors in the drama, that we may know them in later allusions, so he now gives us, in this vision of the war in heaven, a similar preliminary view of the conflict. He shows us what the inner reality of that conflict is, a reality that does not always clearly appear in the development of the story, but must be kept in mind by us; and was to be kept in mind by the early believers, who lived in the first stages of the conflict.

The main point of the teaching is this: that the inward spiritual conflict and the outward persecution or trouble, experienced in the Christian life, although for believers often a very bitter struggle, are part and parcel of a larger conflict in the world of spirits. That unseen conflict is the real thing, and therein a complete victory has been won. The enemy who seems so strong to us is a defeated foe. He has but "a short time" left in which to work out his evil purposes. In principle everything is decided, as Jesus said to His disciples: "In the world ye have tribulation; but be of good cheer: I have overcome the world" (John 16.33). If we are faithful and patient, the victory already gained in heaven will duly and certainly appear upon the earth.

As usual, let us look first that the picture, and then at the meaning of the picture. The apostle sees, in vision, a battle, not on earth, but in heaven, between two great armies. These must be conceived as seen by him in human form, armed with such weapons and fighting such a battle as he might have seen had he been present at a conflict between a Roman army and its foes. One army is led by the Dragon, obviously the same formidable enemy who stood before the Radiant Woman, eager to devour her child; but he is not now necessarily in dragon form. The characters in the visions of the Apocalypse change from the forms of beasts or of natural objects to the human form in the twinkling of an eye. So, as we have seen, the Lamb immediately assumes a human form, so that he is able to take a sealed book and to open the seals thereof; the star in 9.1 is given a key and unlocks the door of the pit, which requires human hands; and the second beast of 13.11 is a beast only when we first see him. After that, he is a false prophet. So here, the dreadful being who was first seen in serpent form, with seven heads and ten horns, is now a mighty warrior, commanding a host. He is the same Satan, whatever his form.

The commander–in–chief of the angelic host is Michael, whose name means: "Who is like God?" We read of him also in the ninth verse of Jude, where he is called an archangel, and is said to have disputed with Satan about the body of Moses. In Daniel 10.13, the prophet is told that Michael helped to overcome the "Prince of the kingdom of Persia." In the same chapter, verse 21, he is called "your prince," that is, the prince of Israel, and in 12.1 further help from him is promised. These passages in Daniel, the one in Jude, and this vision of the Apocalypse, are all the Bible contains about Michael. By some writers he is identified with Christ, but it seems to me without sufficient reason. Some interpreters, also, add to the scene in the chapter before us the dramatic touch that the Dragon ascended to heaven in pursuit of the Man-Child, to drive him from the throne of God; but this seems to me quite out of place. As Bible students, it is our business to interpret the vision, not to add to it.

How long the battle lasted, and what deeds of valor were done on this side or that, we are not told, only that it ended in a complete defeat for the Dragon. His army was routed, and he and his angels were expelled from heaven. "Neither was their place found any more in heaven." Does this mean that up to that time they had had their abode in heaven? Yes, obviously, that is what it means—in the vision. We are now trying to get the picture. Whether it follows that the demons had their home there in reality, until the ascension of Christ, will be discussed later. The Dragon and his army were cast down to the earth, where, furious at their defeat, they set to work to do all the harm they could, while there was still time and opportunity, knowing that they had but a short time. The case is like that of a defeated army, which in its retreat ravages the defenseless country in its path; without, however, gaining therefrom any advantage, so far as the real issues of the war are concerned.

There follows—as always in the case of a victory on earth—a triumph-song. The victors are celebrating; but singularly enough the song does not quite answer to the battle and the victory. It is not the celestial warriors who are praised, but Christian confessors[1] and martyrs; and the victory seems now no longer to be one gained with weapons of war, upon the field of battle, but in a court, where the accuser is put to silence, and the accused go free. The ground of such acquittal is, on the one hand, the death of Christ, and, on the other, the testimony and faithfulness of the believers—faithfulness even unto death.

In any other book but the Apocalypse, such a sudden change of figure would be bewildering; but if we have caught the spirit and understood the method of this book, it is not so here—it is illuminating. It gives us the key to the vision. What do we learn from it? First of all, that it would be a cardinal mistake to think of this war in heaven as something that actually occurred. It is a symbolic vision—a vision only. Is it arbitrary so to take it? By no means. On the contrary, it is in the highest degree arbitrary to think that here a real event of celestial history is disclosed to us. The entire Apocalypse is a series of symbolical pictures, and this twelfth chapter is not less so than the others. Generally this is understood. Every one sees that Satan has not seven heads and ten horns, and that no woman ever had her baby snatched away to heaven in the manner here related. If, then, these are symbols, by what right do we think of this war in heaven as an actual fight?

Yet this mistake is made by many learned commentators. Having made this mistake, they then speak as if one could gather information here concerning the place where the devil and his angels had their abode until the ascension of the Lord Jesus Christ. Auberlen, for instance, says:[2]

> In the next verse it is said: 'Neither was their place found any more in heaven' and this presupposes that hitherto, up to the ascension of Christ,

---

[1] The word "confessors" is here used in a technical sense. In the early church, those who had been brought before the Roman tribunals and had maintained their Christian confession in the face of torture and the threat of death, were called "confessors," if their lives were spared. They were honored in the church together with the martyrs.

[2] p. 254.

the demons were in heaven like the other angels, and that, like them, they influenced earth from their abodes in heaven, in which there are many mansions. As heaven was not yet opened to man before Christ, so it was not yet shut against the devils.

So Seiss, of course, and all the literalists. Even Alford and Mauro, who usually discern symbols without difficulty, appear here to think of actual warfare, and a real expulsion of the demons from their heavenly home.

Against this, Lenski appears to me to be emphatically right, when he says:[3]

> Because John writes: 'There occurred battle in the heaven,' the impossible did not take place—the eternal bliss and peace of the actual heaven was not turned into battle tumult. ...These figures and events form visions, and thus 'were seen' and 'occurred' in the heaven. The wicked angels had long lost their 'proper habitation' (Jude 6) among the good angels in the actual heaven, nor did they try to storm heaven after the Savior's enthronement. Let us keep our exegetical balance.

Duesterdieck, in Meyer's Commentary, well says:[4]

> This idea... is gathered from the text only by the ascription of objective reality to what is indeed improperly regarded as pure fiction; yet to which only the reality of the vision belongs.

To understand what this writer means by its not being pure fiction, and yet not actual, let us think of the vision of St. Peter on the housetop at Joppa. (Acts 10.9–16) That is not a fictional story. He truly was there and saw the vision, which conveyed to him very important instruction; yet no one believes that there was really a sheet let down from heaven. If we did so take it, we should be obliged to draw the inference that such animals as were in the sheet are kept in heaven, for only so could they be let down out of it! The sheet, and the four-footed beasts in it, existed in the vision, but in the vision only. So here. John saw a vision of a war in heaven, and it has a meaning; but this does not in the least make it necessary or reasonable for us to believe that there ever was such a clash of weapons in heaven, or is ever going to be. Hence nothing is to be learned here about the abode of

---

[3] p. 373.

[4] p. 345.

evil angels before the time of Christ. They did have their home there, in the vision, but this tells us nothing about the reality.

Let us settle it firmly in our hearts, and stick to it consistently, that the Apocalypse is a book of spiritual cartoons, the pictures not in any case to be mistaken for the reality, no matter how vividly drawn. As already pointed out, the rest of this chapter, concerning the Radiant Woman, the Red Dragon, and their adventures, is clearly seen by all interpreters to be symbolic, although they do not agree on what is symbolized. Is it not, then, to introduce confusion into the interpretation to suppose that the apostle suddenly shifts from symbolism to reality when he tells of the war in heaven?

Taking the whole, then, as symbolic teaching, what is the spiritual reality embodied in the picture? It seems to me that the vision is intended to teach us the following very important things: (1) That the struggle between good and evil in this world, in which we Christians are personally engaged, and in which we suffer the attacks of Satan, is not something that stands by itself, but is a part of a much larger struggle going on in the world of spirits. This is a moral universe, full of morally intelligent beings, and the conflict concerns them all. It is a struggle, "not against flesh and blood, but against the principalities, against the powers, against the world rulers of this darkness, against the spiritual hosts of wickedness in the heavenly places" (or, "the heavenly things," the world of spirit) (Eph 6.12).

(2) That with the coming and atonement of Christ, the age-long struggle between good and evil did reach a crisis, with a victory on the side of the good more complete and permanent than was possible before.

This was because now at last two great questions could be answered, and because those answers were essential to a satisfactory solution of the problem of a morally disturbed universe. These questions were: "How can a just and holy God forgive sin?"; and "If a way be found to reconcile forgiveness and justice, will men accept it?" The triumph-song indicates that the solution of these problems and the victory of the heavenly host are one and the same thing. The thing rejoiced over is that "the accuser of our brethren is cast down, who accuseth them before our God day and night." Here we are reminded of the scene in Zechariah 3.1–5. In both passages, the presence of an accuser is a concrete symbol to indicate that there is an unanswered accusation; and the silencing of the prosecutor is equivalent to the acquittal of the accused. Now, before the coming and atonement of Christ, the sins of God's people were indeed forgiven, but they were forgiven on the ground of something that was to take place in the future, not because of something that had already taken place. Hence, the problem of forgiveness was not solved; it was only, so to speak, laid on the table. As St. Paul puts it, in Romans 3.25, this was "the passing over of the sins done aforetime, in the forbearance of God." Since we are expressly told that the angels take an interest in these things (1 Pet 1.12) we can readily believe that during all the ages prior to the atonement it was to them a dark and difficult question, how the holiness and justice of God could be reconciled with this "passing over" of sin. Abraham was called the friend of God, yet he lied; and David was "the man after God's own heart"; yet he was guilty of the blackest crimes. That these accusations stood against all of the redeemed is here symbolically expressed by the statement that Satan accused them before God day and night. The good angels could find no solution, for the truth of the said accusations could not be denied. Symbolically speaking, they could not cast out the accuser. When however, the Son of God had died upon the cross, thus atoning for sin, this while problem was cleared up. Against those thus redeemed, no accusation could any longer stand. This is pictorially shown by the scene in which the good angels, under the leadership of Michael, expel those who accuse the brethren. What is here dramatically presented is the truth so eloquently voiced by the apostle Paul:

> Who shall lay anything to the charge of God's elect? It is God that justifieth. Who is he that shall condemn? (Rom 8.33)

> Christ Jesus, whom God set forth to be a propitiation, through faith by his blood, to show his righteousness, because of the passing over of the sins done aforetime, in the forbearance of God; for the showing, I say, of his righteousness at this present season: that he might himself be just, and the justifier of him that hath faith in Jesus. (Rom 3.25–26) (RV)

We can see that such a thing as this marked a crisis in the world of superhuman moral intelligences, appropriately symbolized here by battle and victory.

The second question was this: would there be men who would lay hold on this salvation by faith? Without that, even so great a solution must fail. Would any human beings really be willing to sacrifice all things for the sake of reconciliation with God through Jesus Christ? From the viewpoint of the divine fore-ordination and fore-knowledge, this was, of course, at no time in doubt; but the angels must have watched with the keenest interest for the manifestations of such love and faith. Hence they are here represented as rejoicing with great joy to see that their brethren on earth, redeemed by the blood of the Lamb, steadfastly held fast "the word of their testimony," and "loved not their life even unto death." Thus did the holy angels learn new and inspiring lessons with regard to the power of redeeming grace, and thus were they supplied with weapons to repel finally and for good the assaults of evil. Thus was fulfilled that which is written: "That now unto the principalities and powers in the heavenly places might be made known through the church the manifold wisdom of God." (Eph 3.10) What now was left of victory for Satan and his hosts? Why should their sneers against the divine righteousness and their accusations against the blood-bought brethren be any longer tolerated? All this is pictorially presented to the eye of the seer when in the vision the good angels arise and triumphantly sweep the accusers from before the throne of God.

Timbrel states this interpretation in the following passage:[5]

From the hour when the first saved sinner took his place in heaven, by virtue of a system of credit, piling up its obligations in the great clearing house of eternity, Satan's accusing voice had, up to this hour, broken discordant upon the chant of the Zoa. The holy character of God is thus impugned; and his impartial justice, in the presence of the rattling chains of Tartarus, made the occasion of the Satanic sneer. But now, in the presence of the whelming fact of the blood-stained cross, the ground of this impeachment of the divine character is swept from beneath his dragonic feet, while the voice of accusation is hushed forever.

Weiss, less dramatically, says the same thing:[6]

Since Satan has been hurled out of heaven, he has been deprived of the possibility of coming before God with his accusations; or, stated in plain language, the believers, as we can already see by the results of their lives, have overcome Satan, i.e., have put to naught all attempts to mislead them, because the blood of the Lamb, which has made them free from sin, and thereby delivered them from the accusations of Satan, has given them the joy and the power to begin a new life.

---

[5] p. 236.

[6] Commentary on the New Testament, Vol. IV, p. 449.

Greijdanus puts it this way:[7]

> Now, however, the Lord Jesus Christ has made reconciliation for all
> the sins of those who were his, and were God's elect, and there was
> no longer any appearance of justice in demanding their punishment.
> ...The work of atonement is now complete. Satan is defeated, and ex-
> pelled from heaven for good. Everything is, in principle, decided. What
> remains is but the working out of this victory, which will now certainly
> follow to the full extent.

Thus the early Christians, to whom this book was addressed, if they
understood the meaning of the vision, were prepared to face with confidence and courage the worst that the Red Dragon and his henchmen
could do. Such attempts on his part, in the "short time" left before his
final destruction, are foretold in the remaining scenes of the Apocalypse.

---

[7] pp. 194–195.

XVI
THE ANTICHRIST

Before we go further in the study of the Revelation, it is desirable that we should turn aside and briefly consider a subject that is interwoven with the interpretation of the following chapters in many works on the book, namely, the subject of the Antichrist. Immediately after the apostolic era, we find in the Christian church an expectation that before the Second Advent there would arise a great figure, a man who would be, so to speak, an incarnation of wickedness, who would cause great distress to the Christians.

Perhaps the very first writing after the Apocalypse is the "Didache," or "Teaching of the Twelve Apostles." This is an anonymous manual of Christian doctrine and order, and many scholars date it from about the year AD 100. It contains the following passage:[1]

> Then shall appear the world deceiver as Son of God, and shall do signs and wonders, and the earth shall be given into his hands, and he shall commit iniquities which have never yet been done since the beginning.

Justin Martyr (died c. 166) says, in his "Dialogue with Trypho":[2]

> Christ… "shall come from heaven, with glory, when the man of apostasy, who speaks strange things against the Most High, shall venture to do unlawful deeds on the earth against us the Christians."

The word "Antichrist" does not occur in either of these first two refer-

---

[1] Hitchcock and Brown: "The Teaching of the Twelve Apostles," p. 29.

[2] "A.N.F.," Vol. I, p. 253.

ences, but appears as a well established designation in Irenaeus and Hippolytus. The former (115–190) was Bishop of Lyons, in France, and tells how, in his youth, he had heard his pastor, Polycarp, of Smyrna, speak of seeing and hearing the apostle John. Irenaeus stands, therefore, very near to the beginning. Hippolytus was, in his turn, a disciple of Irenaeus. The doctrine of the Antichrist is, in the writings of these two men, a definite and well developed conception. Hippolytus even wrote a treatise about him.[3] They identify the Antichrist of the epistles of St. John wholly with the Man of Sin of St. Paul, and with the Beast of Revelation 11 and 13. Also with the prince of Daniel 9.27, and they teach that his reign covers the second half of the seventieth week in that prophecy; exactly as it is found in the Scofield Bible. They are sure that he will come from the tribe of Dan, basing this upon Genesis 49.17. They have the traditional interpretation of the four beasts of Daniel seven, taking them to mean respectively Babylon, Medo-Persia, Greece, and Rome. The "little horn" that proceeds from the fourth beast (Daniel 7.8, 24–26) is the Antichrist. Thus all the distinctive features of what one may call the "Futurist" view of the Antichrist appear in these two early writers.

Irenaeus and Hippolytus belong to the millenarian school in the early church, but this Antichrist idea is not confined to that party. Origen (185–253) who rejected millennialism, says:[4]

Paul, indeed, speaks of him who is called Antichrist, describing, though with a certain reserve, both the manner and time, and cause of his coming to the human race.

Thereupon he quotes 2 Thessalonians 2.3 sq., and Daniel 8.23–25, as prophecies of the Antichrist. Other patristic references may be found in Alford: "Greek Testament," in his "Prolegomena" to 2 Thessalonians.

During the Middle Ages, this expectation of the coming of the Antichrist became more and more vivid, until it became one of the most prominent elements in the popular view of the end of the world. Many details not to be found in the Bible were added by the imagination, as may be seen from the following, quoted from the McClintock and Strong Encyclopedia, Vol. I, p. 257:

---

[3] "A.N.F.," Vol. V, pp. 204–219.

[4] "A.N.F.," Vol. IV, p. 594.

The received opinion of the 12ᵗʰ century is brought before us in a striking manner in the interview between Richard I and the abbot Joachim of Paris, (died 1202) at Messina, as the king was on his way to the Holy Land. 'I thought,' said the king, 'that Antichrist would be born in Antioch or in Babylon, and of the tribe of Dan, and would reign in the temple of God in Jerusalem, and walk in the land in which Christ walked, and would reign in it for three years and a half, and would dispute against Elijah and Enoch, and would kill them, and would afterward die, and that after his death God would give sixty days of repentance, in which those might repent who should have erred from the way of truth and have been seduced by the preaching of Antichrist and his false prophets.

What is very striking is that the Jews, as well as the Christians, cherished this expectation, although, of course, in somewhat different form. It is doubtful whether they took it from the Christians or, what I myself think more likely, the Christians originally from the Jews. The Jewish name for him was Armilus, supposed by some to be derived from Romulus, the legendary founder of Rome, and therefore to contain a veiled reference to Rome, whether pagan or papal. He is represented as being a monster, twelve cubits tall and broad, with red hair, but bald on the top of his head. The "Jewish Encyclopedia" says of him, in Vol. II, p. 118:

> In later Jewish eschatology and legend, a king who will arise at the end of time against the Messiah, and will be conquered by him. …The origin of this Jewish Antichrist (as he can well be styled, in view of his relation to the Messiah) is as much involved in doubt as the different phases of his development and his relation to the Christian legend and doctrine.

This encyclopedia gives also the following quotation from a medieval Jewish writing called "Otot-ha-Meshiah" (Signs of the Messiah):

> This creature, Armilus by name—the Gentiles call him Antichrist—will set himself up as Messiah, even as God himself, being recognized as such by the sons of Esau. (i.e. by the Christians)

We are told that substantially the same expectation of such a coming incarnation of evil is found among the Mohammedans. The Antichrist is not named in the Koran, but there are traditional sayings attributed to Mohammed in which he is referred to, such as the following; taken from an English translation of the Koran and commentary on it, by Maulvi Mohammed Ali, of Lahore, India.

> Sec. 469—"There is a saying of the Holy Prophet to the effect that the Antichrist (and the plague) shall never have access to Mecca."

> Sec. 2195—"Hisham bin Amir relates having heard the Apostle of Allah saying that from the creation of man to the coming of the Hour there is no creation greater in temptation than that of Antichrist."

When the corruption and evils of the Papacy began to multiply, earnest believers were led to ask whether this institution might not be the predicted apostasy, and the Pope the Antichrist. This opinion was held among the Waldenses, Albigenses, and the followers of Wickliffe and Huss. During the Reformation it was universal among Protestants. All the great Reformers believed it, and it found expression in some of the creeds. Being closely connected with the "Continuous Church History" interpretation of the book of Revelation, it prevailed until the middle of the nineteenth century, and is by no means extinct today. A very vigorous and well nigh convincing presentation of it may be found in H. Grattan Guinness: "The Approaching End of the Age," published first in 1878, p. 139–220.

Nevertheless, for more than fifty years this idea has been losing ground. This is due partly to the decline of that "Church History" school, as already discussed, partly to a more objective and historical tendency among interpreters. As a result, the liberal school, ascribing no divine inspiration either to the New Testament or the Old, have readily contended themselves with interpretations that were falsified by history; and, on the other hand, many conservatives have come to favor Futurism, returning, therein, almost exactly to the views of Irenaeus and Hippolytus.

These various tendencies have caused much discussion, which has led to a revival of interest in the problem of the Antichrist, manifested by such books as William Bousset: "Der Antichrist," and Valentinus Hepp: "De Antichrist." The former, which is liberal, has been translated into English: the latter is conservative, but available only in the Dutch. The doctrine of a personal Antichrist, to appear shortly before the Second Advent, and to be destroyed by the Lord at His coming, is one of the most prominent articles in the creed of the dispensationalist, or extreme premillenial school. In their books and popular addresses any amount of information concerning him can be found, painted in colors almost as lurid as those of Medieval times. This is true also of Dr. Hepp's book, which gives an astonishing amount of detail concerning him and the days of his reign, including discussion of the political, social, and moral conditions then to prevail. All this is announced with the utmost confidence, as certainly contained in the prophetic revelation.

What is the ordinary Bible student to do in the face of all this bewildering mass of interpretation, speculation, tradition, and confident assertion? (Dr. Hepp says that the literature of the subject is so immense that no one has ever read it all, or ever can.) Let him do as with other disputed points, take his Bible and look for himself. We will attempt to do that.

The only passages in the Bible where the word "Antichrist" appears occur in the Epistles of St. John 2.18, 22; 4.3, of the first epistle, and verse seven of the second. These few verses are all that the word of God directly says about this subject. If we are to find the Antichrist in other places, it must be because a character going by another name is clearly the same as the one of whom St. John speaks. Whether such another name does point to the same individual, must always be a matter of interpretation, and therefore of individual opinion. Every Bible reader has a right to have his own opinion, but he should be cautious as to stating positively that so and so is the inspired teaching on such a matter.

From these epistles of St. John we learn that there was in the early church a general expectation that some one or something would appear, here called the Antichrist, which, so far as the word itself is concerned, may mean an opponent of Christ, or a substitute and rival for Christ, or both together. Historical study, especially of the "Apocalyptic" Jewish literature of that time, recently discovered, has shown that a closely similar expectation pervaded also the Jewish community of the first century. It may be that the Christians borrowed it from them. St. John does not say that this expectation was well founded, or was his own teaching, or emanated from any authoritative apostolic or spiritual source. One can not gather, from his words, whether or not he himself shared it. He proceeds to call the attention of his readers to the fact that "many antichrists" have already come; and emphatically says that whoever confesses not that Jesus is come in the flesh is the deceiver and the Antichrist. (2 John 7) This looks as if he wishes to substitute, in the minds of his readers, vigilance against doctrinal heresy for concern over the appearance of a personal enemy to the gospel; but whether this spiritualization of the idea was intended by him to supplant or to supplement it, remains uncertain. In short, although the special designation "the Antichrist" is derived from these texts alone, they give us nothing from which a clear and definite idea of the subject can be learned.

The most important scriptural source for the doctrine is 2 Thessalonians 2.1–12. In this passage the apostle Paul gives to the Thessalonian church a sign which must take place before the Second Advent of Christ. There must appear, he says, a "Man of Sin," whose coming is hindered, but the hindrance will be taken out of the way, and then this character will appear. When he comes, he will sit in the temple of God, as being himself God, and will exalt himself above everything that is worshiped; but he will be destroyed by the Lord at His coming.

This passage bristles with difficulties. What is the "temple of God" in which this Man of Sin is to sit? If it means the temple then existing in Jerusalem, the prophecy did not come true, so we exclude this interpretation at once. The early Christian expositors held, as the dispensationalists among us still hold, that it is a new temple, to be built by the unbelieving Jews in the future; but it is almost impossible to believe that St. Paul would call such an edifice the temple of God, if built against the divine will by Christ-rejecting Jews. What he thought of such Jews is to be seen in 1 Thessalonians 2.15–16. The remaining interpretation, which seems to me the right one, is that the Christian church is here indicated. This person, then, will be within the church, and lead an apostasy there. If we take this interpretation, we have made one important expression, "the temple of God" figurative, and shall be prepared not to insist upon strict literalism in the other terms of the prophecy.

The next important question is by what or by whom the revelation of the Man of Sin was hindered in the days of the apostle. It is to be noted that he speaks of that hinder once as a thing,—using the Greek participle in the neuter, and once as a person, writing the same participle in the masculine gender. This is curious, and arouses wonder whether he really means a thing or a person, or both. As to the interpretation, we are all at sea. The church fathers, with unusual unanimity, thought that the Roman government was intended. This would allow the singular use of both genders that we have noted, for one may speak of the Roman Empire or of the Roman Emperor, and in either case mean the same thing. This interpretation occurs so early, is so general in that period, and is so remote from anything in the text itself, that there is a good case for supposing it to be an echo of St. Paul's oral teaching to the Thessalonians.

Others have thought that God, or the Holy Spirit, or the grace of God are the "one that withholdeth," but these are not taken out of the way, except in the modified sense that the restraining hand of God is removed. Dr. Abraham Kuyper takes it in this way.[5] Dr. Dollinger, a great Roman Catholic theologian, thinks the coming of Nero to be here prophesied.[6] In that case, the Emperor Claudius would be the restrainer, and his death would be the removal of the restraint; but Nero, although wicked enough, does not in other respects answer the description of the Man of Sin, for he was not an apostate Christian, and never sat in the temple of God, either literally or figuratively. Neither was he destroyed by the Lord at His coming in glory, but stabbed himself. Dr. Hepp is sure that the archangel Michael is the withholder, and paints a vivid picture of his holding Satan by the nape of the neck until God tells him to let go.[7] This adds to the interest of the reader, but not to his enlightenment. Thus we might go on and present still other interpretations, but with all that we shall get no further than St. Augustine did, who said: "I frankly confess I do not know what he means."[8]

A very vital question is, whether we must necessarily take the Man of Sin to be an individual person, or may understand by this expression some succession of persons, such as the popes, or a personification of the spirit of opposition to Christ and the gospel. The language certainly reads as if a person were intended. If so, we must look for him shortly before the Second Advent, and his appearance will be the sure and certain sign that this event is at hand. Scholars so close together in their general theological outlook as Dr. Abraham Kuyper and Dr. Herman Bavinck take opposite sides here. The former says:

Paul thus has in mind a revelation, an appearance of the Antichrist in a definite human person: not, as it is sometimes represented, in a disposition, a tendency"[9]

The latter, on the other hand, says:[10]

[5] Dictaten Dogmatiek, Locus de Consummatione, Saeculi, p. 212.

[6] "The First Age of Christianity and the Church," pp. 274–277.

[7] p. 102.

[8] "De Civitate Dei," Book XX, Section 19.

[9] Dictaten Dogmatiek, Locus de Consummatione Saeculi, p. 209.

[10] Gereformeerde Dogmatiek, Vol. IV, p. 464.

From this it appears that the Antichrist must be thought of, not exclusively as one person, or as a group of persons, e.g. the heretics of the first centuries, the Roman Empire, Nero, the Jews, Mohammed, the pope, Napoleon, etc.

He regards the whole Antichrist conception as a symbol for general hostility against God and the Lord Jesus Christ.

Between these two views, although not without hesitation, I take my stand with the view of Dr. Kuyper as the more natural, and more probably the correct interpretation. This leads me to expect some great adversary of the truth to appear immediately before the Second Coming of Christ, some one connected with the Christian church and leading a great apostasy within it.

From the earliest times the Antichrist of St. John and the Man of Sin of St. Paul have been regarded as one and the same. This is now so well established that it is assumed in all modern discussions. I have not found any writer who even raises the question. Yet this does seem to me at all a matter of course. St. John's Antichrist was already present in his day. He belongs therefore to the first century: St. Paul's Man of Sin will appear until the time of the end. The former did not remain within the church, but left it: the later remains and takes possession of it. The former is a doctrinal error: the latter a person, working lying wonders. Why should it be so readily assumed that they are the same?

Even accepting this, however, and regarding the coming wicked one as future, we are yet a long way from having arrived at the Antichrist, as pictured by the church fathers, the medieval writers, or Dr. Hepp and other Futurists; for neither St. John nor St. Paul hints at anything but a wicked religious leader, whereas the possession of extensive political authority and the use of such power in the persecution of true believers are the most prominent features of the traditional picture. Where did this notion come from? It came partly from identifying him with the Beast of the Apocalypse, partly from applying to him certain prophecies of Daniel, and partly—which is a very important point—from Jewish apocalyptic ideas in circulation in the first centuries of the Christian era, now to be found in the "Ascension of Isaiah," the Jewish Sybilline Books, and similar writings. The early Christians did not yet distinguish so clearly as we do now between such books and the canonical writings. It is probable that in building up their expectation of the Antichrist they were much influenced by them. It seems to me that Dr. William Bousset is right in saying that the original Antichrist conception of the church fathers rests only partly upon Biblical grounds.

Where such grounds have been assigned, whether by the church fathers or by modern writers, they are all of an exceedingly doubtful character. In the following chapters we shall study the Beast of the Apocalypse, so I will content myself here with saying that it is, in my judgment, quite impossible to regard him as symbolizing a single individual. I think he has nothing in the wide world to do with the Antichrist, considered as a coming person. If we make the Antichrist a mere symbol for all the evil and hostile forces, of course, this Beast does represent him in one aspect of his opposition.

Four passages in the book of Daniel have been supposed to forecast the Antichrist: the seventh chapter, with its vision of the four beasts, the eight chapter, with its conflict between the Ram and the Hegoat, the ninth chapter, with its prophecy of the Seventy Weeks, and the eleventh chapter, in which we find a king who is to be a terrible persecuting enemy to the people of God. Of these, we may most readily set aside the eighth chapter, as irrelevant. It foretells the conflict between Persia and Greece, the death of Alexander the Great, the division of his kingdom into four parts, and the rise of Antiochus Epiphanes, the Greek king of Syria, who profaned the temple and so bitterly distressed the Jews, beginning with 168 BC. There is nothing in it that was not fulfilled in his reign.

In the vision of the four beasts, in chapter seven, the fourth beast is commonly, and I think correctly, taken to mean the Roman Empire. If so, then the little horn that arises on the head of that beast and makes war with the saints, is not Antiochus Epiphanes, but some hostile power arising during the breakdown of the Roman Empire, or immediately after it has passed out of existence. The time harmonizes well with the rise of the Papacy, and the activities of the said little horn are an excellent figurative description of the persecuting policy of the Roman Catholic church. To apply it to that church seems to me, therefore, a natural and sufficient interpretation. This is not to call that church the Antichrist, for there is nothing, so far as I can see, to indicate that this little horn must or can be identified with the Antichrist of St. John or the Man of Sin of St. Paul. It is, I think, an independent prophecy of the Roman Catholic apostasy.

The dispensationalist school of interpreters find the Antichrist also in chapter 9.27. With the rest of us, they interpret the "Anointed One" of verse twenty-six of Christ, and find the predicted destruction of city and temple fulfilled in the events of AD 70; but they say that "the prince that shall come" is not Titus, who then commanded the Roman armies, but the future Antichrist, who will then make the "firm covenant" with the unbelieving Jews, and "in the midst of the week" will play them false; reigning and persecuting thereafter for three and a half years. It is evident that no such thing can be found in the passage, considered by itself. It is imported from elsewhere, because their general scheme demands it. It requires such a separation of the final week from the others, and such an introduction of an entirely new character, in verse twenty-seven, without explanation or warning, as the rest of the Christian world is unable to accept. Dr. Hepp, therefore, while finding Christ in other parts of Daniel, omits this verse, evidently considering that it has no connection with the subject.

Dr. Hepp lays great emphasis upon chapters eleven and twelve, as containing a forecast of the coming wicked one. These two chapters are among the most difficult in the Bible, and have been an exegetical puzzle from the earliest Christian times. It seems evident that St. Paul has 11.36–37 in mind when he says that the Man of Sin will "exalt himself above all that is called God or is worshipped." Dr. Hepp also has a good argument when he points to the prophecy of the resurrection, in Daniel 12.2 as indicating that all these things belong to the end-time. Yet neither of these arguments is conclusive. St. Paul does not expressly quote the prophecy and declare that it will be fulfilled in such and such a manner—as he usually does with other quotations from the Old Testament. Just as he borrows part of his language from Isaiah 11.4, so here he may be merely using a familiar form of words, without wishing to indicate that the prophecy from which he takes them will be fulfilled in the event to which he points. As to the resurrection, it is not uncommon, in the prophetic scriptures, to find two events placed side by side, that, in the fulfillment, fall many centuries apart.

Many interpreters consider that the prophecy, as far as 11.35, must be understood of Antiochus Epiphanes, but after that point, of the coming Antichrist. Dr. Hepp is not satisfied with this. He sees that the revealing angel makes no such break in his discourse, and therefore insists that one person only can be referred to in the entire prophecy. That person, he thinks, is not Antiochus, but the future tyrant, of whom Antiochus was a type. His explanation is that the history of Antiochus supplies a miniature model or portrait of the Antichrist, who will be a greatly enlarged Antiochus. This, also, is very unsatisfactory; inasmuch as the prophecy itself contains no hint that it is to understood in such a double sense.

We find, therefore, that all the supposed predictions of a future personal Antichrist in Daniel ought to be otherwise interpreted, or are, at best, highly doubtful, offering no sound basis for any confident forecast of his coming. Are there other predictions in the Old Testament that present a clearer portrait of such a monster of wickedness? Dr. Hepp lays great emphasis upon the prophesy of Gog and Magog, in Ezekiel thirty-eight and thirty-nine. Yet he also thinks that the Beast of Revelation thirteen and subsequent chapters is the Antichrist. It is strange that he has not noticed that, in Revelation 19.20, the Beast is cast into the lake of fire *before* the thousand years, and remains there (20.10); while Gog and Magog appear *after* the thousand years, and never come into the lake of fire and brimstone at all! Whatever these symbols mean, therefore, it seems clear that they can not refer to one and the same personal Antichrist, as Dr. Hepp would have it.

To supplement the very scanty references to such a supposed future Antichrist, it is very common to have recourse to the doctrine of "types." No doubt there are real types of Christ in the Old Testament. In this sense a type is some Old Testament event, or ceremony, or object, or person, that is divinely intended to be a portrait of Christ, in one or more of His aspects or offices. Thus the paschal lamb was a type of His atoning sacrifice, Moses of His work as redeemer and prophet, Melchizedek as priest, and David as king. For all these it would be easy to supply New Testament proof texts. To extend this "type" idea, however, into another field, where the New Testament does not know of it, is another matter. Yet this is done by those who advocate the doctrine of a personal Antichrist. So Dr. Lange, in the Herzog "Real Encyclopaedie fur Protestantisch Theologie und Kirche," finds in Balaam and Goliath types of Antichrist, while Dr. R. B. Kuiper finds them in Cain, Pharaoh, Saul, and Jeroboam, in addition, of course, to Antiochus Epiphanes.[11] Why not also in Jannes and Jambres, Korah, Dathan, and Abiram, Ahab, Jezebel, Sennacherib, Nebuchadnezzar, Sanballat, etc., etc.? This kind of typemongering may have some value for illustration and exhortation; it is unworthy of serious attention when we are trying to find out whether "the sure word of prophecy" unveils for us the coming of such a monster of wickedness and tyranny as the imagination of Jews and Christians has conjured up.

---

[11] "While the Bridegroom Tarries," p. 120.

My own conclusions, which I submit to the judgment of the thoughtful reader, are these:

1. That it is highly doubtful whether the Antichrist of St. John and the Man of Sin of St. Paul are the same.

2. That the words of St. Paul do, most probably, refer to the coming of some great religious leader, a renegade Christian, who will be the head and front of a great apostasy in the church, immediately before the Second Coming of our Lord, but contain no ground to attribute to him also political power.

3. That the identification of this Man of Sin with the Beast of the Apocalypse is wholly without foundation.

4. That no such character is predicted in the book of Daniel, or in any other portion of the Old Testament.

5. Therefore, that it is very absurd, not to say very wrong, for any one, upon so shaky a foundation, to proclaim it as one of the predictions of the prophetic scriptures, that such an Antichrist is coming. It is at most an opinion, that is at best possibly correct. No doubt every Bible student has a right to form such an opinion, according to his own insight into the scriptures, but the matter is so obscure at best, that it ought to be presented to the public as an opinion, never as one of the clear and undoubted teachings of the word of God.

XVII

THE TWO WILD BEASTS

In chapter twelve we had introduced to us by the seer two great characters, which we interpreted to be the same two actors whom we meet at the beginning of the Bible, the Woman and the Serpent; represented, in the visions of Patmos, as the Radiant Woman, crowned and clothed with light, and the Red Dragon, pursuing, with unrelenting hatred, the course of enmity foretold when it was said to him in Paradise: "I will put enmity between thee and the woman." In the drama of chapter twelve, however, the Red Dragon had no success. The Man-child was caught away from his fury, up to God and to His throne. The Radiant Woman was given the two wings of the Great Eagle, and fled to the wilderness. Although he tried to overwhelm her with a flood from his mouth, the earth came to her aid, and all his efforts were in vain. Not only so, but his defeat at the hands of Michael and the angelic host showed him that he could not possibly win in the end, for the forces of heaven as well as those of earth were on the side of the Woman. Conscious that he had but a short time, but eager to do what damage he could in the little space of time remaining, he gave up his attempt to destroy the Woman herself, but "went away" to make war upon the remnant of her seed.

Where did he go? To this question no answer can be given, if we take the reading of the Authorized Version, for there we read, in the first verse of the next chapter: "I stood upon the sand of the sea." Thus we hear no more of the Dragon, except later, that he gave his kingdom and great authority to the Beast. In the Revised Version, however, we have: "And he stood upon the sand of the sea." In this form we get the impression that the Red Dragon went to the sea to summon from its depths an ally, or allies, to help him in his warfare. The difference between the two versions rests upon a difference of one letter in the Greek manuscripts. Both readings are well attested, and it is not certain which is correct; although most modern scholars take it as in the Revised Version—"He stood." This certainly makes the connection more vivid and dramatic.

As the Red Dragon stood there, the apostle saw something rising out of the sea. It was a wild beast. In Greek he is called a "therion." This fact is worth noting, for in the Authorized Version, most unfortunately, two different Greek words have been rendered by the same word in English, the word "beast." One is found in chapter four of that version, where, in verses 6–9, we read of "four beasts" around the throne, and the other is here, in chapter thirteen, also translated "beast." In the former passage the word in Greek is "zoon," meaning anything that is alive. It is the equivalent there of the "living creatures" of Ezekiel 1.5 and other passages; which are glorious forms that stand as body-guards to the divine majesty. In our chapter, the word used is "therion," meaning a savage jungle brute. It is the same word that is used in the Greek Old Testament in Genesis 37.33, of the animal that was supposed to have devoured Joseph. The use of this word in this vision is intended to fix our attention at once upon the savage, cruel and brutal nature of that which now comes upon the stage.

This wild beast looked a great deal like the Dragon himself. The shape of the body, to be sure, was different—he had not the serpentine form; but, like the Dragon, he had seven heads and ten horns, and on the horns ten diadems. The Red Dragon had diadems too, but on his heads, not on his horns. Why there should be this difference, does not appear. It certainly is not that the heads are not to be accounted royal, for we read later that they represent seven kings. On the heads of the wild beast are names—names of blasphemy, indicating that these heads make claims that are blasphemous, either because they revile God, or because they demand an allegiance that is due to God alone, or perhaps for both reasons combined.

To this beast the Red Dragon gives power and his throne, and great authority. That is, he gives to this beast exactly what he once offered to the Lord Jesus Christ. He gives him what "He That Sitteth on the Throne" gives to the Lamb. It looks like a deliberate parallel. This feeling that we have here a Satanic parallel of the things of Christ, is strengthened when we find the remarkable expression: "I saw one of his heads as though it had been smitten unto death, and his deathstroke was healed." Here we can hardly help recognizing an echo of an earlier passage in which the apostle saw, "A Lamb as it had been slain." As the Dragon is the antithesis to God, so this beast seems to be the antithesis to Christ.

The Beast is given world-wide authority. Every one worships him, except those whose names are written in the book of life, namely, all true Christians. He makes war against the saints, who are, of course, "the rest of the seed" of the Woman, and overcomes them. His reign continues forty-two months, no doubt the same period of time we found in chapter twelve, during which the Radiant Woman is in the wilderness. During that period, it is vain to attempt to resist by violence, and not only vain, but impious, seeing "it is given" to the Beast to overcome during this period. In verse ten (Revised Version) the saints seem to be warned not to try it. Further very important details concerning the Beast are given in chapter seventeen, which we shall consider later. Now we must have a look at the second beast:

> And I saw another beast coming out of the earth: and he had two horns like unto a lamb, and he spake as a dragon. And he exerciseth all the authority of the first beast in his sight, and he maketh the earth and them that dwell therein to worship the first beast, whose death-stroke was healed." (13.11–12) (RV)

We notice at once that this second brute does not play an independent part, but is subordinate to the first. He looks gentle, having only two horns, and those of a harmless kind—like the horns of a lamb. Also, he has no diadems on his horns, indicating that he has no political sovereignty. When he speaks, however, he speaks like a dragon; and for all his harmless appearance he is a true "therion," a savage and cruel jungle brute. In all things he heartily seconds the activities of the first beast.

Such is the picture. The interpretation of the picture is, in some respects, and to a certain extent, easy enough. In other respects it is one of the most difficult in the entire Bible; so that, in spite of the extraordinary labor and learning expended upon it, the full meaning remains undiscovered with such a degree of agreement that the ordinary reader is satisfied. Hence the service I can hope to render to the readers of this book falls far short of complete interpretation. Some features I can interpret with considerable confidence; and on others I can quote the views of distinguished Bible students, thus putting him in a position to recognize that much popular exposition of these symbols (i.e. popular in certain circles) is unreliable in direct proportion to the confidence with which it is put forward.

In other words, although I can not hope to deliver the reader completely from ignorance, in regard to many of the things said about these two wild and savage brutes, I can help him to attain a condition of intelligent ignorance, i.e. ignorance based upon study, and upon a fair knowledge of the solutions that have been attempted.

To prepare ourselves for this inquiry, it is very useful to turn to the book of Daniel, chapter seven, and read carefully the vision of the four beasts, there recorded; for it is obvious that the vision of the Revelation rests upon it. Four wild beasts were seen by Daniel to rise out of the sea, not a calm sea, but a stormy sea, one after another. The first was like a lion, the second like a bear, and the third like a leopard, with four heads and four wings. The fourth beast is not named, for he is like nothing ever seen on the earth or in the waters under the earth, and he is much more terrible than all the others put together. The time honored interpretation of these beasts is that the first represents the Babylonian Empire, the second the Medo-Persian, the third the Greek, and the fourth the Roman. This view dates from the earliest Christian writers, and even earlier, from the rabbis. There is also a modern interpretation, accepted by many, in which the second beast is made to mean the Median kingdom, the third the Persian, and the fourth the Greek, thus leaving the Roman Empire out of consideration entirely; but it seems to me that we may lay aside this view without much hesitation. It is scarcely open to doubt that the vision of the four beasts is parallel to that of the great image seen in Nebuchadnezzar's dream, in the second chapter of Daniel. This agrees with the vision of the four beasts in placing the kingdom of Nebuchadnezzar himself first; and we know that his kingdom was succeeded by the Medo-Persian combination under Cyrus the Great, not by a Median kingdom. There was, of course, a Median kingdom before that time, but it does not belong in the order of the vision, it was not comparable in any way to the others in glory and power, and it was not an oppressor of God's people. Besides this, the four heads and four wings of the leopard point unmistakably to the four parts into which the empire of Alexander the Great was divided, and as such are parallel to the four horns on the head of the he-goat, in chapter eight of Daniel. Finally, there was no such marked and terrible difference between the Greek dominion and those which preceded it as is indicated by the special character of the fourth beast; which fits Rome precisely.

Taking, then, this vision of Daniel's, with the traditional interpretation, as the basis, we see at once that the vision of Revelation 13 contains the same elements, although with two significant variations: they are presented in reverse order, and they are in combination, making one composite brute, not four in succession. But it comes out of the same stormy sea, which it usually, and I think correctly, taken to mean that it emerges through war and by violence. Another interpretation, that "from the sea" has direct reference to Rome as seen from the direction of Asia, across the sea, seems to me less suitable, being inapplicable to Daniel's visions.

In the beast that St. John saw, the features of the four of Daniel are united. "The beast which I saw was like unto a leopard, and his feet were as the feet of a bear, and his mouth as the mouth of a lion"; while the horns are like those of the unnamed terror. In Daniel, however, there is only one head to the fourth beast; the brute in Revelation has seven. By these resemblances and differences we are taught, it seems to me, that what St. John saw was the *in essence*, that is, in its origin, nature, and activity, the same thing that Daniel saw; yet that it was not the same in its historical embodiment. Daniel was shown what was still to be—four empires in historical succession; St. John saw the underlying unity of opposition to the Kingdom of God that was present in all of those empires, and saw it as active and terrible in his own day,

That the second beast arose, not out of the sea, but out of the earth, indicates, by contrast, that he comes in time of peace, and is the product of the quiet life. His horns, like those of a lamb, make us think of the Lamb of God. His activities are largely religious activities, working miracles, causing men to worship, etc. This, even if we had no hint from the author of the Revelation, we should come to the conclusion that the second beast symbolizes a religious force or leader; and the correctness of this inference is placed beyond doubt by the fact that he is called, in later chapters, "The False Prophet."

That these brutes symbolize forces hostile to the church is evident, both from their resemblance to those which Daniel saw, and from their position in the story, having been summoned to the aid of the Dragon in his fight with the Woman and her seed. We have, therefore, before us symbolic pictures of two great antichristian powers, the one rough, secular, and violent; the other apparently peaceful and religious, but at heart as much an enemy to the gospel as the first.

So far the interpretation is easy enough, and this much is generally agreed upon, but when we ask whether these powers are personal or collective, whether they have already appeared or are still to come, we find the different schools divided along their characteristic lines.

1. For the "Continuous Church History" school of Elliott, Barnes, Guinness, and others, the Beast is the Roman Catholic Church, and the priesthood of that church is the False Prophet. After the discussion of principles of interpretation given in previous chapters of this book, the reader will hardly expect me to enter upon a formal refutation of this view in this place. It is so thoroughly artificial, so completely out of touch with the circumstances of the age in which the Revelation was written, and so tied up with time calculations which the event has falsified, that I think we may quietly allow it to die a natural death—which it seems to be in process of doing.

2. More formidable, at present, are the Futurists, who hold that these two wild beasts symbolize two individual men, who will appear on earth immediately before the Second Advent of Christ. Usually they look upon the ten horned beast as the personal Antichrist, who will bear rule over all the earth, and persecute the saints for three and a half years. The second, they think, will be his subordinate and helper, also an individual man. So Dr. Hepp. Others of this school, however, including the Scofield Bible, take the two horned beast to be the Antichrist. This is more easily reconciled with the teachings of St. John and St. Paul, in whose writings the Antichrist and the Man of Sin, whether the same person or different, seem to be only false religious teachers, not universal and wicked rulers.

Dr. Theodor Zahn says:

This is as little as all his predecessors a spirit or a phantom, but a mortal man of flesh and blood, drawn from the world of nations, and inspired by an evil spirit. He is a caricature of Christ. (Vol. II, p. 451)

Dr. J. A. Seiss comments:

The Beast is finally damned. He goes into perdition, into the lake of fire. ...We would therefore greatly err from Scripture, as well as from the unanimous conviction and teaching of the early church, were we to fail to recognize in this Beast a real person. (Vol. II, p. 395)

This argument of Dr. Seiss at first looks convincing, but if we look at Revelation 20.14, we see that Death and Hades are also cast into the lake of fire. These are not real persons, but personified for the sake of the symbolism. It may be, and I think it is, equally so here. Another argument used by this school is that since the Dragon represents a person, Satan, this Beast, which is his instrument, or ally, must be a person too; but this argument is untenable. The Dragon is introduced as the enemy of the Radiant Woman, who is not understood by any one to be an individual person.

The reasons why I can not accept the Futurist system have already been set forth, and I see nothing in this vision of the two beasts to require any reconsideration. On the contrary, the position of these brutes in the story, and their evident connection with those of Daniel, which were not persons but kingdoms, leads me to believe that it is a fundamental error to find here any personal Antichrist of the time of the end.

3. The Philosophy of History school, or, as Preusz calls them, the "Kingdom History" interpreters, in accordance with their general principles, find here no definite person or power, whether in early church history or at the end of the world, but a symbol of the secular persecuting and opposing power in general, whenever and wherever it manifests itself. So Auberlen, Alford, Benson, Morris, and many others. By all means read this explanation in Morris: "The Drama of Christianity," p. 81.

Hengstenberg says:

"The Beast, in the passage before us, is a compound of the several beasts in Daniel. If by these the more prominent phases of the ungodly power of the world are represented, the Beast here can be nothing else than that power in its entireness." (Vol. II, p. 17)

Auberlen says:

"The Beast of the Apocalypse is a comprehensive representation, in one figure, of the world power which, in Daniel, is symbolized by four beasts. ...Even as John does not understand by the Woman merely the New Testament church, so the Beast does not refer exclusively to the world kingdom of that period, the Roman, much less to a previous or subsequent phase of the Roman Empire." (p. 263)

Alford says:[1]

---

[1] Vol. IV, Part II, p. 678.

"I believe the interpretation of the second beast to be, the sacerdotal persecuting power, pagan and Christian, as the first is the secular persecuting power, pagan or Christian."

This interpretation has much to commend it. It does justice, in the first place, to the largeness of the vision and of the symbols in chapter 12, of which this chapter is a continuation. We found there the Radiant Woman, as a symbol for the whole People of God, not in any one period of its history, but in the whole; and in the Red Dragon we found a picture of the Devil. To go on and consider this wild beast to be his tool for a brief period only, whether at the beginning or at the end of Christian history, seems out of proportion to the scale upon which the rest of the picture is drawn. Further, this view does justice to certain manifest references to the situation existing when the book was written, and yet does not confine the symbol to that situation; but enables us to include in our conception other manifestations of the same hostile powers arising at various times in history. The Russian Soviet is then the most recent manifestation of the Beast that arises out of the sea. This view can find room even for the Futurist idea, for if there is to be such a future Antichrist as they expect, he will be the final and supreme incarnation of this secular persecuting and opposing power.

Yet we feel that in one respect this view does not satisfy. It is not sufficiently concrete and definite to account for the passion that throbs in this book. However deep and clear was his insight into the permanent underlying principles and forces that make history, the man who wrote this book, when he wrote it, was not thinking in a detached way about the philosophy of history. He was himself suffering from the fury of the Beast in his Patmos exile, and the members of the Christian flock he had left behind him were as sheep in the midst of wolves. The danger of their being forced or cajoled into apostasy was already great, and he foresaw that it would be greater still. He was anxious to arm them for the conflict, and to strengthen them in the present terrible crisis, by revealing to them, on the one hand, the Satanic nature of the forces brought against them, and on the other, the certainty of the ultimate triumph. This aspect of the matter requires us to supplement the truth in the above interpretation by something further.

4. The Preterist school, which is coming to be more and more prevalent, regards the Beast definitely as the persecuting Roman Empire, with especial reference to the institution of Emperor worship. That was one of

the most prominent elements in the religious life of the Empire for the first two or three centuries of our era; and recent investigation, by enlarging our knowledge of it, has thrown much light upon this portion of the Apocalypse. To look upon the reigning monarch as a descendant of the gods, or as himself a god, was not peculiar to Rome. One of the constant tendencies of paganism, in every form, is to deify great men, and, of course, those great enough to be kings or emperors are the very best candidates for such deification. Ancient history is full of it, and it goes on today, in Japan. What the Roman emperors did, was to make of this worship a political instrument for the unification of the empire, just as the Japanese government today is seeking to weld the people together through Emperor worship. Among all the provinces, there was none where this worship was more carefully fostered, and accepted with greater enthusiasm, than the province of Asia, where the Seven Churches were located, and where this book originated. The "Asiarchs," mentioned in Acts 19.31 (RV margin) as protecting the apostle Paul, were in direct official charge of all that pertained to this form of religion. If it be asked how, then, they could be his friends, the answer is that the question at issue on that occasion was not the worship of the Emperor, but the honor of Diana of the Ephesians, with which they had no concern. Moreover, at that time the Christian religion was not yet distinguished from Judaism. Paul was, in their eyes, the leader of a Jewish sect, and the Jews were exempt from the obligation to worship in the Roman fashion. Theirs was a "religio licita," a licensed, permitted form of worship. No emperor, except the insane Caligula, attempted to force the worship of the Imperial statues upon the Jews.

Gradually, however, as more Gentiles came into the church, this situation was changed, and this was especially true after the destruction of Jerusalem in AD 70. Greeks and Romans who became Christians were then clearly seen not to be Jews, and any refusal to do homage to the Emperor in the established way—by burning incense before his statute—was ipso facto evidence of disloyalty, punishable by death. This brought about the irrepressible conflict with the Christian church, since to do that was idolatry. This conflict was a life-and-death struggle for the infant church, and it is this crisis that is portrayed symbolically in the second half of the Apocalypse. The conflict raged, with varying degrees of intensity, for two hundred years, until the time of Constantine the Great. The faith and patience that enabled the church to win were inspired in no small degree by this very book.

The Preterists are the only interpreters who take this element adequately into account, and they are quite right, it seems to me, in insisting that the Beast here means primarily the Roman persecuting power, centered in this required Emperor worship. To think here of some personal Antichrist at the end of the world is to miss the point completely, while it is too vague to speak only of general principles. Yet I can not believe that the vision is exhausted in this primary meaning, and in so far I agree with the "Kingdom History" men. The fact that Daniel's four beasts are combined into this composite brute of Revelation must mean something. It indicates, I think, that while thinking primarily of the Roman persecution and its cause, we must think also of hostility to God and violent attempts to overthrow His kingdom, in a wider sense, as a permanent element in human history. The Beast was the contemporary form of what Daniel had seen in the vision of the four great empires: namely hostility to God, emanating from the Dragon, changing its forms but not its essence. That hostility existed before the Roman Empire came into being, it continued after that empire fell, and it exists today. Whenever and wherever the People of God are opposed by violent means, there we find, in essence, the ten horned brute, and wherever they are opposed by false religion, particularly a corrupt priesthood urging on the secular power to a persecuting policy, there we find the brute that looks like a lamb but speaks like a dragon. We are not wrong if we apply the prophecy to any such situation; we are wrong only if we think that any such later historical development was the thing directly in view when the Apocalypse was written.

We come, therefore, to the following conclusions:

1. The ten horned beast is primarily the persecuting Roman Empire, insisting upon Emperor worship.

2. It is this empire, however, not considered merely in and by itself, but as the contemporary form of the secular hostile power, whenever and wherever violently active against the Kingdom of God.

3. The two horned beast is the persecuting priestly power, primarily that of the Asiarchs, supporting and enforcing Emperor worship; but like the other, also to be considered in a broader sense, as any religious or priestly influence inspiring and upholding the persecuting secular power.

Having arrived at these conclusions in regard to the significance of the vision in general, we are in a position to consider some of the intricate problems connected with the details.

XVIII

THE PROBLEMS OF THE BEAST

In taking up for study the problems of the Beast, we include what is said of him in chapter 17.3, 7–18, assuming that the one spoken of there is the same brute as came up out of the sea in chapter 13. This is questioned by a very few commentators, but is generally accepted and requires, I think, no elaborate argument here. Beginning with chapter 11.7 where he is mentioned by anticipation, until "finis" is written over him in 19.20, we find frequent reference to "The Beast," as one of the chief characters of the drama. This word is held to be a sufficient designation, and it would throw the story into confusion if there were two, both going by the same name. So careful is the author to avoid this kind of misunderstanding that, although the vision at first did include two beasts, the second one in chapter 13 is afterwards referred to as "The False Prophet," in order that the designation "The Beast" may be reserved for his chief. (Compare 13.13–17 with 19.20 and 16.13)

So understanding the matter, the chief problems to be solved with regard to the Beast are his mark, his heads, his wound, his number, and the length of his reign.

I. The Mark of the Beast

We do not know whether the mark by which the boycott of Christians is made effective, in 13.16–17 is intended to be understood as a literal visible mark or not. So far as the boycott is concerned, it has often been practiced, and is practiced today, in many communities in non-Christian lands, against those who profess Christ. A village in Japan, China or India usually reacts violently against the first cases of conversion that appear in it, and it is not uncommon for some form of boycott to be instituted, sometimes an agreement of absolute non-intercourse, sometimes a prohibition to draw water from the village well, or in other ways. It is very likely that similar things went on in the time of St. John. To have a mark on the forehead designating the god one worships is common in India, but I have not heard of it elsewhere, and have no reason to think that it was common in the Roman Empire at that time. It seems likely, therefore, that it was something else that identified the loyal subjects of the Emperor, here symbolically called a mark on the forehead and the hand. Sir William Ramsay, our foremost authority on conditions in Asia Minor at that time, says:[1]

> That the mark of the Beast must be impressed in the right hand or the forehead is a detail which remains obscure: we know too little to explain it with certainty. If it had been simply called the mark on the forehead, it might be regarded as the public proof of loyalty by performance of the ritual; this overt public proof might be symbolically called 'a mark on the forehead.' But the mention of an alternative place for the mark shows that a wider explanation is needed. The proof of loyalty might be made in two ways; both were patent and public; they are symbolically described as the mark on the right hand or on the forehead; without one or the other no one was to be dealt with by the loyal provincials....
>
> How much of grim sarcasm, how much of literal truths, how much of exaggeration, there lies in those words—'that no man should be able to buy or sell, save he that had the mark of the Beast on his right hand or upon his forehead'—it is impossible for us now to decide."

The Seventh Day Adventists have a peculiar explanation of this passage. To them the Beast is the Roman Catholic church, and the mark of the Beast is keeping Sunday instead of Saturday! They assert that the day was changed from Saturday to Sunday by authority of the apostate church, and that every one who keeps Sunday therefore bears the mark of apostasy. The assertion is incorrect, to begin with. The observance of Sunday as the Christian day of rest goes back to the earliest and purest days of the Christian church, long before anything that may be called The Roman Catholic Church existed. As to Sunday keeping being the mark of the Beast, consider what it means. The Beast in the Revelation is the special representative on earth of the devil, and rages, full of satanic hatred, against Christ and the church. Now, according to the Seventh Day Adventists, the more piously and conscientiously one observes the first day

---

[1] pp. 106–107.

of the week, the more plainly he bears the mark of the devil. For venom-
ous denominationalism, this is unsurpassed.

II. The Heads of the Beast

In chapter thirteen, where he first appears, no explanation is given of
the heads of the Beast, but we find it in chapter 17.9–11.

> Here is the mind which hath wisdom. The seven heads are seven moun-
> tains, on which the woman sitteth: and they are seven kings; the five are
> fallen, the one is, the other is not yet come, and when he cometh he must
> continue a little while. And the beast that was, and is not, is himself also
> an eighth, and is one of the seven, and he goeth into perdition.

Notice that the heads have a double meaning—they are mountains, and
they are kings. Probably the meaning is as Alford puts it: "With respect
to the woman, they are seven hills, on which she sits; with respect to
the Beast, they are seven kings." [2] This shows us at once one reason for
the difficulty in interpreting the symbols of Revelation—that the writer
does not use them consistently. He has a Lamb, and yet makes the Lamb
take a book and break the seals thereof; he shows us a star from heaven,
but immediately a key is given to that star and he unlocks the door of the
pit. No consideration is given to the question how a star can handle a key.
The Radiant Woman flies away on eagle's wings, and yet the Red Dragon tries to drown her by casting a flood from his mouth. In 13.3 it is one
of the heads that was wounded with a sword and was healed; but lest we
should make too much of a distinction between the Beast and his heads,
we are told in 13.12, 14, that it was the Beast himself that was wounded
unto death. Of course, you say, if the head of a beast is wounded, the
beast is wounded: yet if the beast stands for an empire and the heads for
emperors, it should be quite possible for a head to be slain and yet not
the beast. Again, in 17.8 we read: "The beast that thou sawest was, and is
not, and is about to come up out of the abyss." This seems plainly enough
to assert that he belongs to the past and the future, not to the present;
but what then shall we say of 17.10: "The seven heads are seven kings,
the five are fallen, the one is, and the other is not yet come"? What shall
we make of an existing present head, if there is no beast to which the
said head is attached? It is almost like the scene in Alice in Wonderland,
when the Cheshire cat disappeared, but the grin remained! Finally, we

---

[2] Vol. IV, Part II, p. 709.

have this: "The beast that was, and is not, is himself also an eighth, and is of the seven, and he goeth into perdition." Was there ever such a bewildering set of statements concerning any thing? It looks almost as if the author deliberately set himself to mystify the reader. For this reason, as soon as we have thought of an interpretation that fits pretty well in some respects, we find that it is impossible to apply it on other respects. We must do the best we can, but a perfectly satisfactory explanation can hardly be expected.

"The seven heads are seven kings" (17.10); but in what sense? The answer to this question divides interpreters into three camps:

1. Those who take it as meaning *seven forms of government* in the history of Rome: namely, kings, consuls, dictators, decemvirs, tribunes, and emperors. So far they are agreed, and this makes six. The seventh is by some explained to be the imperial government under Diocletian (reigned AD 284–305) "Which had more of an oriental character." Then the eighth, they say, will be the Antichrist, when he comes.

There is, in my judgment, not much to be said for this interpretation. Dr. Patrick Fairbairn seems clearly in the right when he points out (Fairbairn on Prophecy, p. 312) that any changes in the form of government of Rome, occurring long before that empire came into any kind of contact with the people of God, "lie entirely outside the territory" in which prophecy is interested.

2. Those who take the seven heads to be, not individual kings, but kingdoms, world powers hostile to the people of God. This use of the word "kings" for "kingdoms" find justification in Daniel, by comparison of 7.17 with 7.23: "These great beasts, which are four, are four kings": 7.17; "The fourth beast shall be a fourth kingdom." (7.23)

Dr. Patrick Fairbairn, among others, takes this view. So understood, the five kings that are said to have "fallen" are Egypt, Assyria, Babylon, Medo-Persia, and Greece. All these occupied a position of hostility to Israel, but all had "fallen" by the time of St. John. Then the sixth "that now is," means the Roman Empire, which fits very well. What, then, is the seventh, which had not yet come, and when it came must "continue a little while"? We are tempted mentally to insert the word "only"—"He must continue only a little while," but it does not say that. Perhaps the meaning is just the opposite, to inform us that there will be some considerable continuance of that power: "He must continue a little while." Calling it "a little while" does not necessarily mean only a few years in human reckoning of time. It is from God's standpoint that the continuance of evil, although it may seem long to us, is for "a little while."

What is the power so designated? Some make it the nominally Christian Roman Empire, beginning with Constantine the Great; others understand it to be a collective title for the Germanic nations that overwhelmed Rome and established themselves upon its ruins. They remained "a little while," not that they were, as governments, short lived, but because they were soon Christianized, and therefore remained but a short time as wild beasts, namely hostile powers. Finally, in this interpretation, the eighth beast, which is in some sense the whole beast—that is, concentrates in himself all the ferocity of the entire brute—must be the kingdom of the Antichrist, to be established at the end of time. This kingdom it is that, in spirit and power, will come up out of the abyss (17.8) and, when its course is run, will go into perdition.

3. Those who take the word "kings" literally, and therefore refer it to individual emperors of Rome. This is the most natural meaning of the word "kings," to be preferred if it will fit, but the trouble is, that it is almost impossible to count the heads, in this sense, so that they will agree with the known facts of history. To have before us the necessary material for judgment, let us first set down here the list of Roman emperors, from the beginning as far as the reign of Domitian, with their dates:

Julius Caesar, died 44 BC

Augustus Caesar, reigned 31 BC to AD 14

Tiberius Caesar, AD 14–37

Caius Caesar (Caligula) AD 37–41

Claudius Caesar, AD 41–54

Nero Caesar, AD 54–68

Galba, Otho, Vitellius, all in AD 68–69 (The line of the Caesars had come to an end with Nero, and these three men in succession attempted unsuccessfully to seize and hold the throne.)

Vespasian, AD 69–79

Titus, son to Vespasian, AD 79–81

Domitian, brother to Titus, AD 81–96 (The family name of these three was Flavius, hence this is called the Flavian dynasty.)

The problem is to find the sixth, reigning at the time when this book was written, and to identify the seventh, who must remain "a little while," and the eighth, who should go into perdition. The first difficulty is the question whether Julius Caesar is to be counted in. He was not really emperor, but he had all the power of an emperor, and started the rule of the Caesarian family. So some count him in, and some do not. The following are some of the most important solutions proposed:

Moses Stuart begins with Julius Caesar, and has Nero as the sixth head, for he thought that the book was written in his reign. Duesterdieck, in Meyer's Commentary, begins with Augustus, and reaches Vespasian by omitting Galba, Otho and Vitellius. This is not unreasonable, for not one of them succeeded in holding the imperial power. Their period is sometimes called "the rebellion of the three princes." This reckoning applies well to Titus, who is then the seventh head, the one that remained but a little while. He reigned only two years. It applies well, also to Domitian, who becomes the eighth. The objection is, that the Apocalypse was not written in the time of Vespasian.

Swete adopts the same reckoning as Duesterdieck. For him also Vespasian is the sixth head, the one that "is," and Titus is the seventh, with Domitian the eighth. He "comes out of the abyss," (17.8) in the sense that the policy of Domitian towards the Christians is the same as that of Nero. Nero was dead, but in the acts and attitude of Domitian he has come back—back from hell. Nero was the first persecuting emperor, and Domitian the second. In this sense, therefore, the Beast was dead during the reigns of Vespasian and Titus, but came back to life under Domitian.

This interpretation looks good, but Swete himself dates the Revelation under Domitian, and so how can what is said to him of the sixth head, that "is," be applied to Vespasian? Swete's reply is, that the writer goes back, "in thought," to the time of Vespasian, and speaks as if he were living then; but why should he do so strange a thing?

Beckwith, in view of all these difficulties, thinks that the seven kings are not to be reckoned numerically, but symbolically; indicating that the Roman Empire must have its full tale of kings, but that the end is coming. In a total (symbolically stated) of seven, the suffering church has already reached No. 6, and may therefore take courage. After the seven allotted to Rome have all come, (no matter what the actual number may be) there comes the end of the empire, for the Antichrist will come from hell, and will destroy Rome, making himself the eighth ruler.

The Problems of the Beast | 161

Thus the interpretation of this point is, to be frank, a jumble of confusion, and the best I can do myself is to go back to the older view of the "Kingdom History" men, that the heads represent the great world empires, of which five were past, and the sixth was flourishing when the book was written. The question is, whether we can, on that basis, find a satisfactory solution of the remaining problems, the deadly wound, the number of the name, and the period of supremacy of the Beast.

III. The Wound That Healed

In chapter 13.3 we read:

> And I saw one of his heads as though it had been smitten unto death, and his death-stroke was healed.

This wound is referred to again and again, and is evidently considered by the author to be a point of very great importance. What does it mean? Various commentaries offer us a choice of ten different interpretations, and I am far from saying that this is a complete list.

1. The assassination of Julius Caesar. (Zuschlag, Bruston, Gunkel, Clemen, Porter. Taken from R. H. Charles, Vol. I, p. 349.)

2. The illness of Caligula. (Weyers, Holzman, Erbes, Spitta. Taken from R. H. Charles, Vol. I, p. 349.)

3. The conversion of the Germanic tribes to Christianity.

So the famous German student of prophecy, Auberlen, explains it. By the conversion of these nations their "Beast" condition of hostility to the religion of Jesus Christ received a deadly wound. In the capacity of a fierce and savage enemy of the kingdom of Christ, pagan Europe died. When such hostility is renewed, it will be the healing of the wound, the coming back to life of the dead "Beast." Auberlen, who died in 1864, though that, in his day, the deadly wound had begun to heal. He would certainly think so still more, if he were living today.[3]

4. The coming of Christ.

So William Milligan, Hengstenberg, and Lenski. Since the wild beast is the symbol of the antichristian power, the coming of the Redeemer into the world was its death-stroke; but yet it seems to continue. The deadly wound is healed. In the days of St. John it was evident that the brute was

---

[3] pp. 298, 304

by no means dead, and this healing of the wound was, no doubt, a sore trial to him and his friends.

5. The Christianization of the Roman Empire.

This ought to have been a deadly wound to the anti-christian secular power. Considered as a jungle-beast, it should have come to an end when a Christian ascended the Imperial throne; but alas, it was not long before it became clear that the wound which should have been its deathblow was healed. The nominally Christian empire turned out to be, in its real character, about as unchristian as the pagan empire had been.

6. The rebellion of the three princes, Galba, Otho, and Vitellius.

This is Duesterdieck's explanation. Taking the Beast to be the Roman Empire, it seemed as if that empire would come to an end, that is, disintegrate, when the Imperial throne, for about a year, found no one who could firmly occupy it. This is what is meant by the deadly wound; but that wound was healed when Vespasian gained the throne, and re-established the Imperial authority.

7. The battle of Waterloo.

At present this interpretation is little more than a curiosity of exegesis, but about the years 1860–70, this was a very popular explanation, especially in the circle of those who were then holding "prophetic conferences." It may be found in the book entitled: "Forty Coming Wonders," published by "The Christian Herald and Sign of Our Times," the forerunner of the very different magazine now called "The Christian Herald." The idea in such circles then was that the Napoleonic family was the Beast with seven heads and ten horns, and that the deadly wound was the battle of Waterloo, in which the power of Bonaparte was overthrown. Later on, Napoleon III was elected Emperor of the French, and this election was pointed to in the edition of 1866 as triumphant proof that the wound was healed. However, the Franco-Prussian war of 1870 again overthrew the Napoleonic family; so that the edition of 1880 speaks of a second deadly wound, received at the battle of Sedan. This wound has not yet been healed.

8. The actual death and resurrection of a personal Antichrist, to take place in the last days.

So the Futurists generally, among them J. A. Seiss and the important German commentary of Theodor Zahn. The latter says:

There can be no doubt that the actual death and resurrection of the Antichrist is intended. (Vol. II, p. 452)

The expositors of this school consider that the Antichrist will, in these respects, be a kind of Satanic copy of the death and resurrection of the Lord Jesus Christ. Dr. Seiss carries this idea so far that he thinks the False Prophet will also come back from the dead, and will turn out to be Judas Iscariot, raised from the dead! In the study of the Apocalypse some degree of imagination is very helpful, but so much as this is a handicap.[4]

9. Nero himself, resurrected from hell.

This is at present the popular theory among those whom we may call the "Left Wing" Preterists. In the first years after the death of Nero, there was a popular rumor, believed by many, that he was not really dead, but had escaped, and had gone to hide among the Parthians who lived near the Caspian sea. During his lifetime these had really been on friendly terms with him, which gave color to the report that he had found refuge among them. It was expected that he would some day lead a Parthian army, and with their help would take the city of Rome. When many years had passed, and he could not well be supposed any longer to be alive, the story became, that he would rise from the dead, and armed now with hellish powers, would be the aid of barbarian tribes, destroy the city.

Since there is this legend, some recent commentators, who do not accept the Apocalypse as an inspired book, seize upon it, and find references to it in the language of chapters 13 and 17. The death of Nero was then the deadly wound, and his resurrection, when it took place, would be the healing of that wound. As risen from the dead, he would be the eighth head, of which the seer says that: "He was, and is not, and is to come"; which, being in one sense the Beast himself, "is the eighth, but is of the seven."

We must admit that this explanation, if acceptable, fits pretty well in some respects; but it does not fit in others. It is, of course, wholly incompatible with any believing acceptance of the book as a genuine prophecy; for the things foretold, if this interpretation is correct, did not take place. Moreover, there are excellent reasons, which may be found in the works of Benson and Zahn, for believing that no such superstition concerning Nero's resurrection was in existence, or could well be in existence at the date when the Apocalypse was written—AD 95. Nero was born in AD 37, therefore in AD 95 he would, if living, be only fifty-eight years old.

---

[4] Vol. II, p. 423.

At such an age the notion that he was among the Parthians, still living, was not out of date. Why should it at that time be thought that he had died and would come back from hell? Dr. A. S. Peake (p. 125) quotes a Roman orator, Dion Chrysostom, early in the second century, as saying; of Nero: "To the present time all men desire him to be alive, and the majority even trust that he is." If the date of this utterance, "early in the second century" is correctly given, it is at least ten or fifteen years after the Revelation was written.

10. The persecuting policy of Nero, revived by Domitian.

This is the interpretation of H. B. Swete. He thinks that the death of Nero was the mortal wound referred to, agreeing therein with most of the modern Preterists; but he differs from them in not thinking that the writer of the Apocalypse himself shared the superstitious expectation of Nero's resurrection. Yet he is certain that St. John was familiar with that notion. He says; (p. XCVII) "It is impossible to doubt that the legend of Nero redivivus is in full view of the Apocalyptist in more than one passage," and also (p. 161) "The legend has been used by St. John to represent the revival of Nero's persecuting policy by Domitian."

Thus he thinks that, the legend of Nero's return being already current, and known to the apostle John, he made use of it, turning it from its original meaning into a figure of speech. Since Nero's immediate successors, Vespasian and Titus, had not persecuted the Christians, the Beast had suffered a mortal wound in the death of Nero; but when Domitian resumed the persecution, the Beast revived. Domitian was thus, in a figurative sense, a second Nero, a Nero redivivus.

This is certainly possible, but it rests upon the assumption that the superstitious expectation was current as early as AD 95, of which proof is lacking. If there is any connection between the expressions used in the Apocalypse and that legend, is it not just possible that it is the other way around, that the legend rests upon this book, not the book upon the legend? To think and speak of Domitian as a second Nero is something which St. John was quite able to originate, without any such popular expectation to suggest the idea to him. After this book was read and discussed in Asia Minor, may it not, through a misunderstanding of these passages, have given currency to the idea that Nero would come back from the under world? Whichever way it may be, this interpretation that the suicide of Nero was the mortal wound received by one of the heads of the Beast, and that the resumption of persecution by Domitian was the healing of the wound, seems to me the best solution that has been offered. It certainly agrees with the hint given in the words: "the stroke of the sword" (13.14) for Nero stabbed himself.

IV. The Number of the Beast

We read in 13.18 that the Beast has a number.

> Here is wisdom. He that hath understanding, let him count the number of the Beast, for it is the number of a man: and his number is six hundred sixty and six.

Here is a definite challenge to figure it out, and numerous indeed have been the attempts to solve the puzzle. From the beginning it has been generally agreed that this expression "the number of a man" refers to an ancient custom of giving a man a number, made up of the numerical value of the letters in his name, added together. The Hebrews, Greeks, and Romans did not have our Arabic numerals. Instead of them they used the letters of the alphabet. We preserve a remnant of this method in our use of the Roman numerals, I, V, X, L, C, D, and M. By this means, we could give a man a number today. Thus in the name Martin Van Dyk, the letters having numerical value are M, 1,000; I, 1; V, 5; and D, 500. His number is therefore 1506. The question of interpretation in our text is to find a name that, in this way, will yield the sum 666. That is not difficult, for such names are only too easily found, among others, Mohammed, Pope Benedict, Martin Luther, Napoleon, and Trajan. Thus it furnishes us with no certain clue.

The earliest attempt to find the right name is by Irenaeus. If the true meaning had been made known to the circle of St. John's intimate friends, one could reasonably expect Irenaeus to give us a hint of it, for he was taught by Polycarp, who himself knew the apostle; but evidently Irenaeus did not know any more about it than we do. He prefers the name "Teitan," or Titan, taken from the ancient mythology, therefore a beast that has Titanic powers. He also mentions the word "Lateinos," or Latins, which will, in Greek letters, add up to the required number. This, he thinks, may be the true solution "because the Latins now bear rule." As he thinks the name is the name of Antichrist, this suggests that he may not have thought of the Antichrist as an individual of the last time. In his discussion he says something of great interest, although without himself attaching any special significance to it, namely, that while the best manuscripts of his day had the number 666, some had it 616. If, therefore, a name can be found that in some way or other can be made to yield both these numbers, the presumption is very much strengthened that it is the right one.

This is the case with the name "Nero" spelled in the Greek and Latin forms, but with Hebrew letters. Such words as "Nero," "Plato," in Latin, become "Neron," "Platon," etc., in Greek. Taking the name "Neron Kaisar," and spelling the same in Hebrew, we have 666. Spelling it in the Latin form, but also in Hebrew letters, we get 616! Many modern scholars, therefore, consider it settled that this is the solution, and it agrees, of course, beautifully, with their idea that the myth of "Nero redivivus" underlies the whole symbolism. Many others, however, including Alford, Zahn, Benson, and Lenski, reject this solution with scorn. One of the powerful arguments they bring against it is that the Apocalypse is a Greek book. When Christ is called "The Alpha and Omega" it is the Greek alphabet that is used. How, then, can we suppose St. John to mystify his readers by expecting them to figure it out in the letters of another language, of which most of them knew nothing?

Zahn comes to the conclusion that we cannot solve this puzzle, and are not intended to solve it. It belongs, he thinks, to the time of the end. When the great Antichrist of the end-time appears, his name will yield this number, and thoughtful Bible students will thus be able to recognize him, long before his acts would lead them to look upon him as the promised incarnation of evil. Most people, and probably he himself will be unconscious that his name betrays him.[5]

A few commentators reject the numerical method altogether, and seek to find a symbolical meaning in the number itself. Thus Lenski says (p. 411).

> This is the number 6, plus its multiple by 10, namely, 60, plus again its multiple by 10x10 (intensified completeness) namely 600—thus 666, falling short three times of the divine 7. In other words, not 777, but competing with 777, seeking to obliterate 777, but abortively, its failure as complete as its expansion by puffing itself up from 6 to 666.

Perhaps he is right, but it reminds me of the church father who found the number by adding the years of Noah's life when the flood began (600) to the height of the golden image Nebuchadnezzar made (60 cubits), and its breadth (6 cubits). This also makes 666!

---

[5] Vol. II, p. 457.

V. The Years of the Beast

One final puzzle with regard to the Beast must occupy us—the length of his reign. In many passages, under various forms, we are informed that he is to have power for three and a half years.

> The holy city shall they tread under foot forty and two months. And I will give unto my two witnesses, and they shall prophesy a thousand, two hundred, and three score days. (11.2–3) The woman fled into the wilderness, where she hath a place prepared of God, that there they may nourish her a thousand, two hundred and three score days. (12.6) She is nourished for a time, and times and half a time, from the face of the serpent. (12.14) There was given unto him authority to continue forty and two months. (13.5) (RV)

Such expressions are evidently taken from the book of Daniel:

> He shall wear out the saints of the Most High, …and they shall be given into his hand, until a time and time and the dividing of time. (7.25) "How long shall it be to the end of these wonders?...It shall be for a time, times, and a half." (12.6–7)

Is this period to be understood literally, as numerical count of days, months and years, or symbolically, and, if so, what does it symbolize?

Here, as often, extremes meet. The Futurists can see here nothing but literal chronology; so also the Left Wing Preterists. The former expect a period at the end of the world, of exactly three and a half calendar years, during which the Antichrist will be in power. The latter suppose that the writer of the Apocalypse expected the return of Nero, the destruction of Rome, and the end of the world to come in that number of years from the time he saw the vision. Of course, that did not happen, but this does not trouble the said school of interpreters, for they do not accept his inspiration. We need pay no further attention to these interpretations, for we do not share their point of view.

The Continuous Church History school found in these figures, for a long time, their chief strength. Understanding them on the "year-day" principle, they thought they could figure out from them when to expect the end of time. This system may be studied in the works of H. Grattan Guinness, especially "The Approaching End of the Age," p. 222–681, and "Light for the Last Days." His calculations are most interesting and instructive, but, alas, the latest date he can find for the end is 1934,[6] and it is now 1946. Why should we give it more space in this discussion?

A favorite explanation is that this mystic period represents the entire period between the first and second advents. This does very well for those who have entirely escaped the influence of the Preterist view, and thus regard the Beast merely as a symbol for the entire antichristian power, but if the Beast in any way refers to the pagan Roman Empire, this period also should have some explanation in connection with it.

Perhaps the best solution is to regard it, as Swete does:

> In Daniel this expression probably represents the three and a half years during which Jerusalem was in the hands of the Syrian oppressor, and the Apocalypse accordingly uses it, or its equivalents, to signify the age of persecution, whatever its duration might be. Other explanations are less probable. (p. cxxxiii)

If this explanation also does not satisfy, we must fall back upon the confession of ignorance of Alford, who says:[7]

> I am driven to believe that these periods are to be assigned by some clue, of which the Spirit has not put the church in possession.

---

[6] "History Unveiling Prophecy," p. 384.

[7] Vol. IV, Part II, p. 252.

XIX
THE WAR WITH THE BEAST

We have had before us the terrible foes which the cause of Christ and His righteousness must encounter in the world. ...But what has the church of Christ been doing? The sealed ones of God have suffered, but have they done more than suffer? Has theirs been only a passive endurance of evils? Have they wielded no weapons against these foes, and used no counter influence for good? The chapter before us will answer. In it the sacred seer takes from our survey of the powers of evil, and shows us the powers of good.[1]

This seems to me a correct statement of the general meaning, not only of chapter 14, but also of the two following chapters. It is characteristic of St. John thus to shift the scene from good to evil, from heaven to earth, and back again; so that we may see both sides of the great conflict: first the scene on earth, where the church seems helpless and her cause hopeless, and then the unseen allies of the church in the spiritual world, fighting with her and for her, certain to attain ultimately a glorious triumph. Chapter 14 gives us this conflict from the earthly point of view, where the church fights, suffers, but also conquers, until the judgment day brings the course of history to a close; while chapters 15 and 16 (to be taken together as one section) show us how God helps the church from heaven by pouring out judgments upon her foes. The description of the powers of evil is resumed in chapter seventeen.

Thus chapters 14–16 are not a digression, taking up a new subject, or an interlude. They are strictly a continuation of the story of the conflict between the Radiant Woman and the Red Dragon, begun in chapter twelve. This close connection is made clear by references to the Beast and

---

[1] W. Boyd Carpenter, in "Ellicott's Commentary," Vol. III, p. 601.

the False Prophet scattered here and there (14.9, 11; 15.2; 16.2, 10, 13) and by anticipatory references to Babylon the Great, which is pictured to us in detail in later chapters. Hence the view which one has taken of the Beast must influence the understanding of these chapters; and the reader will readily see that the interpretation of the Historicists, who re-fer everything to the Roman Catholic Church, and of the Futurists, who believe that the Beast is a personal Antichrist of the last days, can not be ours. The three chapters before us consist of a number of independent scenes, although all bear upon the same general subject, the war with the Beast. They can best be taken up separately.

I. The Embattled Host of the Lamb

And I saw, and behold, the Lamb, standing on the Mount Zion, and with him a hundred and forty four thousand.

The picture is that of a military leader and his army, ready for battle, occupying an impregnable position. This is the meaning of the reference to Mount Zion, the citadel of David. That this is the same company seen in 7.4 is generally agreed, and seems scarcely open to doubt. Therefore the interpretation here must be reckon with that adopted in the former pas-sage. Rejecting the idea that it referred to the converts from Judaism, or to the Israel of the end-time, or to the "tribulation saints" or to any other group within the total membership of the church, we took it there as the entire body of true believers on earth at any particular time, thus the church in the midst of the struggle, the "church under the cross." There-fore, in that passage, they were seen as sealed and kept in the midst of the calamities which the judgment of God brought upon a wicked world. Here we see the same group, and they are in the same position, but they are viewed now as a fighting force, "the church militant," led by the Lord Jesus Christ, doing battle with the Beast and the False Prophet, the allies and instruments of the Dragon. As Dr. Swete says:[2]

> As in 7.4ff., it is the living church which is in the Seer's thought, not the unnumbered multitude of 7.9, i.e., not the church in her final completed glory, but the faithful who are on earth at any given time.

Some, however, take it as the glorified church in heaven. So Kuyper, Alford, Lenski, and many others, influenced therein especially by what

---

[2] p. 174.

is said of this company; that they "had been purchased out of the earth," that they *were* (not are) undefiled, that in them "was found no lie," and that they are "without blemish." Since we know only too well that imperfection cleaves to even the holiest believer in this life, it is held that such statements about the people of God are possible only if they are thought of as those "whose course is ended and looked back upon as a thing past." This is not without force; yet such things are said of all true believers even in this life, from the ideal standpoint. So John says in I John 3.6: "Whosoever abideth in him sinneth not. ...Whosoever is begotten of God doeth no sin, because his seed abideth in him and he can not sin, because he is begotten of God." St. Paul also says of the Corinthians, in whom remained much imperfection: "Ye were washed, ye were sanctified" (I Cor 6.11), and he habitually refers to Christians as "saints." What is said of believers in such passages is true of them in principle, as seen "in Christ." It will be actually true some day, but it may already be said of them by anticipation. Hence the use of such language in this vision of Revelation seems to me no decisive argument for supposing this group of 144,000 to symbolize the perfected church in glory.

Against it, on the other hand, is the identity of this company with that in chapter seven, and also the whole representation here of an armed host, following their Leader. "These are they that follow the Lamb, whithersoever he goeth." It reminds us of Matthew 10.38, John 12.26, and similar passages, and is inconsistent with the state of heavenly rest. Moreover, we find a description of those who have gained the victory in 15.2–4; which seems like a needless and meaningless repetition, if this condition is already shown in 14.1–5.

Since the believers are here represented as soldiers, ready to march and fight, it is natural that they are spoken of as men only, and that their virtues are stated in masculine terms. This belongs to the symbolism, not to the reality, and does not in the least mean that godly women are excluded. Hence their purity from spiritual fornication, namely, idolatry and worldliness, is expressed in the following manner: "They were not defiled with women, for they are virgins." This has nothing to do with sex relations, and indicates no superior holiness in the celibate life. This is almost universally agreed upon among commentators, so that it awakens surprise to find so sober and excellent a writer as Alford giving it here a literal interpretation. He thinks that those who have never known sex relations (in which he includes small children dying in infancy) will occupy a position of special privilege and glory in heaven! The notion is wholly untenable and unacceptable; as it would run counter to the constant teaching, not only of the rest of the Bible, but of this very book, in which the Lamb is represented as marrying a wife!

These 144,000 are spoken of as "first fruits," which seems, at first sight, to favor those who see here only a select portion of God's people, not the whole; but in James 1.18 believers are called the "first fruits of his creatures." Here the contrast is the same: not "first fruits" as compared with the entire body of the redeemed, but as compared with the whole of God's creation, which is eventually to share in the redemption. (Rom 8.19–23)

In connection with this vision of the 144,000, St. John hears a song from heaven, mighty and sweet, which only those can learn who belong to this company on Mount Zion. In accordance with the interpretation which looks upon the whole group as already in the perfected heavenly state, this is sung by them: if we take it that these are still on earth, we lay emphasis upon the word "learn." Those already in heaven are singing it; those still on earth are learning it. Dr. Swete finely says:[3]

> Even the 144,000 have need to learn the Song; it does not come to them naturally, or without effort; every Eucharist, every thankful meditation on the Passion, is an exercise in the art. And only they can learn it; the music of the heart (Eph 5.19; Col 3.16) can not be acquired without a receptivity which is a divine gift.

II. The Three Angelic Heralds and the Voice from Heaven

Three angels, with three solemn announcements, fly in mid-heaven, symbolizing things made known, or to be made known, to all men. The first has "eternal good tidings" to proclaim, and the substance of the said good news is that men should fear God, the Creator of all things, and give glory to Him, since the hour of judgment is near. Some excellent commentators—among them William Milligan and H. B. Swete—can not see that this is the gospel of salvation, in the ordinary sense. They urge that this can not be the case, because the message has to do only with the near approach of judgment, with no exhortation to believe in Christ, and no mention of forgiveness or mercy. Yet it seems to me decisive against this view that the word "gospel" is used, which is a distinctly technical

---

[3] p. 175.

word, elsewhere always designating in one form or another, the good news of salvation in Jesus Christ our Lord. In the original the emphasis upon this word is heightened by the fact that it is used twice, as a noun and as a verb, in a way that can not be translated into good English, but may be imitated if we say that the angel had "a gospel to gospel" to all nations, or that he had "eternal good news, to tell as good news" to all men. What is said in verse seven is, to be sure, not the whole of that good news, but it is in integral part, and the part with which we must always begin when preaching to the heathen. The gospel is always one and the same, but it is presented in accordance with the needs and the spiritual state of those addressed. To the Jews of the days of John the Baptist it was "Repent, for the kingdom of heaven is at hand"; to the careless Christian in the pew it is: "Today, if ye will hear his voice, harden not your hearts"; to the pagan it is: "Fear God and give him glory... and worship him that made the heaven and the earth, the sea and fountains of waters." In the same spirit St. Paul says that the effect of the gospel upon the Thessalonians was that they "turned unto God from idols, to serve a living and true God," (I Thess 1.9). His own summary of his ministry was that he "testified both to Jews and Greeks repentance towards God and faith toward our Lord Jesus Christ" (Acts 20.21), and again, that he had "declared both to them of Damascus first, and at Jerusalem, and throughout all the country of Judea, and also to the Gentiles, that they should repent, and turn to God, doing works worthy of repentance," (Acts 26.20). This is not so different from the gospel proclaimed by the flying angel in the vision. There seems to me, therefore, no sufficient reason to reject the common and natural interpretation that the flight and proclamation of this angel symbolize the world-wide preaching of the gospel, primarily in the apostolic and sub-apostolic ages, but continuing to the day of judgment. This is the first great thing that the followers of the Lamb do in their warfare with the Beast.

The second angel brings the good news that the capital of the enemy has been destroyed. "Fallen, fallen, is Babylon the Great." The words are taken from Isaiah 21.9. If, as we have taken it, the Beast means the persecuting Roman Empire, Babylon, the seat of the Beast, will naturally mean the city of Rome, as we shall see clearly when studying the seventeenth chapter.

The third angel solemnly warns against desertion from the army of the Lamb, by yielding to the temptation to save this temporal life by offering incense to the statue of the Emperor. To escape the wrath of Caesar by apostasy is to come under the much more terrible wrath of a holy and almighty God, to drink the cup of His anger undiluted, and to be tormented with fire and brimstone forever and ever. Symbols these are, certainly, not literal realities, but they are not vain symbols. The truth taught here is the same as that emphasized by the Lord Jesus, when He said: "Be not afraid of them that kill the body, but are not able to kill the soul: but rather fear him who is able to destroy both soul and body in hell" (Matt 10.28).

In beautiful contrast with this solemn and dreadful warning, a voice from heaven speaks to St. John, telling him to put it on record that those who die in the Lord are blessed. This is not proclaimed by an angel, for it is not something to be made known to the world at large; only to those who read "what the Spirit saith to the churches." That the words, "from henceforth" are inserted, is not to intimate that it has not hitherto been so, but to direct the thought of the reader to that which concerns him personally. The time for him has not yet come, but he is to look forward with confidence and comfort, knowing that when it does come, whether quietly, in the ordinary course of human destiny, or by violence at the hands of the persecuting Beast, it is no real calamity, but the gateway to a blessed and eternal rest.

III. The Harvest and the Vintage

The fourteenth chapter reaches its climax in a revelation of the great judgment at the end of the world. Plainly he who sits upon the cloud is the Lord Jesus Christ, appearing as the judge of the living. The dead are not here in view. An account of their judgment is given in Revelation 20.11–15. The figures under which the final judgment is here presented are those of a harvest—the ingathering of the saved—and of a vintage, with the grapes crushed in a winepress—the destruction of the wicked. These symbols are familiar from other portions of the scriptures. From Daniel 7.13 is taken that of the "one like unto a son of man" sitting on the clouds of heaven. The harvesting of the grain is found also in the Parable of the Tares, (Matt 13.30, 39; 24.31). The sharp sickle is simply a detail, required by the harvest symbol. That Christ, as reaper, can not proceed until the word is given by an angel coming forth from the presence of God, dramatizes the truth which He himself taught His disciples, that "That day and hour knoweth no man, not even the angels in heaven, neither the Son, but the Father," (Mark 13.32). The symbol of a winepress, where grapes are crushed, is from Isaiah 63.3–4:

I have trodden the winepress alone, and of the people there was none with me: for I will tread them in mine anger, and trample them in my fury; and their blood shall be sprinkled upon my garments, and I will stain all my raiment. For the day of vengeance is in my heart, and the year of my redeemed is come.

That the winepress was "without the city" indicates that those crushed in it were cast out from "the city of God," the holy community of the New Jerusalem, as also in Revelation 22.15: "Without are the dogs, and the sorcerers, and the fornicators, and the murderers, and the idolaters, and every one that loveth and maketh a lie." It has nothing here to do with the earthly Jerusalem.

By one of those startling changes of figure to which we grow accustomed in the Apocalypse, we are told that "there came out blood from the winepress, even to the bridles of the horses, as far as a thousand six hundred furlongs." Here the symbol of a winepress is suddenly changed to that of a great battle, where the carnage is so dreadful that the cavalry horses wade in a sea of blood, extending for two hundred miles. To think here of geography is entirely out of place. Palestine is not two hundred miles long from end to end, and the configuration of the country is such that no such sea of blood could stand upon it, no matter what happened. We are not even told whether the said distance is the circumference, diameter, or radius of the bloody sea, and the reason for this is simply that it makes not a particle of difference. It is not intended to be measured and calculated. We are simply intended to recoil from the horror of it. This is an attempt to impress the imagination, not to inform the mind. The dreadful nature of the judgment, and the completeness with which the foe is crushed, must be borne in upon the mind by the mental picture of such a sea of blood and of the cavalry riding through it. That is not helped by calculations of length and breadth.

IV. The Bowls of Wrath

The war with the Beast is over. God's enemies have been completely crushed, and his own have been safely garnered in. In 15.2–4 we see them before the throne of God, celebrating the victory. This is the same army which we saw in 14.1–5; then beginning the campaign. Now they are welcomed in heaven as "those who came off victorious from the Beast, and from his image, and from the number of his name."

Yet in chapters 15 and 16 we see the same conflict again, this time as the act of God, sending calamities upon the earth and especially upon the kingdom of the Beast. The Dragon, the Beast, and the False Prophet are still active, as we see in 16.13, and Great Babylon, of which the fall was announced in 14.8, is still to be dealt with in 16.19—not to speak of the fact that all of these characters appear again in later chapters. How is all this to be explained? It seems to me that Dr. William Milligan points out the true meaning to us when he says:

> Nothing can more clearly prove that the Revelation of St. John is not written upon chronological principles than the scenes to which we are introduced in the fifteenth and sixteenth chapters of the book. We have already been taken to the end, as we have seen, in chapter 14, the Son of Man upon the throne of judgment, the harvest of the righteous, and the vintage of the wicked. Yet we are now met by another series of visions setting before us judgments that must take place before the final issue. This is not chronology; it is apocalyptic vision, which again and again turns round the kaleidoscope of the future, and delights to behold, under different aspects the same great principles of the Almighty's government, leading always to the same glorious results.

The great series of judgments symbolized by the outpouring of the bowls of wrath bears a close resemblance to that of the trumpets, in chapters eight and nine. Both are modeled, in the earlier portions, upon the plagues of Egypt. In the latter portion both introduce an invading force from beyond the Euphrates. The most striking difference is that in the former series only one-third of each area stricken was destroyed, while no such limitation appears when the bowls are poured out. Since the symbols are so much alike, why is the presentation repeated? Because the divine judgments in the Great Book section of Revelation are viewed as judgments upon a wicked world in general; while, here, in the Little Book section, they form a part of the conflict begun in chapter twelve, between the Radiant Woman and the Red Dragon, of whom the Beast and the False Prophet are allies and instruments. Dr. Swete says:[4]

> The Seven Bowls are usually classed with the Seven Seals and the Seven Trumpets, and with the latter, especially, they have an obvious affinity; but their relation to the great section of the book which begins in XII:1 is even closer; they belong to the drama of the long conflict between the Church and the world.

---

[4] p. 190.

This general meaning is plain; but so far as detailed exposition of the separate bowls and their happenings is concerned, the confession of ignorance made in connection with the Trumpet series is again in place. It is possible—indeed, very likely—that to the mind of the apostle, as he saw the visions, each one had relation to some definite event in history or fact of experience; but if so, these meanings have not come down to us by any trustworthy tradition, and remain undiscovered to the satisfaction of the most earnest and intelligent students. Literalism is here hopeless. How could any one put the wrath of God into a bowl and pour it out upon the sun? The Historicists find fulfillments in connection with the Roman Catholic Church, and give themselves much trouble to determine which of the bowls is being poured out in our day; but if one considers their whole method wrong—as I do—he can not find any value in their speculations. The Futurists postpone everything to the time of the Antichrist, which saves them from the need of any interpretation, except as they understand the symbols literally, which not even they can do consistently.

Most other interpreters contents themselves with pointing out this or that with regard to the symbols, but do not venture, usually, to say what is the reality symbolized. When they do attempt it, the wide diversity in their expositions shows that they have no solid basis. We may take as an example the various meanings attached to the drying up of the Euphrates and the coming of "the kings of the East," in 16.12. To many they are, as Swete puts it, "the vanguard of the forces flocking to the last war"; to which the nations are summoned by the three evil spirits, like frogs, issuing from the months of the Dragon, the Beast, and the False Prophet. No doubt these frogs represent influences exerted through teaching or propaganda of some sort. The "kings from the sun-rising," however, are spoken of before this summon goes out, and as their way is prepared by God, it is difficult to consider them as a part of the hostile army. Therefore Dr. William Milligan thinks that these kings "are an emblem of the Israel of God, as they return from all the places whither they have been led captive." If we could believe that the Ten Tribes are still to come back across the headwaters of the Euphrates, as prophesied in the apocryphal book of Esdras IV, this would be as good a solution as any, but that fable can no longer be accepted. Dean sees in these kings, "the Parthian rulers, in alliance with whom Nero was to return and destroy Rome." So considered, they might be among God's instruments for the destruction of the Beast, but the Parthians did not come, so, if this is the meaning, the prophecy

178 | *The Lamb, The Woman, and The Dragon*

failed. Dr. Greijdanus looks upon the Euphrates as the symbolical prophetic boundary between Christendom and heathendom. This is to be
dried up and the "yellow peril" will overwhelm the church.

On the whole, it seems clear that the true interpretation has not yet
been found, and probably cannot be found. It is for us, in this situation, to
take to heart and to our imaginations the picture as a whole, rather than
to be over curious about the meaning of every several part. We see here a
vivid dramatization of the fight God puts up from heaven in behalf of His
Church, and we take courage, knowing that whatever His own may need
to suffer for a time, with such a Helper the victory must be on their side.
He is not asleep; neither is His hand shortened that it can not save.

XX

THE TWO WOMEN AND THE TWO CITIES

The section of the Revelation from the beginning of chapter twelve to the end of the book is dominated by a great contrast between two women and two cities. In chapter twelve, we found a radiant and glorious woman, clothed with the sun, having the stars for her crown and the moon under her feet: yet, although she is so radiant and glorious, hated and persecuted. She is given the wings of the great eagle, and flies to the wilderness, where she must remain for a time, and times, and half a time, the standard prophetic formula for a period of trouble.

In chapter seventeen, the guiding angel says to the seer:

> Come hither, I will show thee the judgment of the great harlot that sitteth upon many waters; with whom the kings of the earth committed fornication, and they that dwell on the earth were made drunken with the wine of her fornication.

Then the angel carries away the seer, not to the sea shore, as might have been expected, from the mention of "many waters," but to the wilderness, and there he sees an amazing sight:

> And I saw a woman, sitting upon a scarlet colored beast, full of names of blasphemy, having seven heads and ten horns. And the woman was arrayed in purple and scarlet, (the finest possible cloth, used in the hangings of the tabernacle and in the raiment of kings) and decked with gold, and precious stones, and pearls.

Points of similarity and contrast at once attract our attention. Here are manifestly two symbolic women, and the fact that in each case a woman is chosen as the symbol suggests some relation between the things symbolized. Both, also, are in "the wilderness." On the other hand, the beast upon which the Scarlet Woman rides appears to be the same as the one that came up out of the sea to aid the dragon in his welfare against the Radiant Woman of chapter twelve. The enemy of the one is therefore the friend and servant of the other. Nevertheless, eventually the persecuted woman is safe, while the other is destroyed by her own allies, for we read:

> The ten horns, which thou sawest, and the beast, these shall hate the harlot, and shall make her desolate and naked, and shall eat her flesh, and shall burn her utterly with fire." (17.16) (RV)

The great question of interpretation that confronts us here is whether these are two different women, symbolizing different things, or whether they are really the same woman, considered from different points of view, or in different stages of her existence.

Just as the two women are thus contrasted, there is also a contrast between two cities. One is introduced to us in chapter 16.19, where we read:

> And Babylon the great was remembered in the sight of God, to give unto her the cup of the wine of the fierceness of his wrath. (RV)

Further on, in the eighteenth chapter, the fall of this Babylon the Great is elaborately described, in a very noble and beautiful passage that makes concrete, by the heaping up of details, the greatness and luxury of which the fallen city has been the center. Her fall is final and complete:

> Fallen, fallen, is Babylon the great, and is become a habitation of devils, and a hold of every unclean spirit, and a hold of every unclean and hateful bird. …And a strong angel took up a stone, as it were a great millstone, and cast it into the sea, saying: Thus with a mighty fall shall Babylon, the great city, be cast down, and shall be found no more at all." (18.2, 21) (RV)

In contrast to this is seen the New Jerusalem, of chapter twenty-one, established in eternal and unchangeable splendor:

> Coming down out of heaven from God, made ready as a bride adorned for her husband… having the glory of God, her light like unto a stone most precious.

What do these two cities symbolize? Do they mean something different from what is symbolized by the two women, or is it really the same idea under a different figure? This question is comparatively easy to answer. Unquestionably the harlot on the wild beast means the same thing as Babylon the Great. Verse five of chapter seventeen begins to make that clear by saying: "And upon her forehead a name written, Mystery, Babylon the Great...." The explanation is continued in 17.18, where we are told that the woman represents a great city, and in many expressions throughout the eighteenth chapter, until, in the beginning of the nineteenth, the triumph song over the fall of Babylon is altogether in terms of the Great Harlot.

That the Radiant Woman is also the same as the New Jerusalem, is not quite so clear, but may nevertheless be confidently asserted. We have already seen reason to look upon that woman as a symbol of the church of God, considered in the widest possible sense. In 19.7 we read:

The marriage of the Lamb is come, and his wife hath made herself ready.

This is a familiar language, and causes us at once to think of the parable of the Marriage Supper in the gospels, as well as of St. Paul's references to the church as the bride of Christ, which references, again, merely carry on, in the New Testament, a favorite figure of the Old. The bride is the church, the company of the redeemed, and therefore the same company as was represented by the Radiant Woman. Then, in 21.9–10, this symbolism of the bride, the Lamb's wife, is unmistakably linked to that of the city, the New Jerusalem, for we read:

And there came one of the seven angels, who had the seven bowls, who were laden with the seven last plagues, and he spake with me, saying: Come hither, I will show thee the bride, the wife of the Lamb. And he carried me away in the Spirit to a mountain, great and high, and showed me the holy city, Jerusalem, coming down out of heaven from God. (RV)

Thus it seems quite clear that the holy and radiant woman means the same thing as the New Jerusalem, and that both are representations of the church of God, the former, in her persecuted and afflicted condition—the "Church Militant"—the latter as divinely protected, perfected, and eternally glorified—the "Church Triumphant."

Since we are thus assured that the harlot and Babylon are one thing, and that the Radiant Woman and the New Jerusalem are also one and the same thing, the very important and difficult question is before us whether there is any relation between the one double symbol and the other. That they are, in some sense, antagonistic to one another, is plain enough; but is this antagonism that of the Apostate Church to the True Church, or of the Church to the World? If the former explanation is correct, all of these four symbols refer to the same thing, the church of God; but to that church, now as faithful and pure, the chaste bride of Christ, then as unfaithful, as an adulterous and rejected wife.

There are thus two main lines of interpretation, between which we must choose:

1. That the Great Harlot symbolizes the apostate Christian church, manifested historically in many forms, conspicuously and chiefly in the Roman Catholic Church, but also in other forms of nominal Christianity, especially when in combination with political power. We shall call this the Apostate Church Interpretation.

2. That the Great Harlot symbolizes the city of Rome, considered as the center of vice and luxury, as the seat of "The World," in the unfavorable spiritual sense (James 4.4), as the very embodiment of the lusts and temptations of the flesh. Therefore also, by extension of the idea, any similar city, wherever and whenever found. This is the City of Rome Interpretation.

I. The Apostate Church Interpretation

This view is held by many of the very best expositors, among whom we may mention William Milligan, Auberlen, and Alford. They use, in favor of it, the following arguments:

1. That the figure of adultery, or fornication, is the standard figure used in the Old Testament prophecies for apostasy from the true God. It is used in this way so often that it almost becomes a technical designation of idolatry, as in Judges 2.17; Deuteronomy 31.16; and 1 Chronicles 5.25. In the prophets, this idea is worked out in detail in the figure of a woman unfaithful to her husband. So we find it in Hosea, where the unfaithfulness of Israel to Jehovah, and the wonderful love of Jehovah for Israel, in spite of such sin, are graphically and pathetically set before us in the acted parable of Hosea and his relations to his unchaste wife. In Ezekiel 23, this figure is carried out in almost revolting detail, and in his sixteenth chapter the destruction of Samaria and Jerusalem is likened to the public execution of a wife found guilty of adultery.

It is correct, therefore, that the figure of a harlot is a standard symbol of the Old Testament, and that it usually means apostasy from Jehovah on the part of his people. Since it is the rule to seek the origin and meaning of the symbols of the book of Revelation first in the usage of the Old Testament, the argument has great force that we must so interpret it here. If so, the Great Harlot must be understood to represent some form of false Christianity, of the church of God become unfaithful and found in alliance with the persecuting power. If there were no such phenomenon to be found in church history, the interpretation would fail, but it is only too well supported. We all know the appalling apostasy of the Papacy and how terribly the words of Revelation 18.24 are true of the Roman Catholic Church:

> In her was found the blood of prophets and of saints, and of all that have been slain upon the earth.

2. The second argument in favor of the identification of the Great Harlot with the persecuted Woman, is that she is found in the wilderness. That is the place to which the Radiant Woman fled. Since the guiding angel now leads the seer into the wilderness, we naturally expect that he will find there this same woman. According to this interpretation, it is indeed the same, yet how changed! Instead of being content there, nourished by the heavenly manna, to wait in patience for the return of her Lord, she sought other lovers, and found them, who changed the wilderness for her into a place of drunken debauchery and royal luxury. Again, if this change had never taken place in church history, the comparison would go for nothing, but if the vision be so interpreted, it is, alas, only too true to life. This is exactly what happened to the Roman Catholic Church, and not only to her, but to many Protestant churches. Ever and again the world comes into the church, and pomp and luxury take the place of holy waiting for the coming of Christ. This striking correspondence with the facts of experience is a strong point in favor of the interpretation.

3. In the third place, the extreme astonishment of the seer is best explained on the basis of this interpretation. It was perhaps an astonishing sight, under any circumstances, to see the terrible wild beast of the earlier vision now so meek that a woman can ride him in comfort; but more so still if that be the woman whom the Dragon sought to destroy, the very same woman who originally fled to the wilderness, persecuted and af-

184 | *The Lamb, The Woman, and The Dragon*

flicted, but chaste and faithful. If it is the same woman, how comes she now to be the friend of the Dragon's ally, and to be riding him in drunken revelry? Surely, in such a case, the words are most appropriate: "When I saw her, I wondered with a great wonder."

4. Alford argues also, as a decisive argument, that no such complete destruction befell the material city of Rome as that described in chapter eighteen; but it seems to me that in insisting upon this argument he is straining the language somewhat. The reduction of the proud metropolis of the entire civilized world to the position of a comparatively poor and unimportant city, after the barbarian invasions, may well be poetically described as a complete destruction. She *was* destroyed, in her capacity of ruling city.

5. Another argument, which also seems to me of little weight, is used by Alford, namely, that there were no independent kings left in the Roman Empire, so that the words of 17.2, "with whom kings of the earth committed fornication," could not be true of the actual city of Rome, the only kings left not under her dominion being the kings of the Parthians, who lived near the Black and Caspian seas. Here, again, he seems to me to be too closely bound to the literal sense. In a composition in which a city can be described as a woman, there is surely no difficulty about understanding the "kings of the earth" to be the high and mighty, whatever their actual titles may be. Sir William Ramsay, one of the foremost authorities on the customs and language of the first century, says that "the term 'kings' was not commonly used in the social speech of that period to indicate the wealthy and luxurious."[1] Besides, if we must find actual kings left in the Roman empire, we shall not find it so difficult. Nothing is said here about "independent" kings. We have only to think of Herod the Great, of his sons, and of Agrippa, whether the first or the second. So there were others, kings under the suzerainty of Rome, to be sure, but kings nevertheless.

On the whole, this interpretation certainly has a strong case. Let me quote the summing up, from this side of the argument, as we find it in William Milligan,

> The two cities are the counterparts of one another. But we know that by the first is represented the bride, the Lamb's wife, of the true church of Christ, as, separated from the world, she remains faithful to her Lord, is purified from sin, and is made meet for that eternal home into which

[1] p. 94.

there enters nothing that defiles. What can the other be but the representative of a false and degenerate church, of a church that has yielded to the temptations of the world, and has turned back in heart from the trials of the wilderness to the flesh-pots of Egypt? Every feature of the description answers, although with the heightened color of ideal portraiture, to what such a professing but degenerate church becomes—the pride, the show, the love of luxury, the subordination of the future to the present. Even her very cruelty to the poor saints of God is drawn from actual reality, and has been depicted upon many a page of history.

II. The City of Rome Interpretation

Strong as the case is for the above interpretation, to the other side also is strong, and among recent scholars can claim the greater number of adherents. The arguments are as follows:

1. The identification of the Great Harlot with the city of Rome suits the circumstance of the times.

This argument has great influence upon me. I would not go so far as some of the Preterists along this line, I am perfectly willing, with the "Philosophy of History" school, to see in the symbols of the Apocalypse representations of great principles and abiding forces, rather than definite events, persons, and places; and yet I do feel that for a proper interpretation we must always seek at least our starting point in the immediate age and circumstances of the prophet, and of those for whose instruction and comfort he writes. When I read the introduction and the letters to the seven churches, it seems to me clear that this book was primarily intended to be a veritable "tract for the times"; and how much it did actually, by undergirding the believers of the early church, contribute to their victory through martyrdom can never be adequately estimated.

To interpret this vision of the great apostasy of the Papal system, or of still other earlier or later apostasies, in which the professing but spiritually adulterous church is combined with the wicked secular power to persecute the true saints, is to suppose that the apostle here speaks of something that had no connection whatever with the needs of the churches addressed; something the knowledge of which could be of no benefit to them: nay, more, that, in the precise degree to which they correctly understood it, would tend to discourage them. Perhaps we can not say that this is absolutely impossible, but surely, if there is another interpretation that equally well fits the text, and that does have some connection with the times, such an interpretation is to be preferred.

2. In reply to the argument that adultery and fornication are the standard figures used in the Old Testament for unfaithfulness on the part of God's people (which is admitted to be correct) it may fairly be said that the same figure is used also of heathen cities, when considered as centers of luxury and vice. Illustrations of this are found in Isaiah 23.15–17 and Nahum 3.4. Here the same figure is employed of Tyre and Nineveh, which were, of course, not of the people of God, but great heathen cities, full of the lusts of the flesh. It is therefore not entirely without prophetic precedent, if that figure is used in the Revelation for the heathen city of Rome, without any special religious reference.

3. It is difficult to see how the original readers of the Apocalypse could attach any other meaning to the explanation given in 17.9, 18, except to think of the Imperial city. In the former place they read, or heard read in the assembly of the believers: "The seven heads are seven mountains, on which the woman sitteth," and in the latter. "The woman whom thou sawest is the great city, which reigneth over the kings of the earth." Would they have the slightest doubt—would it even occur to them to inquire—what was meant by the seven hilled city, and by the city that ruled the world? This is as nearly as anything can be a direct naming of the city of Rome. That, in a book of this kind, many things should be left unexplained, is within reason, but not so the introduction of a misleading explanation: and yet such this was to the first readers, if the Apostate Church Interpretation is correct. To say that it means Rome, indeed, but Papal Rome, not imperial Pagan Rome, may do for us, but does not take away its misleading character for them.

4. The final argument on this side is that the identification of the Great Harlot with the city of Rome is in better harmony with chapter eighteen, and with the facts of history.

The eighteenth chapter is an elaborate description of the fall of a great commercial metropolis, with the emphasis from beginning to end laid upon the trade, wealth, and luxury of the city. Read it carefully, especially verses nine to eighteen. Now, of course, we all realize that when a city is taken as a symbol, the poet (for this is what our author is) must be allowed to draw out the symbol in some detail; but if the thing symbolized is really an apostate church, the essential evil of which is that she departs from the true faith, is not such symbolism as this drawn out beyond all reason? Not a hint is given of any religious evil. All the emphasis is laid upon commerce in articles of luxury. This certainly fits the City of Rome Interpretation far better than the other.

This chapter is closely modeled upon the 27th chapter of Ezekiel. There the prophet is speaking of the great city of Tyre, the center of world-wide commerce in his day. It is interesting to know that some expositors believe that, under cover of the name "Tyre," the prophet Ezekiel, who was at the time a captive in Babylonia, was really foretelling the ruin of Babylon. Unable with safety to publish such a prediction openly, he is thought to have veiled it under the name of the other metropolis. Is this is correct, there is a close parallel between his situation and that of St. John.

Hengstenberg affirms that this interpretation was the common one in the early church. He says:[2]

> That by Babylon, and by the great whore, heathen Rome is denoted, was understood even in the earlier ages of Christianity during the dominion of Rome itself, and while the fulfillment was in progress: and that not merely here and there, but by all who followed generally the historical exposition.

This, therefore, is the interpretation for which I give my vote, not without hesitation and yet with a considerable degree of confidence. The Great Harlot, on the scarlet beast, identical with the Mystery Babylon, is not the apostate church, but the city of Rome, as existing in the apostle's day; the center of luxury and vice, the embodiment of "the world," with which to be contaminated is to be guilty of spiritual adultery and to become the enemy of God (James 4.4). She was the very embodiment of "the lust of the flesh and the lust of the eyes, and the vainglory of life" (1 John 2.16). In her markets the saints of God were bought and sold as slaves, and in her circuses they were torn to pieces by wild beasts, for the amusement of her ladies and gentlemen. The bottomless moral degeneracy which prevailed, from the palace of the emperor to the huts of the proletariat, cannot with decency be described. Pagan Rome deserved every word of the terrible indictment here brought against her, and well merited the fate she ultimately met.

Dr. Swete says:[3]

> The Woman on the Beast represents, is the symbol of, Babylon the Great, while Babylon itself is a mystical name for the city which is now mistress of the world. Her gaily attired, jeweled, gilded person, and her cup of

---

[2] Vol. II, p. 296.

[3] p. 214.

abominations proclaim her to be the Mother-Harlot of the Earth. All the harlots of all the subject races are her children; all the vices and superstitions of the provinces were suckled at her breasts.

Sir William Ramsay gives this interpretation:[4]

The Woman of 17.1, sitting on a scarlet colored beast with seven heads and ten horns and names of blasphemy, decked in splendor and lapped in luxury and drunk with the blood of the saints and the blood of the martyrs, is the Imperial city, which attracted to her allurements and her pomp the kings of the nations, the rich and distinguished men from all parts of the civilized world.

We find, then, in the story of the Radiant Woman, that she has three enemies; perhaps, more accurately stated, two enemies and a rival, although the rival is precisely for that reason the most dangerous enemy of all. All these operate under the guidance and by inspiration of the Dragon, but he himself remains out of sight. Her first enemy is the Wild Beast from the Sea, symbolizing the persecuting power that attempts to overthrow her by violence, that puts to death her children, and, usurping the powers of government, defies her Lord. This is, in the first place, the pagan empire of Rome, contemporary to St. John: by extension of the idea, any such opposing and persecuting power, whether before or after Rome.

Her second enemy is the Wild Beast from the Land, having two horns like a lamb, but speaking like a dragon. This is the opposing religious and intellectual power: in the first place, the pagan priesthood and philosophy of the Roman empire, but, by extension of the idea, any false teaching that seeks to oppose and corrupt the true church.

Her third enemy is the Great Harlot on the Beast, primarily the great city that was supported and fed by the Roman empire, namely, Rome itself, considered as the embodiment of the lusts of the flesh and the pride of life. Again, by extension of the idea, every such great city, in any age of the world, where luxury and vice abound, and where lurk the terrible dangers to religion and virtue which make such a metropolis their lair.

Looked at in this way, we can see that these three enemies were precisely those against which the early church needed to be warned. What would be the chief anxieties of a faithful bishop in those days with regard to his flock? First, that they should be afraid of persecution, and fail to

[4] p. 94.

remain faithful unto death; second, that they should be led away by false doctrine; third, that they should be enticed by the lusts of the flesh, failing to withstand the allurements of the great city.

Against all of these dangers the book of Revelation strengthened and warned the believers: against persecution by assuring them that the Beast could continue only the prophetic period of forty and two months, a "short time" fixed by God and known to Him, not to be over passed: against the False Prophet, by showing them his end in the lake of fire: against the Great Harlot by showing them how the great city which she symbolizes is presently to be destroyed. Thus we get, by this interpretation, a book thoroughly suited to the times in which it was produced, and yet full of warning and instruction to the end of the world.

Accepting this line of interpretation, I get from the Apocalypse no definite prediction either of a personal Antichrist to appear shortly before the coming of Christ, or of the Pope; which, I fear, will be a disappointment to some of my friends. The nearest approach to a prophecy of the Papal apostasy that I find is the Wild Beast from the Land. Considering this as a religious priesthood cooperating with the wicked secular power in the persecution of true believers, whenever and wherever found, I do think that the Roman Catholic Church is its most conspicuous historical counterpart, although not its primary or only fulfillment.

XXI

THE BATTLE OF ARMAGEDDON

In the first part of the nineteenth chapter of Revelation we are the audience, or are spectators, at a great celebration. It has to do with the Two Women we have been studying, and therefore looks both backwards and forwards. It celebrates first the victory over the Great Harlot, Babylon, and then proceeds to celebrate the approaching marriage of the Bride to the Lamb. As remarked in the beginning of this discussion, to get the full value of such scenes we must imagine ourselves seated in an audience, with a magnificent panorama, or pageant, enacted before us. Now and again, as an important point in the drama is reached, there is a pause. While a new act is being prepared, the choir sings an anthem, to the accompaniment of stately music, from an organ, or orchestra. These doxologies form one of the finest features of the Apocalypse, and serve as a means of expression for the emotions aroused by the tremendous things we have seen. There is nothing flabby or colorless about these anthems. They ring with stern joy at the judgment executed upon Babylon and with exceeding gladness at the coming marriage supper of the Lamb. This is the same marriage feast of which the Lord Jesus Christ spoke in Matthew 22.1–14; the completed union of the Redeemer with the perfected Church. The time for it was not yet, in St. John's day—it is not yet fully come in our day, but the invitations are out and the time is drawing nearer. Let us be ready. "Blessed are they that are bidden to the marriage supper of the Lamb." Christ is the bridegroom, the church is the bride, and the individual members of the church are the guests.

With the eleventh verse of chapter nineteen, the action is resumed, and a magnificent vision meets the eye. Heaven is opened, not merely a door in it, that one may look in (as in 4.1) but the great gates of Heaven itself swing wide, that the heavenly cavalry may ride forth to war. At the head of the host rides one upon a white horse, whose eyes are as a flame of fire, and whose head is crowned with many diadems. He has four names. First He is called Faithful and True, for men know Him to be such by His acts. He is also called the Word of God, which we know by revelation. He was in the beginning with God, and He was God. He became flesh and tabernacled among us, and we saw His glory, the glory as of the only begotten Son of God. The third name is the ineffable secret and mysterious name of His eternal deity, and this no mortal knows, or can know; for however much of Him is revealed, there always remains a depth that is not made known, and can not be, to the sons of men. Finally, where all can see, is written the name of royal majesty: "King of Kings and Lord of Lords." We need not here ask of which kings He is King, and of which lords He is Lord. The expression is a Hebraism, for intensification of the idea. So Solomon said: "Behold the heaven of heavens can not contain thee." (1 Kings 8.27) So in Deuteronomy 10.17: "God of gods and Lord of lords," and in Psalm 136.3: "Give thanks unto the Lord of lords."

The garments of this Warrior are stained with blood, and we must not here think of His own blood, shed for our redemption, but of the blood of His foes, as in Isaiah 63.3. If we ask how this can be, since the battle has not yet begun, we have only to remember that this is not the first battle He has fought. He is a seasoned fighter, this Christ of ours. He came of old, again and again, to strike down the enemies of His people. Isaiah saw Him and sang of His blood-bespattered raiment, in 63.1–8, a passage that was clearly in mind when our chapter was written. As with most of the supreme passages of the Apocalypse, this description is a mosaic of great utterances from the Old Testament. Even the sharp sword that goes out of His mouth, which we saw also in 1.16, is probably a pictorial version of Isaiah 11.4: "He shall smite the earth with the rod of his mouth, and with the breath of his mouth shall he slay the wicked."

He comes not alone this time, as He did when Isaiah saw Him. "The armies which are in heaven followed Him upon pure white horses, clothed in fine linen, white and pure." Because fine linen is the raiment of the saints (Rev 19.8) it is not an unnatural idea of some commentators that these are the redeemed, and yet it seems to me better to understand it here of the angels. They also are usually spoken of as clad in white. The saints while on earth are often spoken of as warriors, and Christ as their leader in the fight, but it is an idea alien to the scriptures to speak of them as going forth again to wage war upon evil, after attaining a heavenly rest. Of the angels, on the other hand, similar things are often said. They issue forth from the heavenly citadel to carry messages for God, to protect or punish His people, or to strike down their foes. According to scriptural analogy, therefore, "the armies which are in heaven" must be angelic armies.

No weapons are spoken of as borne or wielded by this host of celestial cavalry; whence many Bible students conclude that they do not fight at all, but merely witness and rejoice in the victory of their leader. This, however, seems to me an untenable inference from such silence. They are expressly called: "The armies which are in heaven"; and when their foes advance, it is not only against "Him that sat on the horse," but also "against His army" that they fight. When a writer speaks of an army, is it necessary also to say that the soldiers composing it are armed? Is not that understood? Is an assembly of unarmed witnesses in any sense an army? That the prowess which leads to victory is ascribed to the leader alone, is natural in all such writing, and is peculiarly appropriate here, in view of His unequalled majesty.

The place where the battle is fought is not here named; but in 16.14–16 we read that unclean spirits, like frogs, went out of the mouths of the Dragon, the Beast, and the False Prophet, "unto the kings of the whole earth, to gather them together unto the place which is called in Hebrew Har-Magedon." Since this is the only battle subsequently spoken of, and since in this battle also "the kings of the earth" fight against the heavenly army, (19.19) it is agreed, almost unanimously, that this is the battle of Armageddon. In the King James, or Authorized Version, the form of the name is "Armageddon" and in the Revised Version it is "Har-Magedon," a difference that rests upon variant readings in the Greek manuscripts, and is of no consequence for the meaning. As "The Battle of Armageddon" it has passed into current English speech as a synonym for any final and decisive conflict. So Theodore Roosevelt used it, when, at the convention where he organized his short-lived Progressive Party, he said: "We stand at Armageddon, and we battle for the Lord."

The meaning of "Har-Magedon" is obscure, because the word is found only in the one passage, 16.16. Various interpretations have been given, but the one generally preferred by scholars is that the word "Har" means "mountain" or mountainous district, and the "Magedon" refers to the biblical Megiddo, a city in northwestern Canaan, near the plain of Esdraelon, the scene of many memorable battles. It is used here, probably, not as a place name, but as a symbolic term for a decisive conflict.

Before the slaughter begins, an angel, standing in the sun, issues an invitation to all the carrion eating birds of heaven to come and feast upon the bodies of the slain, which reminds us of David's words, when about to slay Goliath, (1 Sam 17.46) and still more of Ezekiel 39.4; 17–20, where a similar invitation to a similar gruesome feast is issued. The battle itself is not described only the result, which is complete victory for the Heavenly Warrior and His army. The forces of the foe are utterly destroyed, the two leaders are taken prisoner, and they are cast alive into the lake of fire. Here again what was said above of the weapons seems in place. We must not, I think, infer from the lack of any description of the fighting that no real struggle took place, that the army of the foe fell down dead at a word from the one who sat upon the white horse. Some commentators take this view, but the whole setting of the scene is against it. Nothing so easy as this would be worthy of the combatants and the occasion. Although the fighting is not described, we are to understand that the conflict was real, and that the result was so glorious because forces so mighty were so completely overthrown.

So far the picture: what does the picture mean?

Of necessity, the divergent schools of interpretation follow here their characteristic lines. Only on two points is there unanimity. All are agreed that the heavenly leader is the Lord Jesus Christ. The names attributed to Him and the other indications place this beyond dispute. Every one sees, also that this is the final scene in the history of the Beast and the False Prophet, who are introduced as allies of the Dragon and enemies of the Radiant Woman in the thirteenth chapter. Whatever these figures mean there and in the intervening chapters, they must mean here also. Thus, in one very important point, the interpretation of the nineteenth chapter is determined before we reach it.

Those who belong to the Continuous Church History school, and we have seen in the Beast the Roman Catholic Church, must, to remain consistent, find here some great final struggle, by which that power is overthrown, and since it is not yet overthrown, they must teach that the Battle of Armageddon is still future, or at least, if already in progress, has not yet been won. So Barnes says:[1]

> The Beast here, as all along, refers to the Papal power, and the idea is that of its complete and utter overthrow.

---

[1] p. 455.

Carroll is more specific:[2]

What, then, is the war of the great day of God the Almighty, culminating at the place called in Hebrew Har-Magedon? Laying aside all figures
of speech, it is the war against the declarations of the Council of Trent,
against the dogmatic degrees of the Vatican Council, and against the
various Papal utterances embodied in various encyclical letters and in the
Syllabus of Errors.

The Futurists, especially the literalistic element among them, have no
difficulty with the interpretation, or, rather, they see no need of any interpretation at all. To them this is a description of what is to take place exactly as described, not a symbol that teaches in veiled form some spiritual
fact. To what astonishing lengths this literalism can go will appear from
the following quotations: Dr. J. A. Seiss,[3]

It is hard to find room in the record for any other conclusion than that
the horses are as literal as the sitters on them. …There is a reality in the
powers on which these heavenly armies ride forth to the battle of the great
day; and I know not why these powers should not be in the form of real
horses, of the character of the world to which they belong.

So, then, he believes that the Lord Jesus Christ will come down from
heaven riding on a horse, and that the angels or saints with Him will also
be mounted upon actual horses, albeit of a heavenly, not an earthly, breed!
How he reconciles this with other statements of scripture, that the Lord
will come upon the clouds of heaven, is not stated.

As to the vultures, devouring the dead, Ottman says:[4]

It may well represent the literal vultures that shall batten on the bodies
of the slain.

Writers of this school uniformly consider the Beast to be the personal
Antichrist of the last days, and think that his army will be a literal military
force, brought to the land of Palestine for warfare against the Jews, who
will by that time have repossessed the land.

---

[2] p. 282.

[3] Vol. III, p. 250.

[4] p. 421.

Some writers of the Continuous Historical school, although identifying the Beast with the Papacy, come to much the same conclusion with regard to this battle, since the history of the Papacy is regarded by them as culminating in the person of the last Pope. So Fysh and Elliott, having understood chapter eighteen of the destruction of the city of Rome by volcanic fire, make the bold supposition for which the text gives no hint that this last Pope will be away from home leading the antichristian army in Palestine, when that catastrophe occurs.

Fysh says:[5]

At the time of the overthrow of Rome by volcanic fire, it would seem that the Pope and his adherents are absent on an expedition to the Holy Land.

Lord, who belongs to the same school as Elliott and Fysh, in the same manner holds the battle and the slaughter to be a real future event.[6]

As the armies are to be literal armies, and the slaughter a literal slaughter, so the birds that fly in mid-heaven are to be literal birds, and carnivorous.

He does not say anything about the angel standing in the sun, or explain in what language the literal angel standing in a literal sun will make the literal vultures to understand and accept his literal invitation to a literal feast on literal carrion of a literal army.

The reader will understand that the above quotations are adduced only as terrible examples of how not to understand this vision. The whole method is, in my judgment, utterly out of harmony with the nature and purpose of the book of Revelation. If any man think otherwise, he is free to accept such exegesis. "Let every man be fully persuaded in his own mind." For me, at least it is impossible.

The point of highest importance in this chapter is whether it represents, in some form or other, the Parousia, or Second Advent of the Lord Jesus Christ. That He is here represented as coming down from heaven is clear; but does this vision, in this place, mean to describe the Second Coming itself, or does it symbolically represent His coming to the aid of the hard pressed church with heavenly assistance in her spiritual struggle? The former is the prevailing view, not only of the Futurists, and of some of the

---

[5] p. 301.

[6] p. 512.

Continuous Historical school, but also of many who belong to what I have called the "Philosophy of History" interpretation. So Auberlen, Greijdanus, Alford, Lenski and many others. They can and must so regard it, because to them the Beast and the False Prophet stand respectively for the whole antichristian false religious propaganda, whenever and by whomsoever wielded. This can not be supposed to come to an end except by the appearance of the Lord to judgment.

It is only the Preterists who can not join in seeing here the Second Advent, for they identify the Beast very definitely with the Roman pagan persecuting empire, and as this came to an end three or four hundred years after the birth of Christ, no battle with that Beast is possible later. Hence, this battle of Armageddon must be explained as a vivid symbolical representation of that struggle and the resultant victory. This is not a very recently invented explanation. De Wette, writing in 1843,[7] remarks that the Roman Catholic Jesuit commentator, Alcazar, (died 1613) "finds in the entire symbol nothing but the conversion of a great mass of heathen to Christianity." De Wette himself inclines to this view, for he interprets the sword from the mouth of the conquering Christ to be "the conquering and judging might of His word or His truth: by which it appears probable that he (St. John) has been thinking of the entire victory as a spiritual one."

This interpretation seems to me to be the correct one. In accepting it, I am influenced by the following considerations:

1. It is in accordance with the nature and design of the book of Revelation.

I have written in vain if I have not by this time succeeded in convincing some of my readers that the Apocalypse is a book of symbols, which, in every one of its chief visions, must *always* be understood to mean something other than it says. A literal interpretation of any part of this book stands condemned by the very fact that it is literal, for literal interpretations have no place here. There are, to be sure, exceptional expressions, outside the structure of the visions, such as that the apostle was in the isle called Patmos, that must be literally understood, and in some of the visions, (as in that of the final judgment) there is less than usual of the symbolical element; but these exceptions do not affect the principle.[8]

---

[7] Vol. III, p. 182.

[8] Compare the following from an eminent pre-millenarian, Dr. H. Grattan Guinness, in "The Approaching End of the Age," pp. 103–104:

"Plain predictive sentences and literal explanatory clauses are interspersed here and there, amid the signs of this book. They stand out from the general text as distinctly as a few words of English introduced here and there in a page of a Greek book would do; it needs no sign-post to say, 'adopt a

2. This description of our Lord coming down from heaven is too far out of line with other scriptural predictions of the Second Advent to be readily accepted as referring to that event. Elsewhere He comes upon the clouds of heaven, to judgment, not to war. He is, as here, accompanied by holy angels, but they do not come to fight, rather to gather the elect (Matt 24.31) or to bind together the tares to burn them (Matt 13.41–42) or to separate the evil fish from the good. (Matt 13.49–50) Nowhere else are either they or the redeemed saints spoken of as an army that must do battle with powerful foes before the reign of Christ can be established.

3. To regard this battle as a symbolical representation of the victory over Roman paganism, is required by the identification of the Beast with the persecuting Roman imperial power. That identification has already been discussed, and seems to me unshakable. It is adopted by many—if not most—modern students. The False Prophet is best understood of the antichristian religious priesthood and propaganda connected with that Roman paganism. If these identifications are accepted, it follows that the battle of Armageddon means the victory of the Christian church over these foes, and that the riding forth of Christ and the angelic army symbolizes the heavenly assistance by which that victory was won. Some point to the fact that the Beast and the False Prophet are cast alive into the lake of fire and triumphantly ask whether hostile systems can have such an experience; but this offers no more difficulty here than the same statement made in Revelation 20.14 about death and hell. When systems or abstract conceptions are personified, they must be spoken of as persons, and suffer the fate of persons.

If this view is adopted, we must interpret in harmony with it the instruments and processes by which the victory is won. Prominent among these is "the sword which came forth out of his mouth." We are accustomed to this figure, and elsewhere it almost invariably means the gospel, the revealed word of God. So in Ephesians 6.17 and Hebrews 4.12. That the soldiers of the army of the Beast were "killed with the sword of him that sat upon the horse, even the sword which came forth out of his mouth," then means that they were converted, and thus were casualties, so far as

---

literal interpretation here.' ...The system that says: 'Babylon means Babylon, and the literal ancient Babylon will, we are bound to believe, he revived' must be false. In the Apocalypse, Babylon does **not** mean Babylon, nor Jerusalem, Jerusalem, nor a Jew a Jew, nor the temple the temple... the system that says the New Jerusalem is a literal city, 1,500 miles square and 1,500 high, made of gems of gold, **must be** false. The New Jerusalem is a sign, the thing signified is the glorified Church of Christ as comparison with other Scriptures prove."

their support of the persecuting policy is concerned: or, if not all personally converted, were at least, as a result of the wide spread conversion of others, rendered disinclined or unable any longer to lend that policy their support.

An objection of real weight, against this interpretation, is the severe and warlike character of everything in this vision. There is no angel flying with "the eternal good tidings" as there was in a previous vision, and there is no grace or mercy of any kind. On the contrary, the flaming eyes, the drawn sword, the rod of iron, the trampling of the winepress of wrath, the blood-stained garment, etc., are all features better in keeping with destruction and judgment than with the preaching of the gospel of peace. This is true; but we gain help in the understanding of such figures from our own use of battle symbolism in our hymns. We sing:

Onward Christian soldiers,
Marching as to war.

Stand up, stand up for Jesus,
Ye soldiers of the cross,
Lift high His royal banner.
It must not suffer loss.
From victory unto victory
His army shall He lead,
Till every foe is vanquished,
And Christ is Lord indeed.

Encamped along the hills of light,
Ye Christian soldiers rise,
And press the battle ere the night
Shall veil the glowing skies.

Lead on, O King Eternal,
The hour of march has come.
Henceforth, on fields of battle,
Thy tents shall be our home.
Through years of preparation,
Thy grace has made us strong,
And now, O King Eternal,
We raise our battle song.

In all this we mean nothing more than a spiritual conflict, consisting of the preaching of the gospel and resistance to every form of temptation and sin; but we express ourselves in such vivid military terms that it is no wonder that the Japanese police, hearing the Korean Christians sing such hymns, concluded therefrom that they were plotting an uprising!

In the nineteenth chapter of Revelation, this familiar military symbolism is simply carried to the utmost limit. The entire Christian enterprise is here pictured from one side only—the overcoming of all opposition. Hence the severity of the picture, even to the revolting feature of the vultures feasting on the decaying carcasses of the slain. Nor can we say that such severity is wholly alien to the gospel, for if it is a "savor of life unto life" for some, it is not less true that it is a "savor of death unto death" for others. (2 Cor 2.16)

My conclusion, therefore, is that this vision of the battle of Armageddon must be understood as symbolizing and foretelling the complete victory of the Christian faith over the pagan religion and the persecuting policy of the Roman empire. This all came to pass in the course of time. The accession of Constantine the Great, in AD 306, and his edict of toleration, in AD 312, marked the conclusion of that struggle. That we apply the vision primarily to this conflict with paganism in the Roman empire does not, however, exclude its application to any similar conflict to the end of time. In so interpreting it, the vision must be taken *as a whole*, and no separate meaning must be sought in the details, such as the angel standing in the sun, the vultures, etc. These belong to the scenery of the vision, to the vivid working out of the central symbolism of battle and victory, and have no distinct significance of their own.

Let me, in conclusion, fortify this interpretation by the following quotations from writers of the first rank:

Dr. Swete says:[9]

> The Beast and the False Prophet are not cast into a bottomless dungeon, to be kept in safe custody, but into a pool of blazing sulphur, where they will be consumed. It is the utter destruction and consumption of the two systems which is in view; like Babylon, they are to be burnt with fire; not a vestige of them will be left in the new order.

> The rest of the enemy, the kings and their hosts, were not cast, like the Beast and the False Prophet, into the Lake of Fire, but slain outright with the sword of the Word. ...That this wholesale slaughter is to be understood in a purely spiritual sense, is clear from the words, 'that proceedeth

---

[9]p. 255.

from His mouth,' which follow. The sword is that of which St. Paul speaks, in Ephesians 6.17, and the action of the living Word who wields it may be illustrated by Hebrews 4.12. ...In interpreting, room should be allowed for punitive as well as for restorative operations: the Word slays by pronouncing judgment, as well as by reducing to the obedience of faith. But it is probably the latter process which is chiefly in view.

(P. 251) The Word of God fights with the sword of the word; His weapons are spiritual, and not carnal; He smites the nations, not with judgments only, but by the forces which reduce them to the obedience of faith. ...The whole course of the expansion of Christianity is here in figure: the conversion of the Empire, the conversion of the Western nations which rose on the ruins of the Empire; the conversion of the South and the Far East, still working itself out in the history of our own time.

Dr. B.B. Warfield, the late noted theologian of Princeton Seminary, says in his "Biblical Doctrines," p. 647, of this passage:

It is a vivid picture of a complete victory, an entire conquest, that we have here: and all the imagery of war and battle is employed to give it life. This is the symbol. The thing symbolized is obviously the complete victory of the Son of God over all the hosts of wickedness. Only a single hint of this signification is afforded by the language of the description, but that is enough. On two occasions we are carefully told that the sword by which the victory is won proceeds out of the mouth of the conqueror. We are not to think, as we read, of any literal war or manual fighting, therefore: the conquest is wrought by the spoken word—in short, by the preaching of the gospel.

XXII

THE THOUSAND YEARS

It has been our habit, throughout this discussion of the Apocalypse, to endeavor, as we entered upon a study of each new vision, to see clearly, first of all, the picture as presented to us, and after that to determine, as far as possible, what is symbolized by it. We shall follow this course also with the twentieth chapter, although we shall find it unusually difficult to know exactly what is the painting on the canvas.

The seer beholds an angel coming down out of heaven, carrying a key and a great chain. With the latter he binds the Dragon, Satan. Then he opens the door to the abyss, thrusts his prisoner in, locks the door over him, and, for extra security, seals it, so that it can not be secretly tampered with without discovery. It is not appropriate here to ask how Satan, being a spirit, can be bound with a chain or shut up behind lock and key. In an apocalyptic vision this offers no more difficulty than it would in a cartoon, no more than for a lamb to take a book and open the seals thereof, or for a star to handle a key, or for clothes to be washed white in blood. It is the idea only to which attention is directed.

This imprisonment of Satan is for a special purpose, "that he may deceive the nations no more"; but must the word "nations" here be understood of national organizations, in their national and international acts and policy, or of the individuals who compose those nations, or must the Greek word be rendered here, as often in the Bible, the "Gentiles"? The question will be discussed later. Satan having been thus disposed of, the apostle sees "thrones, and they sat upon them." Who sat upon them? The judges, of course, but who are these judges, and over whom do they exercise jurisdiction? It is not said, which is a very remarkable and astonishing omission. After that he sees "souls." This is not the first time he has seen souls. He saw them also in 6.9, beneath the altar; not necessarily these same souls. There we saw reason for considering them to be, not real souls, but a symbol of martyr blood that had been shed upon the earth. Is it so here also, or are we to think of them here as persons? "They lived and reigned with Christ a thousand years." It does not say that they lived in the body. Souls can live outside the body, as both the Lord Jesus Christ and the apostle Paul have taught us. (Matt 10.28; 2 Cor 5.6–8) Yet we cannot forget that in 1.18 of his book "to live" certainly means to live in the body, for reference is there made to the resurrection of Christ. This also agrees best with the comment: "This is the first resurrection," for "resurrection," elsewhere in the scriptures, except when employed by an obvious figure for regeneration, always means the reunion of soul and body. I take it, therefore, that the same thing is intended here. Remember that we are now studying only the picture. Whether a physical resurrection in the picture does not symbolize something else in the reality, is another question, which will come before us when we seek the interpretation of the vision as a whole.

"They reigned with Christ"—It does not say where. Usually, perhaps invariably, in this book, and in the rest of the New Testament, Christ is spoken of as reigning in heaven, "where Christ is seated, on the right hand of God." (Col 3.1) This reigning with Him must also be there, unless it can be shown that He has begun a reign on earth, of which nothing is here said. Some will think of 5.10, where it is said of the saints that "they reign upon the earth" but the verb is in the present tense, and the passage is from the beginning of the visions, when Christ is clearly represented as in heaven. In that passage it must, therefore, mean that the saints reign spiritually, in such a sense that they are not under any external spiritual dominion or constraint. If we could accept the reading of the King James Version in that passage: *"we shall reign* on the earth," we should feel justified in thinking of some reign of the saints in the body upon the earth at some future time, but that meaning is excluded by the form of the Revised Version.

Those thus privileged are a very limited, and definite group, consisting of two classes. First, "those that had been beheaded for the testimony of Jesus and for the word of God"; and then, with these, "such as worshipped not the beast, neither his image, and received not the mark upon their forehead and upon their hand." This points us back to 13.15–16, and shows us clearly that we are still within the circle of ideas and events connected with that vision. Some of the believers resisted the Beast, and were put to death. Others, faced by the same imminent danger, also resisted; and yet, for some reason or other, were spared. Both have the same standing before God. The question is not whether this or that physical suffering was endured, but whether the believer was "faithful unto death." This faithfulness was found as well in those who defied death and lived, as in those who did so and died. The two classes were later called, in the church, "martyrs" and "confessors," and the second were held in honor with the first. These two classes together are "the overcomers of the Beast," in 15.2. We need not be too closely bound to the letter, with regard to the mode of death. The text says: "those beheaded with an axe," for so it reads in the original. There were other and more dreadful modes of death suffered in those days. Some were burned alive, some crucified, some thrown to the wild beasts, some put to death with various tortures. All of these may be accepted as included here, by the familiar figure of "synecdoche," whereby a part is put for the whole: in this case, one form of death for all. We can not very well help so understanding it, as there appears no reason why those who suffered this particular form of death should be a distinct group. This liberty of interpretation cannot be extended, however, so far as to include all of the redeemed; for the mention of the Beast, his image, and his mark, are clearly intended to point us back to a specific struggle with a definite foe.

The period of a thousand years in due course comes to an end, and then Satan, having served his allotted term, is let out of prison; but alas, it is with him as with so many other ex-convicts. No sooner is he free than he is at his old evil ways. His former associates in crime, the Beast, the False Prophet, and the Great Harlot are no more, but he seeks other allies, and find them, here called Gog and Magog, from the prophecy of Ezekiel (chapters 38–39). These are assembled from the ends of the earth, for one more desperate battle. In vain: they are consumed by fire from heaven. Then the devil is cast into the lake of fire, and from this dreadful fate there is no reprieve.

Such is the drama enacted upon the stage before us: what is the interpretation?

As usual, the most prominent line of cleavage among interpreters is between those who, with due allowance for figures of speech, take the vision literally, and those who consider it a symbol. The former see here a description of events that must come to pass substantially as written, at some future time: the latter understand it to be a symbolical presentation of some spiritual truth, or of events that happened long ago. The former group are historically known as "chiliasts," or "millenarians," now often as "premillenarians." These words are taken respectively from the Greek and Latin words for one thousand.

The controversy is a very old one, running back to immediately sub-apostolic days, while men still lived who had known the apostle John. Some of the greatest, wisest, and best Christian men are to be found on each side. The first to mention the matter is Justin Martyr (d. c. 166[1]). He was himself a chiliast, but tells us frankly that many good Christians of his day were of a different opinion. It is often said that the early church was prevailingly of this view, but the evidence does not substantiate this assertion. Rather it indicates that then, as now, there was a difference of opinion. Justin's views were shared by Papias (d. 155), Irenaeus (d. 190), Tertullian (d.c. 230) and Hippolytus (d. 235). On the other side were Caius (d. 235), Origen (d. 253) and Dionysius (d. 264). Caius was so much opposed to chiliasm that he said it had been invented by Cerinthus, the first great heretic. In this he was probably mistaken, but it indicates how he felt about the theory. Origen and Dionysius the Great, his successor in the theological seminary at Alexandria, engaged in a vigorous polemic against it, and it appears from the writings of the latter that in his days it was held in Egypt only by a small group of separatists.[2]

It is also often said that the church did not abandon the hope of Christ's coming to set up an earthly kingdom until after external peace and prosperity had been brought about by the union of church and state, after the accession of Constantine the Great; but this assertion, too, fails to stand the test of history. The edict of toleration, under Constantine, is dated AD 312, but the early church fathers named above as opposing chiliasm all lived and died long before that, in the age of persecution.

It is common for millenarians to say that they are led to their convictions purely from Biblical teaching; but this was not the case with the ancients who held the same opinions. Papias betrays the fact that he has other sources in the following remark, quoted from him by Irenaeus:[3]

The days will come, in which vines will grow, each having 10,000 branches, and in each branch 10,000 twigs, and on each twig 10,000 shoots, and

---

[1] The letter "d" stands for "died," and "c" for "circa," "about." It is added when the date is somewhat uncertain. The works quoted were usually, of course, written some years before these dates.

[2] See the interesting account of his discussion with the followers of Nepos, a millenarian bishop. "A.N.F.," Vol. VI, pp. 81–82.

[3] "A.N.F.," Vol. I, p. 563.

in each shoot 10,000 clusters, and on every one of the clusters 10,000 grapes, and every grape, when pressed, will give five and twenty metretes of wine. (About 225 gallons)

It is at any rate clear that Papias, expecting such a millennium, was not a prohibitionist! Where did he get this idea? Irenaeus says that it came originally from Jesus, and Zahn thinks that this is quite credible, but my own agreement goes to the remark of Lenski:[4] "The very language betrays the contrary, to say no more." That the source was in the Jewish apocalyptic literature becomes quite clear when we compare the words of Papias with the following quotations:

The Apocalypse of Baruch:[5]

The earth will bring forth fruit, one producing 10,000; in the vine there will be a thousand branches, in every branch a thousand clusters, in every cluster a thousand berries, and every berry will yield a cor of wine. (36 gals.)

The Book of Enoch:[6]

In those days will the whole earth be tilled in righteousness... and vines will be planted on it. The vine which is planted thereon will yield wine in abundance, and of all seed which is sown thereon will each measure bear 10,000.

Thus it appears clearly that at least one of the sources of chiliasm in the early church must be found in Jewish imagination, which originated the "Jewish fables" against which the apostle Paul warns Titus (1.14). For Tertullian another source was the Montanist movement of the second century, the equivalent for that day of Irvingism, Seventh Day Adventism, and similar movements of our times, in claiming prophetical gifts and divine inspiration outside the written scriptures and supplementary to them.

By the time the first great Christian council met, at Nicaea, in AD 325, chiliasm was definitely on the wane, as is clear from the attitude of Eusebius, the church historian, who, himself, was a member of the said Council. Whether this was because the church was losing its pristine

---

[4] p. 576, note.

[5] J. E. H. Thomson: "Books Which Influenced Our Lord and His Apostles," p. 260.

[6] R. H. Charles: "The Book of Enoch," p. 76.

purity, as the millenarians say; or, on the contrary, because it was being purified from Jewish accretions, is an open question. St. Augustine (d. 430) gave it what was apparently its deathblow. He was at first a millenarian, but gave it up. His views became dominant in the church, and remained so until the Reformation, when millenarianism revived. It was condemned in the Augsburg Confession, of the Lutheran Church, but in no other of the great Protestant creeds: although it must be added that their ideas on the resurrection and the last judgment are inconsistent with it. Some of the members of the Westminster Assembly were millenarians, and in Germany the work of the very learned and pious Johann Albrecht Bengel (d. 1752) gave it a great impulse and a high standing. He has been called the father of modern premillenarianism. Early in the eighteenth century there came an important development through the work of Daniel Whitby (d. 1726), who originated the theory called "postmillennialism." He agreed with the millenarians in thinking that this vision in the twentieth chapter of Revelation predicts a period of great religious prosperity and happiness, but placed the Second Coming of the Lord *after* it instead of *before* it. Therefore his view is called "postmillennialism," from the Latin "post," after. From that time on the chiliasts, who had until then been called millenarians, began to speak of themselves as "premillenarians," from "pre," Latin for "before," inasmuch as they expect the Second Advent to take place before the millennium. It seem to me better, however, to retain the historic designation, inasmuch as the postmillennial idea of a millennium is so far from what chiliasts have always believed that it is a misnomer to call it a millennium at all. Disciples of Whitby do not look upon the millennium as a visible reign of Christ on the earth, which is the heart of ancient chiliasm, but as a period when the entire world will have been converted to the Christian religion, and all social relations will have been adjusted in conformity to it; which is regarded as a spiritual reign of Christ on earth. This view has become very prevalent, but the constant exhortation in the Bible to watch for the Lord's coming seems an insuperable objection to it; for if we believe that He can not come until the end of a period of a thousand years, the said period having not yet begun, how can we possibly watch for His advent?

During the first half of the nineteenth century, a learned and godly Englishman, John Nelson Darby, ex-lawyer and ex-clergyman of the Church of England, made a contribution, and a very important one, to the development of the millenarian doctrine, in his peculiar theory of the

Christian church and its relation to prophecy. He taught that the church, the Bride of Christ, must be limited to those true believers who lived between the first and second comings of Christ. Old Testament saints, and those saved during the period or periods after the Second Advent, do not belong to it. With this Bride of Christ prophecy has nothing to do. It is a "parenthesis in history." Prophecy has to do only with the fortunes of Israel, considered as a racial and national unit. Christ came and offered Himself to the Jews as their king, but since they rejected Him, the offer to set up His kingdom and become their king was withdrawn. It will be renewed and accepted at the time of the end. This is called the "postponed kingdom theory." It is most important to note that those who hold it deny that Christ set up any kingdom at all at His first coming. Dr. I. M. Haldeman, one of the foremost exponents of this teaching, says emphatically that[7] there is no such thing as the kingdom of God on earth today.

During this "parenthesis" period, they say, Christ is not fulfilling prophecy, He is calling out a church from among the Gentiles. Darby had not a low opinion, but a very high opinion of the church, which, however, was for him not the "visible church," but strictly the "invisible church" of the truly regenerate only. He had not much use for the outwardly organized church, as historically manifested; and his views have everywhere been a source of division and disintegration in the organized church life; as is illustrated by nothing more clearly than by the body with which he allied himself, the Plymouth brethren, whose record has been well nigh an unbroken history of dissension and separation.

The distinctive and important Darbyite contribution to the millennial discussion was that prophecy is silent concerning the church age. This is often illustrated by a sketch of a man standing and looking at a landscape, with low hills in the foreground and high mountains in the distant background. He can see the tops of the hills near by, likened to the first coming of Christ, and he can also see the tops of the distant mountains, the Second Advent, but he cannot see anything of the great valley between, which is the age of the Christian church. This theory of Darby's, if accepted, gives great aid to the millenarian position. The Old Testament prophecies are full of glowing visions of a good time coming, and all of these promises are, of necessity, couched in terms of Israel. It has always been the standard faith of the Christian church that this good time coming, foreseen by the prophets, began to be fulfilled with the birth of

---

[7] I. M. Haldeman: "The Kingdom of God," p. 232.

Christ, and is being progressively realized in the Christian dispensation. The Christian church is thus looked upon as the heir to the promises. Formerly, millenarians, as well as others, held this view. Joseph Mede, a very eminent millenarian of the seventeenth century, says:[8]

> The Church… succeeded in the room of Israel, and was, as I may so call it, 'surrogated Israel.'

In this view, predictions not yet literally fulfilled must be either understood of the church, or must be considered to have lapsed, under the rule laid down in Jeremiah 18.9–10, or because they belonged to the age of the childhood of the people of God. Nothing remains to form the content of the millennial age. Hence, formerly, millenarians who held such views were much embarrassed to answer their opponents. They certainly could not get their millenarian expectation wholly from the 20th chapter of Revelation, for nothing is there said as to the condition of the world during the thousand years. They must get it from the Old Testament prophecies; but since they themselves believed that the said predictions were largely fulfilled in the Christian church, they could not point out any consistent principle whereby to differentiate between one class of predictions, already fulfilled and to be understood of the church; and, another, to be fulfilled in the Millennium.

From this embarrassment John Nelson Darby delivered them, and present day millenarianism could scarcely survive without his assistance. He boldly cut the Gordian knot by denying that anything at all of the prophetic scripture was fulfilled after the death of Christ. What we see now, and have seen in Christian history for eighteen hundred years, is not referred to in any way, shape or manner in the Old Testament. It is all something new, a mystery, belonging to the church age, as completely hidden from the prophetic eye as the valley, in the illustration above, is beyond the sight of the man looking at the hills near by.

It is not my purpose at present to refute this Darbyite doctrine, but to point out emphatically its novelty, and its relation to the millenarian discussion. If he is right, the whole Christian church, for eighteen centuries, very seriously misunderstood the word of God. Dr. C. I. Scofield, who popularized Darbyism in this country, through his annotated Bible, says that the idea that the Church is the true Israel must be rejected, although

---

[8] Part I, p. 72.

he says also that such an idea is taken from post-apostolic and Roman Catholic theology. (p. 989)

Here he admits that this was the post-apostolic doctrine, and his reference to the "Roman Catholic theology" is an unfair appeal to Protestant prejudice. Of course the "post-apostolic" doctrine has come to us through the Roman Catholic Church—how else could it reach us? That it was truly the post-apostolic view is clear, as it was taught by the early millenarians, to whom the present day adherents of the same school take so much pleasure in referring, to show that theirs is the original and unadulterated Christian doctrine. If this is good proof with regard to millenarianism, let them give the same heed to their ancient predecessors when the latter proclaim the church to be the true Israel.

Justin Martyr says:

Since God announced that He would send a new covenant... we will not understand this of the old law and its proselytes, but of Christ and His proselytes, namely us Gentiles.[9]

As, therefore, Christ is the Israel and the Jacob, even so we who have been quarried out from the bowels of Christ are the true Israelitish race.[10]

"What then?" says Trypho, "Are you Israel, and speaks He such things of you?"

"If, indeed," I replied to him, "We had not entered into a lengthy discussion on these topics, I might have doubted whether you ask this question in ignorance, but since we have brought the matter to a conclusion by demonstration and with your assent, I do not believe that you are ignorant of what I have just said, or desire again mere contention, but that you are urging me to exhibit the same proof to these men." And in compliance with the assent expressed in his eyes, I continued, etc.[11]

Irenaeus says:

But... the King has actually come... and has bestowed upon men the good things which were announced beforehand. ...By His advent He Himself fulfilled all things, and still does fulfill in the church the new covenant foretold by the law."[12]

---

[9] "A.N.F.," Vol. I, p. 260.

[10] "A.N.F.," Vol. I, p. 267.

[11] "A.N.F.," Vol. I, p. 261.

[12] "A.N.F.," Vol. I, p. 511.

Now I have shown a short time ago that the church is the seed of Abraham.[13]

Hippolytus, quoting from Isaiah, says:

For it is not of the Jews that He spake of old, nor is it of the city of Zion, but of the church.[14]

In thus understanding the prophecies of the Old Testament, these early fathers believed themselves to be in line with the teachings of the apostles, and in this the whole church, millenarian and antimillenarian, agreed with them until the rise of John Nelson Darby. If heresy is to be defined as any doctrine that contradicts the historical universal Christian faith, then this Darbyite doctrine is entitled to the name. Millenarianism as such is not a heresy; for it had the right of citizenship in the Christian church from the beginning, but this denial that Christ set up a kingdom at His first coming, and this denial of the continuity of Israel and the church, are very serious heresies, which introduce inextricable confusion into our conception of the New Testament. These ideas ought to be earnestly opposed wherever they obtain a foothold in the churches. It is most astonishing that they were popularized in this country by a Presbyterian minister, with the aid and approval of other distinguished Presbyterians, and that a Presbyterian writer could call the Scofield Bible, a "God-planned, God-guided, God-illuminated, and God-energized work."[15] Can any one say anything more about the inspired scriptures?

This brief statement of the history of the discussion seemed desirable that the ordinary reader may understand the points at issue and the present situation. Turning back, now, to direct study of the twentieth chapter of Revelation, we can distinguish four main schools of interpretation, which we may call: the Millenarian, the Augustinian, the Post-Millenial, and the Preterist interpretations. We shall take them up in that order.

I. The Millenarian Interpretation

The outstanding feature of this interpretation is that the thousand years are taken to mean a literal period of time of precisely the indicated length,

---

[13] "A.N.F.," Vol. I, p. 563.

[14] "A.N.F.," Vol. V, p. 243.

[15] Charles Gallaudet Trumbull, "The Life Story of C. I. Scofield," p. 114.

to follow the Second Advent of our Lord. During this period He will set up a visible earthly kingdom, with a capital, where His personal residence will be—usually placed at Jerusalem—and where He will discharge all the functions of a supreme political executive, either directly or through His appointed officers. This will include the making of laws, the setting up of courts of law, levying taxes, maintaining an army and navy and a police force, building and repairing roads and bridges, regulating commerce, industry, education and agriculture, supervising and safe guarding the public health, etc., etc. In short, anything that a good government may be supposed to do. He will be primarily and personally the King of Israel, reassembled in Palestine and reconstituted a nation. Herein will be fulfilled the promise of the angel to Mary, Luke 1.32–33. His dominion will, however, at the same time extend to all nations of the world, which will exist as vassal states to the kingdom of the Jews.

During these thousand years there will be a state of great prosperity and happiness over the entire globe. The knowledge and profession of the true religion will be universal, so that all false religions will disappear. There will still, to be sure, remain sin in the human heart, but all of its outward manifestations will be sternly and promptly suppressed. The laws of Moses will again come into force, and the Levitical sacrifices will be offered. Death will not be unknown, but longevity will be very great, so that, if a person dies at one hundred years of age, it will awaken surprise that he died so young. (Isaiah 65.20) Conditions in the animal world will be literally as described in Isaiah 11.6–9. The curse will be removed from nature, so that the fertility and beauty of the earth will be beyond anything the world has ever experienced. War will be no more, as prophesied by the prophet Micah. (4.3)

Millenarians differ more or less among themselves as to the details, but they all agree on the general picture, as above. It is a very alluring prospect. There is nothing (except, perhaps, sex) more fearfully abused than government. Indispensable to human life and welfare, it has commonly been made an instrument of injustice and cruelty. That before the end, for at least one thousand years, the world should see a period of perfect peace and righteousness, under a government of unimpeachable integrity, justice, benevolence, and wisdom, is something we would all like to believe. If it can be supported from the Holy Scriptures, let us take it to our hearts with delight: if not, it remains a beautiful piece of "wishful thinking."

In this system, chapter nineteen is interpreted as a presentation of the

Parousia, or Second Advent, and since the twentieth chapter is the description of the millennial reign of the returned Savior, the closest possible connection is maintained between the two chapters—a very good feature. The binding of Satan is, of course, recognized to be figurative, and symbolizes his being put under complete restraint. The "nations" whom he must deceive no more, are understood to be all men everywhere. That he can deceive them no more does not mean the cessation of all moral evil, for there are other sources of sin, especially the depraved human heart, but the great incitement to every form of wickedness which emanates directly from the Prince of Darkness will be unknown. The "first resurrection" is not a symbol, but is understood as an actual resurrection of the body, and is interpreted as the resurrection of all true believers, as prophesied in 1 Thessalonians 4.16. The "second resurrection," not mentioned in the chapter by that name, but implied in the designation "first resurrection," is the one spoken of in Revelation 20.13, and is limited to the wicked dead. The reigning of the saints with Christ is on earth, and is an actual participation in the discharge of political functions: probably holding office as judges in the courts which Christ will set up for the administration of justice. If it is asked how those with resurrected bodies can thus associate freely with men in the flesh, the millenarians have an answer that is hard to refute, namely, that this is what Jesus did during the forty days between His resurrection and ascension; and that, since our bodies are to be on the model of His, (Phil 3.21) there is no reason why the risen saints should not do the same.

Attractive as this whole scheme is, it is, in my judgment, and not in mine only, but in that of the vast majority of believing Bible students of all the ages, entirely untenable for the following reasons:

1. Because it takes the thousand years and the resurrection literally. That we must look upon the vision of the Apocalypse, not as literal information of something that is to come to pass, but as symbolical pictures, meaning something else than they say, is the principle upon which all our exposition has proceeded, and we cannot abandon it here. Granting that there may be an exception (as we shall find there is, in the prophecy of the last judgment) we must nevertheless give our preference to a symbolical interpretation if there is one that fits.

2. Because it rests upon the view that the nineteenth chapter portrays the Second Advent. This is essential to the millenarian exposition and has already been discussed.

3. Because, in this interpretation, the "first resurrection," as interpreted

by millenarians, is extended to all believers who died before the Second Advent. This also is essential to their system, but it is hopelessly in conflict with the text, which speaks only of those who had been faithful during the conflict with the Beast. This binds the present passage very closely to that in chapter thirteen. No one has a right to find here the resurrection of any but believers who endured and triumphed in that particular conflict. Since millenarians believe that the Beast is a personal Antichrist of the last days, they must, if they are to be consistent, and faithful to the plain sense of the prophecy they interpret literally, confine this "first resurrection" to the martyrs and confessors of the last fateful three and a half years. But this would be fatal to their scheme, for "the rest of the dead" must then include all other believers as well as the wicked. This would leave but an inconsiderable handful to reign with Christ during the thousand years, and would be inconsistent with St. Paul's prophecy in 1 Thessalonians 4.16–17. Some, seeing this, speak of the "first resurrection" having two stages, seven years apart, those raised at the beginning of the seven years being all believers then dead, and those at the end of the period being the martyred "tribulation saints": but this is too plainly a subterfuge. Our passage, Revelation 20.4–5, speaks of something that happens at the same time as the binding of Satan, thus *after* the Parousia, and then says: "this is the first resurrection." Under the millenarian scheme it is the second, not the first: the first took place seven years before.

4. Because this interpretation reads into the twentieth chapter of Revelation an immense amount of material that does not belong there. Millenarians cannot find, and do not pretend to find, their entire programme here. They find it chiefly in the Old Testament prophecies, the fulfillment of which they assign to this period of a thousand years. By what right? Not a whisper in the twentieth chapter, not a hint, however obscure, links this period with the great promises of a good time coming which we find in the utterances of the prophets. To accept the Darbyite notion that the clock of prophecy stopped ticking at the death of Christ, leaves us orphans, so far as any share in the prophecies is concerned. Instead of being "fellow-heirs" with the Jews of all this prophetic inheritance, as St. Paul says we are, (Eph 3.6) we are heirs to nothing.

One has only to enumerate the chief points of the millenarian expectation to see how alien the whole thing is to the twentieth chapter of Revelation. When they tell us of Christ's personal return, of the "rapture" of the saints, of the resurrection of all believers, of Christ's personal residence in Jerusalem, of the restoration of law and sacrifices, of the return of the Jews to Palestine, of the rebuilding of the temple, of the renewal of nature during the millennium, of the age of universal peace, etc., etc., they introduce a whole series of ideas which, whatever their basis in the scripture elsewhere, are conspicuous by their absence here. Whatever we may think of the author of the Apocalypse, he was certainly no Scofield millenarian, or he could never have kept still about these things.

5. Because their scheme leaves an immense number of the dead unaccounted for. The believers who are raised at the return of Christ, (even if we allow them to speak of two stages of the first resurrection) belong to the "Bride of Christ," and do not include the Old Testament saints. The "second resurrection" described in Revelation 20.13 is, they say, limited to the wicked dead. Where, then, do the Old Testament believers come in, and the believers who die during the millennium? There surely will be death during that time, for death and hell are not cast into the lake of fire until the war with Gog and Magog. (Rev 20.14) Moreover, Isaiah 65.20, (believed by them to refer to millennial conditions) contemplates the death, not only of the sinner, but of others contrasted with him. When are such believers to be raised? This difficulty has led some millenarians to conjecture an unnamed resurrection of the just at the close of the last conflict, the one with Gog and Magog, but this is wholly a work of the imagination, and would give us three resurrections, not two.

6. Because this interpretation is bound up with an entirely untenable and unacceptable view of the last judgment. This will be discussed in detail in our next chapter.

II. The Augustinian Interpretation

The distinguishing feature of this interpretation is that the binding of Satan in this chapter is identified with that mentioned in Mark 3.27. Since that took place at the first coming of Christ, this binding and imprisonment in Revelation twenty must also be referred to that point in history, and the thousand years are understood to symbolize the entire period between the first and second advents. This view, with variations in detail, is accepted by many modern scholars for whose expositions, on the whole, one cannot help having the greatest respect. It is accepted, with others, by Morris, Lenski, Warfield, Masselink, and, with an important modification, by Wm. Milligan. They take the twentieth chapter to be a new beginning, unrelated in any very close connection, to the nineteenth.

This is in accordance with the "recapitulation" principle of expounding the book, according to which each of the several visions—usually considered to be seven in number—goes over the same ground, each beginning with the first coming of Christ and extending to the second. This is well stated and defended by Morris. There is truth in it. The visions cannot be held to any rigid chronological order. Sometimes a series of events is presented in summary, to the very end; and then one or more features of the series are selected for more detailed development. Yet there is also a forward movement of the thought as a whole; and in the present case the mention of the martyrs and confessors as having fought their good fight and received their reward before the thousand years begin, seems to me decisive against this interpretation. To start the thousand years with the birth of Christ, is to leave this feature of the symbolism without any meaning.

The weakness of this view also becomes apparent when its advocates attempt to explain the details. To St. Augustine the "first resurrection" is regeneration, whereby men spiritually dead are made spiritually alive; to Warfield it is the blessed "intermediate state" of all true believers in heaven before the resurrection of the body. The former interpretation is excluded by the fact that those who share in this "first resurrection" have already been faithful unto death. To William Milligan the "first resurrection" is, as with Augustine, the beginning of the Christian life here on earth. That those who have part in the first resurrection reign with Christ is an ideal description of their spiritual victory. They reign over sin. With all the imperfections that cling to them, yet "already they live a resurrection and ascended life, for it is a life hid with Christ in God." He differs from Augustine, however, in his view of the thousand years.

> They are not a figure for the whole Christian era, now extending to nearly nineteen hundred years. ...They embody an idea, and that idea, whether applied to the subjugation of Satan, or to the triumph of the saints, is the idea of completeness, or perfection. Satan is bound for a thousand years; that is, he *is* completely bound."

Then he goes on to say that the "little while" during which Satan is loosed, "is the historical period of the Christian dispensation." He is bound with respect to believers, but loosed with respect to the rest of the world. At this point Warfield agrees, followed therein by Masselink. That Satan is bound, says Warfield, means simply that he cannot harm the saints who have gone to their rest.

There is, indeed, no literal binding of Satan to be thought of at all. What happens, happens not to Satan but to the saints, and is only represented as happening to Satan for the purposes of the symbolical picture.[16]

Against the views both of Milligan and of Warfield the objection is crushing that it is expressly said that the binding takes place "that he should deceive the nations no more." It is possible to understand this as excluding the saints, for this word "nations" may legitimately be translated "Gentiles" or "heathen," or it may include the living saints, as being also men in the flesh, but by no possibility can this *exclude* unbelievers and apply only to saints, much less to saints already in glory. Symbolism must not be narrowly construed, but such extension as this would make it absolutely arbitrary.

To Lenski the binding is as Augustine has it, restraint put upon Satan through the incarnation and the work of Christ upon earth, and he gains encouragement to hold this view from the fact that, after chapter twelve, Satan, being cast out of heaven, seems to disappear from the story as an active agent.[17] He is said to "give his power" to the Beast. Thus the commentator infers that the devil is in prison, and cannot act directly. He seems to have overlooked 16.13, where the Dragon is active, along with the Beast and the False Prophet, showing that although the latter two appear to the eyes of men and play their part on the stage of human history, the Dragon is the inspiring and efficient force all the time.

Every form of this Augustine interpretation is open to the same decisive objection we have already brought against the millenarian exposition, that it makes the "first resurrection" to apply to all true believers; although in 20.4 those who partake in it are clearly stated, and are a small and definitely limited group. Let us keep our eye on that, and demand an interpretation that shall reckon with it. Milligan says with respect to this, that those named include "all faithful ones, …for in the eyes of St. John all the disciples of a martyred Lord are martyrs." Warfield, quoting this, remarks that it is "beautifully said." Yes, it is beautifully said, but it doesn't make sense. All Christians are in the conflict with the world, the flesh, and the devil; but do they therefore all suffer persecution and death under tyranny of the Beast? The vast majority of them die peacefully in their beds, attended with loving care, and mourned by their neighbors and

---

[16] "Biblical Doctrines," p. 651.

[17] p. 597.

friends. To call such people martyrs is to empty the word "martyr" of all meaning. Whatever the Beast means elsewhere, the word must mean here. If the persecuting world power, then only those who suffer persecution are intended; if the Roman Catholic church, then those who defied that church when it was a persecuting power; if the Antichrist of the last days, then those who triumph in that last dread period. It cannot in any case mean something that all believers experience.

The symbolism of numbers also, in this exposition, runs into utter confusion. Lenski believes, with Warfield, that the thousand years symbolize the entire Christian dispensation: yet when we turn back to his interpretation of chapter twelve, we find that the three and a half years during which the Radiant Woman is in the wilderness symbolize exactly the same period! No doubt there is a symbolism of numbers in the Apocalypse. I could accept the three and a half years as representing the entire period named, or I could accept the thousand years in that sense, but I cannot understand a symbolism of numbers in which three and a half means precisely the same thing as one thousand; not even with Warfield's explanation that it is a brief period of three and a half years to the saints in affliction, and a long and peaceful period of a thousand years to those at rest; for to those in trouble time always seems to drag more slowly.

III. The Postmillennial Interpretation

In the postmillennial interpretation, as given by Barnes, Carroll, and others, the thousand years are a real period of historical time, of that length, not yet begun. The binding of Satan means his being restrained in the exercise of his evil power, not so much by anything done to him directly as through the great success and universal acceptance of the gospel. The "first resurrection" is symbolical of the triumph of the principles for which the martyrs died, primarily those who suffered at the hands of the Papal power, for in this system the Beast is closely identified with the Roman Catholic Church. Some interpreters of this school make the "second resurrection" the general resurrection at the last day, but Carroll, feeling the force of the objection made by Alford, that if one resurrection is symbolic the other must be so too, finds the second resurrection in the revival of evil for a short time after the millennium, symbolized in the text by the conflict with Gog and Magog.

This exposition of the twentieth chapter of Revelation seems to me to have greater merit than either of those already discussed, as it deals more adequately with the various elements to be considered, and does not make the mistake of thinking that all believers can have part in the "first resurrection"; but it rests upon the postmillennial theory and the system of Continuous Historical interpretation, to both of which there seem to me to be fatal objections. It cannot be accepted by any but those who are already committed to those views. Its merits are, that it furnishes a symbolical, not a literal, interpretation, and that it does justice to the terms of the prophecy with regard to the restraint of Satan, the participants in the "first resurrection," the period of the thousand years, etc., in which the Augustinian interpretation notably fails.

IV. The Preterist Interpretation

This naturally places the beginning of the thousand years in the past, but it is not definite about the end of that period. As adherents of this view look upon the Beast as the pagan Roman persecuting power, they agree with the millenarians in preserving a close connection between this chapter and the preceding one. They emphasize the purpose for which Satan was imprisoned, "that he might deceive the nations no more" and the word "nations" is understood to mean the heathen nations, the "Gentiles," by a perfectly good and well established meaning of the Greek word. This binding, therefore, means that the pagan power having been overthrown, in the Battle of Armageddon, in the nineteenth chapter, Satan was divinely restrained from re-establishing it. His other activities continue, but he can no longer "deceive the Gentiles" in that special point in which he did deceive them before, as compared with the Jews of the New Testament period, namely, idolatry. In other respects he abundantly incited the Jews also to sin, but in this respect he deceived the Gentiles, not the Jews, and this is the point at which he is henceforth restrained.

The "first resurrection" and the reigning with Christ, in this view, just as in that of the post-millenarians, represent the triumph of the principles for which the martyrs gave their lives. Hence it is an actual resurrection in the picture, but this symbolizes the revival of those things for which they stood. Thus the "first resurrection" is strictly limited, as in the text, to those who remained faithful in the conflict with the Beast, understood to be the pagan persecuting power of the Roman Empire. The beginning of the thousand years must therefore be located at the point in history when paganism ceased to be a menace to the Christian church. If looked at from the standpoint of the Roman Empire, this was at the accession of Constantine the Great. If the barbaric nations to the north are included in the view, it comes some centuries later, in the time of Charlemagne. This is of minor importance.

The thousand years are taken to mean a period of great length, but not necessarily a thousand times three hundred and sixty-five natural days, for the figure is symbolic, and means the whole time during which the Christian religion, as compared with paganism, enjoys uninterrupted triumph. This view has the great advantage of providing a suitable contrast between the three years and a half and the thousand. The former means the period during which Christianity had its bitter conflict with paganism, and the latter its time of triumph. The former is very brief as compared with the latter. Herein the interpretation has the support of history. At the end of the period there will be a revival of the conflict with paganism; whether formal and acknowledged pagan religion, or some form of opposition that is essentially the same as paganism, remains to be seen. Possibly the present godless opposition in Russia and the shameless proposal in Germany to restore the old gods may be the beginning of such a revival; but it is too early, and we are too near to these events, to speak confidently.

As for the "second resurrection," Swete makes it the actual resurrection at the last day, and brushes aside the objection of Alford, already noted, with the remark that "this is to interpret apocalyptic prophecy by methods of exegesis which are proper to ordinary narrative." Here I am not satisfied with his exposition, which otherwise looks good to me. That objection of Alford's seems to me very weighty, and I like Carroll's plan of making both the first resurrection and the second to be symbolical, the former of the triumph of the gospel, and the latter of the revival of evil in the last days, the war with Gog and Magog.

This is all the more in place, because in Swete's interpretation the expression "the rest of the dead" does not stand in contrast with the "first resurrection," as the text evidently intends it to do. If the second resurrection is the general resurrection of all men at the last day, the saints and martyrs have part in it, and it forms no antithesis to them. The meaning of both groups, those intended here as participating in the "first resurrection" and those called, by contrast, "the rest of the dead," becomes intelligible if we transfer ourselves in thought to the days of the apostle John, and remember that he was thinking in terms of himself and the men of his generation. There were then, in the Roman Empire, in his eyes, and in those of his fellow Christians, just two classes of men, those siding with the Beast, and those standing out against him. In the course of time both classes passed away from the land of the living, and formed "the dead," that is, not all the dead of all generations, but the dead of that time. Of them all, the martyrs and confessors would (symbolically) come to life again when the Christian religion triumphed: the rest would not have such a revival so long as that triumph lasted (the thousand years) but would likewise (symbolically) revive when the final conflict should come. This seems to me the best interpretation. So understood, neither the first resurrection nor the second has anything to do with the mass of mankind, or with the general resurrection at the last day. The section beginning with 20.11 is then a new vision, with an entirely independent meaning.

Allow me now to summarize this Preterist interpretation, which is the one I commend to the reader, and then to conclude with one or two quotations from expositors who hold it.

1. The Battle of Armageddon, in the nineteenth chapter, means the victory of Christianity over the Roman paganism, in the first three centuries of our era.

2. The binding of Satan is the divine restraint put upon the devil, so that he was unable any longer to "deceive the nations," that is, to bring about a restoration of that paganism.

3. The "first resurrection" and the "reigning with Christ," symbolize the triumph of Christianity, as if the ancient martyrs had come back to life and were in power.

4. The three and a half years stand for the period of struggle with paganism, and the thousand years for the succeeding period of uninterrupted triumph of Christianity over it.

5. The "rest of the dead" are the rest of the dead in the generations of the struggle. These will revive, in the same symbolical manner as the martyrs, when the last conflict comes.

6. The war with Gog and Magog is a renewal, in some form or other, of the ancient conflict with paganism, either through missionary work in pagan countries, as it present, or through some movement in opposition to the gospel that is essentially or openly the same as the ancient heathenism.

Greijdanus says:[18]

> A thousand years indicates a complete period of time. A thousand is also at present a symbolical number, that points to a perfect fullness. How long a time is represented by it, we cannot more closely determine. It

---

[18] pp. 296–297.

indicates a period of considerable length, entirely sufficient for the purpose which God has in mind.

From the significance of this binding and imprisonment of Satan it follows, that it began with the close of the period during which paganism attacked the Lord's church, to destroy her from the earth, in the first centuries of our Christian era. During those first centuries, Satan repeatedly made the attempt to destroy Christianity, by causing the pagan world to throw itself upon the church in terrible persecutions. But at last this was no longer possible. The persecution of Diocletian was the final persecution of the Lord's church by the Roman world power. Presently Christianity came into power, and became the state religion, in the fourth century. Afterwards, through all the ages, there have been dreadful persecutions against the true servants of the Lord and the pure preaching of the gospel, both within Christendom and outside of it; but these were only partial persecutions, that afflicted the Lord's believers in a particular country or district, larger or smaller, not Christendom as a whole, the entire church of the Lord and His gospel throughout the whole world. Such a general persecution by the pagan power, threatening all Christendom, all the Lord's believers and servants, His entire church on earth, took place only in the first centuries, through the Roman world empire.

With the breakdown of that pagan supremacy and with the victory of the gospel and Christendom over paganism in the fourth century, and in the Roman empire—no matter how partial that triumph was, and how much heathen corruption still reigned—the general persecution of the whole church of the Lord and of all gospel preaching throughout the world, came to an end, and this binding of Satan, with his imprisonment in the abyss, for a thousand years, began. And they shall come to an end when Satan again has opportunity to arouse the entire pagan power, the non-Christian peoples, entire nations, who in number far surpass the Christian nations, to undertake the annihilation of the gospel from the earth.

The interpretation of H. B. Swete is as follows:[19]

If the 1,260 days symbolize the duration of the triumph of heathenism, the 1,000 years as clearly symbolize the duration of the triumph of Christianity. ...How short the age of persecution would be, when compared with the duration of a dominant Christianity, is shown by the adoption of a term of three and a half years in the one case and of a thousand years in the other. Blessed and holy indeed were those who by their brief resis-

---

[19]p. 263.

tance unto blood secured for the Church so long a continuance of peaceful service; they would live and reign with Christ as kings and priests in the hearts of all succeeding generations of Christians, while their work bore fruit in the subjection of the civilized world to the obedience of the faith. …The question remains at what epoch the great chapter in history represented by the Thousand Years began. An obvious answer would be, with the conversion of Constantine, or of the Empire. …But possibly the question, like many another raised by this Book, admits of no precise answer. …That the age of Martyrs, however long it might last, would be followed by a far longer period of Christian supremacy, during which the faith for which the martyrs died would live and reign, is the essential teaching of the present vision.

It will be seen that of the four forms of interpretation we have studied, only one provides for an earthly reign of Christ, a millennium in the proper sense of the word. Another provides a sort of millennium, but not the kind contemplated by chiliasm as a historical system. The other two, the Augustinian and Preterist systems, look for no future period of special blessedness at all. Recently, those who take this view have begun to call themselves, or to be called "amillenialists." The prefix "a" here is from the Greek, and means a denial of the existence of the thing to which it is prefixed, as "a-theist" means one who denies that there is a God. The word is not well compounded, as it uses a Greek prefix for a Latin word, but it is the term now in use, and we cannot help it. Because the term employed is new, there is danger that people will think the idea is recent also, but this is not the case. The Augustinian interpretation dates, of course, from St. Augustine, who died in AD 430, but even before that the millenarian conception was stoutly opposed, and those who rejected it were true "amillenarians." Thus this view is historically as old as chiliasm, and it has been far more prevalent in the church. For twelve hundred years there was scarcely any other view. Up to the time of Daniel Whitby, who died in 1726, there was no alternative to millenarianism but amillenarianism. All of the creeds of the Christian church, ancient or modern, Catholic or Protestant, are amillenarian, for chiliasm has not found recognition in any one of them. It is historically the standard form of the Christian faith in regard to the last things.

XXIII
THE LAST JUDGMENT

The section of Revelation found in 20.11–15, differs from almost every other portion of the book in that it is not, as a whole, a symbolical picture. There is much symbolism in it, but the truth conveyed by the whole is exactly what it seems to be, not, as usual, something else, to be discovered by interpretation. It professes to be a prophecy of the final judgment, and so it is. Every reader, learned or unlearned, sees at once that this is so, and on this point there is no difference of opinion. This is an excellent illustration of a remark made by H. Grattan Guinness, in "The Approaching End of the Age," p. 107. After having pointed out clearly that, as a rule, the Apocalypse does not mean what it says, but something quite different, he adds:

> It is hardly needful to say that there are exceptions, in the Apocalypse. Plain predictive sentences and literal explanatory clauses are interspersed here and there, amid the symbols of the book. They stand out from the general text as distinctly as a few words of English introduced in the pages of a Greek book would do; it needs no sign-post to say, 'adopt a literal interpretation here.' They speak for themselves; common sense dispenses with literary canons, and recognizes them unaided.

The symbolism of this vision is not difficult to understand. The great white throne symbolizes the majesty, authority, and holiness of God in judgment. No one supposes that God actually occupies a seat like that, which is conceivable only if we attribute to Him a human form. It is not important to decide whether this judgment is by God directly or by Christ in the name and by authority of God. The two are one in the mind of the writer of the Apocalypse, and they should be so in our minds. That this is a symbolical picture of the idea and certainty of the General Judgment,

226 | *The Lamb, The Woman, and The Dragon*

not a description of the very manner in which it will take place, is further evident from the statement that the heavens and earth fled away before the face of the one who sat upon the throne. Yet all the dead are raised and stand before Him. Where do they stand, if there is neither heaven nor earth? You cannot have such a thing in reality, but you can have it in a symbolical picture, as in a dream or vision. The books evidently stand for the omniscience of God the Judge, to whom nothing is unknown, and by whom nothing is forgotten. He needs no actual record books or files. This feature of the vision is taken from a human necessity, and helps to make the certainty of an accurate and just judgment plain to our minds. The Belgic Confession interprets the books as the consciences of men; which also makes good sense, but my own preference is for the other meaning. The Book of Life is the roll of those who are redeemed by the grace of God, as in Luke 10.20, Philippians 4.3, and Revelation 3.5. The lake of fire stands for utter destruction and eternal condemnation: destruction for those things that can be destroyed, and eternal condemnation for immortal souls. The things to be destroyed are Death and Hades, personified here as a wicked pair who have captured and held prisoners all the generations of men. Their power is broken and their reign is over, as St. Paul foretold. (1 Cor 15.26)

The only important point of difference in the exposition of this vision is, whether this is to be understood as a judgment of all the dead, or of the wicked dead only. William Milligan takes the second view, and supports it by the following four arguments:

1. That this judgment is the same as is mentioned in 11.18, and that since in that passage the servants of God are distinguished from "the dead," it must be so here also.

Turn back to that text and see whether you can agree with the learned expositor. I can not. It is not at all clear to me that the servants of God are there a distinct group from the dead, rather it seems to me that they are one class among them.

2. That since the dead are gathered from Hades, and since this word stands for the powers of evil and the place of punishment, those who are summoned to judgment from there must be the wicked only.

It is true that the word often has that meaning, but it is not always so. It also means simply the grave, or the state of being dead, as in Acts 2.27, 31, and commonly throughout the Old Testament, as the equivalent of the Hebrew Sheol.

3. That "the 'books' mentioned in the passage are clearly books containing the record of evil deeds alone."

How does this appear? There is no hint of it, unless we translate verse 13, "and they were condemned every man according to his works"; but the Greek does not require such a translation, even if it permits it; and it is not so rendered in any standard version.

4. That in the general teaching of St. John the redeemed do not come into this judgment. (John 5.24, RV)

This is true, but applies to the passage in question only if this General Judgment is understood as confined to the single point of determining eternal weal or woe. As we shall see presently, there is no reason why it should be. The judgment of rewards may very well be included in it—as I think it is.

This view has found no acceptance among commentators in general. The whole picture is against it. With elaborate and carefully wrought details, the author seeks to impress the universality of the judgment upon us. All the dead, both small and great, stand before the throne. How does this admit of any exception? The sea, the grave, and the underworld give up their dead. Every place that might possibly hide a dead man is explored, and all are emptied of their occupants. Could universality be more vividly and forcibly expressed? Hence those who are not committed to the millenarian system almost unanimously see here an absolutely universal assize of all who shall have passed through death when the Lord comes. That the millenarians do not agree, is because they have misinterpreted the "first resurrection" to include all of the saints, which leaves only the wicked dead to participate in this resurrection and judgment; although even so, as pointed out, there ought to be some righteous dead during the millennium. The only way to avoid having them present in this resurrection and judgment is to be wise above what is written and imagine a special resurrection for them. It is no small argument against the position of the millenarians that they are thus obliged to pile one imagination upon another, and are forced to give so arbitrary an interpretation to this last judgment scene.

In addition to the universality of the expressions used, the mention of the "Book of Life" is decisive against all such views. It is not, to be sure, expressly said that any of those judged were found written in this book; but neither, for the matter of that, is it said that none were so found. The form of verse 15, "If any was found not written in the book of life, he was cast into the lake of fire," rather conveys the suggestion that such cases are contemplated as exceptional. If none of those judged are written in that book, why is it mentioned? It seems a mockery of the worst kind to have this precious record of God's redeeming love brought into court if it is known beforehand that not a single name of those on trial will be found written there.

For these reasons we accept this passage to be, as the overwhelming majority of all Bible readers have always felt it to be, a description of the final judgment, involving all men who ever lived upon the face of the earth, except those who remain alive at the coming of the Lord. Their judgment is, I believe, described in the twenty-fifth chapter of St. Matthew's gospel. I heartily agree with the following comment by Philip Mauro: (p. 615)

> That these were not the unbelieving dead only is evident from the fact that, conspicuous among the books out of which they were to be judged was 'the book of life,' and from the statement that 'whosoever was not found written in the book of life was cast into the lake of fire.' For manifestly there would be no use for the book of life at this judgment if all the believing dead had been raised, clothed with their resurrection bodies, and made sharers of Christ's throne and glory, a thousand years previously.

The general system of the millenarians forces them not only to explain this vision in the foregoing untenable fashion, but to do still worse violence to the judgment scene in the twenty-fifth chapter of Matthew, the well known passage of the sheep and the goats. With regard to this see Scofield Bible, p. 1036.

Substantially this interpretation is given by Henry W. Frost, in "The Second Coming of Christ." (p. 115)

> The judgment of the nations described in Matthew twenty-five, it is to be recognized, is at a particular time, and has reference to particular circumstances. It takes place at the end of the present age, just subsequent to the seven years' reign of the Antichrist, and thus it is the outcome of that time and event. Antichrist has hated and persecuted all godly persons, particularly godly Jews; these last have been driven from Palestine broadcast among the nations; multitudes of persons among the Gentile nations have joined the Antichrist in his persecution of the Jews, while some have opposed him by showing compassion upon them; and in this way individuals have made definite choices in respect to Christ and Antichrist. …The judgment is in respect to what the nations have or have not done to the King's 'brethren,' namely, godly Jews. The result of the judg-

ment is, on the one hand life and the kingdom, and on the other hand, death and everlasting punishment. It is to be observed that the 'kingdom' spoken of is not the heavenly one, because the nations as such will have no place there, but the earthly one, that is, the millennial, into which those who are spared from death will enter as living persons, to be nationally recognized therein under Christ's benignant reign.

Let us examine this conception.

1. The subjects of the judgment, they say, are "nations" in their national capacity. Thus England, Germany, Russia, the United States, Japan, China, etc., are to stand before the Lord in judgment; possibly through their representatives. The acts that form the subject-matter of the judgment are, of course, the acts of the respective governments, for only so do nations act "in their national capacity"; but the sentence passed is to everlasting fire, which can be suffered only by individuals. Who are these that go into the eternal fire? Not the nations as such, for they have no existence apart from the people that compose them. Are, then, all the citizens to be held personally and individually responsible for the acts of their governments? Let us fervently hope not! Thus, as soon as you try to think it through, this whole idea of a national judgment breaks down in your hands. God can certainly judge nations, and does judge them, through national calamities, famine, flood, and war; but such a judgment as this, with such a sentence, is wholly inconceivable in the case of a nation.

Dr. Frost says that the kingdom into which the just are invited is not the heavenly kingdom, "because the nations as such will have no place there, but the millennial one"; but is it not clear that the sentence pronounced in verses 34 and 41 must be the same as the result of the judgment, stated in verse 46? The latter speaks beyond question of the heavenly kingdom—why not the former also? To drag in the millennial conception here is wholly out of harmony with the context. That the word "nation" is used, is no argument in favor of this interpretation, nor does this confine the meaning to Gentiles instead of to Jews, or Christians for the expression is precisely parallel to Matthew 28.19: "Go, therefore, and teach all nations." This means that the gospel is to be taught to the people of all nations, not to the nations as such.

2. The acts commended in the saved, and the lack of which is the ground for the condemnation of the lost, are such as no nation, in its national capacity, ever performs, or can perform, especially to visit the sick and those

in prison. This stamps the whole judgment as dealing with individual persons, not in any way with "nations as such."

3. The significance attached, in this interpretation, to the words "my brethren" is out of line with New Testament usage. Dr. Scofield describes them as "the Jewish Remnant," and Dr. Frost calls them "godly Jews." Neither says that they are believers in Christ. They are at any rate not believers as such, but Jews. No such usage of the word "brethren" is found in the New Testament anywhere. Especially is it out of place in the mouth of the Lord Jesus, who expressly disowned earthly relations when He defined the word "brethren" in connection with Himself. (Matt 12.48–50)

It is true that we can not wholly identify this judgment in Matthew with the one in Revelation; but that does not oblige us to accept the Scofield view. The fact is simply that the two are supplementary to one another, at no point in conflict, but both required for a complete account of what is to happen at the return of Christ. The "Catholic Christian Church" has from the beginning confessed, in the Apostles' Creed, that Christ will come again, "to judge the quick and the dead." Apply this clue, and the differences between these two scenes cease to trouble you. The description in Matthew tells us what happens to the living, that in Revelation to the dead. Hence it is natural that we find no mention of a resurrection in the former passage, or of any living in the latter. Hence, also the surprise of both classes in the judgment scene in Matthew; which we do not find in Revelation, and would be impossible to those raised from the dead, inasmuch as their experiences in the intermediate state have abundantly shown them what is in store for them.

That in both descriptions the ultimate sentence turns on works and not on faith and the grace of God, need form no stumbling block to even the most ardent evangelical Christian. It is the established thing, in the scriptures, to say that judgment is according to works. It could not be otherwise here. We must remember that, in one sense, to believe in Christ is itself a "work" (John 6.28–29). Further, we all know that there is no true faith without works resulting from it. These also are on record, and while no salvation can issue from them, as meritorious, they do confirm the reality of the grace of God in a man's life, and the sincerity of the faith by which he has laid hold on Christ. Since the judgment scene in Revelation 20.11–15 employs the figure of two sets of books, we may extend the symbolism a little, and imagine the clerk of the heavenly court calling off a name. One angel looks in his book to see what the works were of the one named. He finds, in the midst of a sad and shameful record of failures and offenses, as a precious jewel in the rubbish, this entry: "He believed on Jesus Christ as his Savior." He looks further, and finds works on record in accordance with this faith. Then he turns to the angel with the Book of Life, and asks: "Is his name written there?"—"It is!"

Thus, as Alford finely says:[1]

> Rather we should say that those books and the book of life bore independent witness to the fact of men being or not being among the saved: the one, by inference from the works recorded: the other by inscription or non-inscription of the name in the list. So the 'books' would be, as it were, the vouchers for the book of life.

It is often asked, with regard to the General Judgment, what occasion there is for it, since we are taught that at death a person immediately enters upon a state of conscious blessedness or suffering, and how John 5.24 is to be reconciled with the idea of the believer's also taking his place before the great white throne. In seeking the answer to such questions, we are to be guided by the general principle that we must base our doctrinal conceptions, not on this or that utterance, taken by itself, but upon the whole scriptural teaching on the point involved. Also, let us often remind ourselves that the final judgment is an event in another world than this, an unseen and spiritual world, of which we have no direct experience. Therefore the scriptures speak, and we must also of necessity speak, in terms and pictures taken from this present life, although we know perfectly well that these pictures fit only in certain respects. They must therefore be cautiously interpreted, and must not be pressed in every particular. For instance, the chief thing to be done when a prisoner stands before an earthly court, is to determine his guilt or innocence; an idea that can have place when we have an omniscient God in the seat of the Judge.

Considering all the various teachings of the Bible on this subject, and seeking to find the underlying unity in them, it seems to me helpful to analyze the idea of "judgment" into its elements, and to see how these are dealt with. We find the following:

1. A determination of eternal destiny.

2. A manifestation of that determined destiny, for the individual, and an individual beginning of the experience of it.

---

[1] Vol. IV, Part II, p. 733.

3. A determining of degrees of merit and demerit, corresponding to differences of reward or punishment.

4. Such a declaration of reasons for the decisions arrived at as shall make the justice and love of God clear to all moral intelligences.

Let us consider these points in order.

1. The determination of eternal destiny.

This takes place at the moment when a man is united to Christ by true faith. God then and there forgives his sins and adopts him into His family as a returning prodigal, a redeemed son. By this his destiny is fixed: he has passed from death into life (John 5.24; 1 John 3.14). He is justified, and there is no more condemnation for him. This is in the deepest sense a "crisis," as the Greek has it, a judgment. Therefore we may truly say that for such a one the judgment is past already. He is "justified," which can take place only as the result of a judgment. This is the most important of all judgments: it is "the real thing," of which all subsequent judgments are but results and manifestations. It is worth noting, from John 3.18, that the unbeliever, as well as the believer, is spoken of as already having had a judgment. "He that believeth not hath been judged already, because he hath not believed on the name of the only begotten Son of God." This judgment, of course, is not irrevocable, for the man may yet repent and believe, but it is a judgment that stands against him unless changed. The unbeliever has been found guilty. He is under condemnation, and the wrath of God abideth upon him. If this judgment of the unbeliever does not render a final judgment day superfluous, neither does the justification of the believer have that effect. This is what we may call the secret judgment, or the inward judgment. It is real, and decisive of the believer's eternal state, but it is not yet made manifest.

2. A manifestation of that eternal destiny, and a beginning of the individual experience of it.

This takes place at death, and is referred to in Hebrews 9.27, "It is appointed for men once to die, but after this the judgment." From this time on men begin to experience the destiny to which they were adjudged from the time when they believed in Jesus Christ or rejected Him, but this is only the beginning. There are important questions not yet decided. These are held, so to speak, in abeyance, until the last great day.

3. A determination of degrees of merit and demerit, of rewards and punishments.

The judgment when he first believed placed the Christian forever among the redeemed; and the judgment at death caused him to be "absent from the body and present with the Lord"; but within the number of those who are saved, and equally so of those who are lost, there are many degrees of difference; whether, on the one hand, of glory and reward, or, on the other, of punishment. This is clearly stated in 1 Corinthians 3.11–15, and Luke 12.47–48. For this reason those who, as explained above, hold strongly that the believer is excluded from the judgment of the great white throne, yet are obliged to speak of another judgment, which they call the judgment of rewards, quite distinct from the general judgment usually taught by the church. Dr. Frost thinks that this judgment is the one referred to in 2 Corinthians 5.10:

> For we must all be made manifest before the judgment seat of Christ; that each may receive the things done in the body, according to what he hath done in the body, whether it be good or bad.

He thinks also, although he does not affirm it positively, that this judgment will be instantaneous, and that it will occur in the air, at the time and place of our meeting with Christ (p. 99). He goes on to find confirmation of this view in the meaning of the Greek word used for the judgment seat of Christ, saying:[2]

> It is interesting to note that the Greek word which the Holy Spirit uses to describe the judgment seat of Christ, as related to the saints, is a peculiar and differentiating one, inasmuch as it is not connected with any other judgment. This is the word 'bema,' which was used in classical Greek to signify the judgment seat located in the arena of the Isthmian games, where the judge sat, not to punish contestants, but to give his rewarding of this or that kind of prize to the victors. So Christ will seat Himself upon His 'bema,' not to punish Christians, but to reward them according to their works.

If this remark on the meaning of the word "bema" were correct, it would be very interesting, and perhaps important, but it would not stand examination. Whatever may have been the use and force of this word in classical Greek (which is no safe guide in the New Testament period) it is repeatedly used in the New Testament for the judgment seat of an official

---

[2] p. 99.

who hears criminal cases. It is so in Matthew 27.19, and John 19.13, where Pilate takes his seat on the "bema" to judge the case of Jesus Christ. It is so also in Acts 18.12, 16–17, where we have to do with the "bema" of Gallio, pro-consul at Corinth, and Acts 25.6, 10, 17 where mention is made of the "bema" of Festus, and Paul appeals to the "bema" of Caesar. The meaning, in this period, therefore, certainly includes a judgment seat that pronounces acquittal or condemnation in criminal cases. Whatever merit the millenarian case may have on other grounds, it derives no strength from the use of this word.

We find no reason, therefore, to depart from the general Christian conviction, that wherever judgment is spoken of, it is the General Judgment of the last day. Thus Acts 17.31, Romans 2.16, and 2 Corinthians 5.10, with similar passages, all refer to the same event. If this is correct, the final judgment will not be limited to the question of eternal salvation or perdition; but will include all other questions that require to be publicly judged and settled, especially the question of rewards and of degrees of punishment.

4. Finally, the judgment of the great day is needed, not only for the determination and final settlement of all kinds of questions, but as a public manifestation and vindication of the ways of God. God made this a moral universe, created for moral ends, and peopled by moral intelligences: angels, men, demons, and whatever other moral intelligences there may be. All that we know of God leads us to think that He wishes to govern the world, not by sheer power, but in such a manner that His ways will be vindicated before the moral sense of His creatures. Therefore it is necessary that there should be, some time, somewhere, a grand assize, in which all the facts shall be laid bare, and in which the reasons for God's judgments shall be made manifest. This is one of the deepest demands of our moral nature, and it fully met only by the church doctrine of the General Judgment.

XXIV

THE GOLDEN CITY

In the last two chapters of the Apocalypse, two sections are easily distinguished, the second beginning with 22.8. This is the "Epilogue," a closing statement about the book, rather than a continuation of the book itself. The unveiling of the future, promised in the first chapter, has been completed in 22.5. For the second time (the first was in 19.10) St. John, overcome with wonder at the things revealed, falls down at the feet of the angel to worship him, and for the second time he is strictly forbidden to do so. Is it not amazing that, in the face of a twice repeated prohibition of this kind, the worship of angels should nevertheless have obtained a foothold in the Christian church?

The apostle is told that the time is near, the eternal issues are fixed. Jesus declares that He will soon come, and will bring His reward with Him. There follows an invitation by the Spirit and the church to whomsoever will, to take of the water of life freely. Then comes a warning to every man neither to add to nor to take from the book as written, and the final benediction: "The grace of the Lord be with the saints, Amen." In all this there is nothing hard to interpret, and there are no great differences among commentators. The difficulties of the book lie behind us, by the time we come to this epilogue. It need not further claim our attention.

From the beginning of the twenty-first chapter on, most readers feel that we have before us a description of the eternal state. Dr. Milligan, to be sure, does not acknowledge this, but understands everything spiritually, as applicable, in an ideal sense, to the church in this present age; but I cannot follow him in that. Without seeking to find any succession of historical events or any hidden chronology in the Apocalypse, the order of the visions in the latter portion does seem to me to correspond to a broad order of events in time. The story of the Radiant Woman, beginning in chapter twelve, starts with the birth of Christ; and the record of the afflictions, conflict, and triumph of the church goes forward until all her enemies are destroyed. After that, what can come but exactly what does come, a description of her eternal state of glory and blessedness? We have seen in chapter nineteen the triumph of Christ and the gospel over the paganism confronting the church in the early period, then a long rest from this conflict with the heathen, then a renewal of the fight with distant, dimly apprehended foes, the final victory, and the General Judgment. Now fitly comes the consummation of all things. These chapters are an unveiling of that which was spoken of by the apostle Paul in 1 Corinthians 2.9–10.

Things which eye saw not, and ear heard not, and which entered not into the heart of man, whatsoever things God prepared for them that love Him. But unto us God revealed them through the Spirit. (RV)

So we have first of all a vision of the new heavens and the new earth.

And I saw a new heaven and a new earth, for the first heaven and the first earth are passed away, and the sea is no more. (RV)

In that new world God dwells with men:

And I heard a great voice out of the throne saying: Behold the tabernacle of God is with men, and he shall dwell with them, and they shall be his peoples, and God himself shall be with them, and be their God, and he shall wipe away every tear from their eyes; and death shall be no more, neither shall there be mourning, nor crying, nor pain anymore; the first things are passed away. And he that sitteth on the throne said: Behold, I make all things new. (RV)

This is all that is told us of conditions in the new earth, as distinct from the New Jerusalem, the city that is to be the metropolis of it. To appreciate this wonderful brevity and restraint of the Revelation, one needs to turn aside and see what other men, very good and great men, too, have allowed themselves to think about the perfect state. Dr. J. A. Seiss sees the new earth peopled with men in the flesh, ever begetting children, and thus fulfilling the earth "by ceaseless augmentation... throughout unending generations."[1] We must in all charity believe that he wrote this without stopping to think what this would mean: eternal production of children, without death, and all this confined to this planet! Dr. Abraham Kuyper even makes provision in the new earth for animals,[2] led thereto, I suppose, by the idea that he must find a place for the literal fulfillment of Isaiah 11.6–9, which he can not place in the millennium, because he does not believe that there will be any millennium. Here, also, he places the redemption of suffering nature, spoken of poetically by the apostle Paul, in Romans 8.19–22.

For my own part, I love to turn from such speculations to this passage of the Revelation, where, in picturing the new heaven and the new earth, nothing at all is said about such things. It seems to me unsatisfactory, and even dangerous, to speak on such matters, where the scriptures are silent. Once a person starts this kind of thing, it is very easy to fall into conceptions unworthy of eternity. What is promised us here is the fulfillment of Isaiah 65.17 and 66.22, passages wrongly ascribed by the millenarians to the thousand years.

> Behold, I create new heavens and a new earth. ...The new heavens and the new earth, which I will make, shall remain before me, saith the Lord. (AV)

The apostle Peter reminds us of this promise, and urges us to look forward to its fulfillment: (2 Peter 3.13):

> According to his promise, we look for new heavens and a new earth, wherein dwelleth righteousness.

Here, in the Apocalypse, we find a description of the new earth, but whether this picture is in every respect real, or is partly symbolical, needs to be considered. The mention of the sea, in the sentence: "The sea is no more," is against its being real, for so far as we now understand natural law, there could not be a fruitful and beautiful earth without the sea. Therefore it is likely that this is to be understood in a symbolical sense, the sea meaning, as in other portions of this book, the turbulent and unruly nations that rage against God and His people, the element from which came forth the Beast. In this sense, the absence of the sea is necessary

---

[1] Vol. III, p. 443.

[2] In "De Heraut," June 7, 1912; quoted by G. H. Hospers, in "Three Views of the Millennium," p. 10.

in a perfect world; but if this is the meaning of "the sea," then the whole picture must be taken as a symbolical presentation, not as a description of something that shall exist in the form described.

To my mind, it is quite permissible to think of this planet as the final and eternal home of God's people, after the resurrection; but if it should be otherwise, if God should provide us with an eternal home in some other portion of His great universe, the promise will not fail; for that new home will surely be, to us, a new heaven and a new earth. That is the great thing for us to take our hearts from this description of the new earth, that God will surely provide for us an eternal dwelling place, beautiful, peaceful, satisfying, and glorious. It does not much matter where it will be.

In the new earth there is, of course, a new city, a great metropolis for the inhabitants of the said new earth, a center of their activities. The first thing we notice about it is that it is not produced upon this earth, or constructed with any earthly materials. Twice we are told that it comes down out of heaven, from God.

> Verse 2. "And I saw the holy city, new Jerusalem, coming down out of heaven, from God... verse 10. And he carried me away in the Spirit to a mountain great and high, and showed me the holy city, Jerusalem, coming down out of heaven, from God." (RV)

So let us carefully remember this, that whatever else may be true of this city, it is both heavenly and divine in its origin. This is the city which by faith the patriarchs saw and longed for, "the city which hath foundations, whose builder and maker is God." (Heb 11.10)

The next thing indicated with equal repetition and emphasis is that this is a symbolic city; it represents the church of Jesus Christ. We have already read of the marriage supper of the Lamb, at which the church is the bride, and the members of the church are guests. With this thought fresh in our minds we can not mistake the meaning when it is said that this heavenly city was "made ready as a bride adorned for her husband." (21.2) And lest this hint should not be sufficient, we read again:

> Come hither, I will show thee the bride, the wife of the Lamb. And he carried me away in the Spirit to a mountain great and high, and showed me the holy city, Jerusalem, coming down out of heaven from God. (RV)

The angel promises to show the seer the Bride, and he shows him this city. What is meant by the Bride, the wife of the Lamb? The entire company of those redeemed by the blood of the Lamb, from the first man who believed the promise of God in paradise, to the last one believing, before the curtain of eternity shall fall. At many points in this interpretation I have confessed my inability to expound the text, or have given my interpretation with hesitation, but it is not so here. With the utmost confidence do I set aside any view of the Bride, the Lamb's wife, that falls short of including the entire true and invisible church, as defined in answer 54 of the Heidelberg Catechism:

> What believest thou concerning the Holy Catholic Church of Christ?
>
> That the Son of God, from the beginning to the end of the world, gathers, defends, and preserves to Himself, by His Spirit and Word, out of the whole human race, a Church chosen to everlasting life, agreeing in true faith.

When we read the parable of the Marriage Supper of the King who makes a marriage for His son; when St. Paul tells us of the mystery of the wedded union between Christ and His church; when we see the Radiant Woman, clothed with the sun; when we hear a great multitude, in chapter nineteen, singing:

> The marriage of the Lamb is come, and his wife hath made herself ready, and it was given unto her that she should array herself in fine linen is the righteous acts of the saints; (RV)

and when here again we are told that St. John was shown the Bride, the wife of the Lamb; then I think we can not exclude from this symbolism any soul redeemed by the blood of the cross. Periods, dispensations, and various other manifestations there must needs be, in this earthly and imperfect state, but when that which is perfect is come, they have place no more. As there is but one God and one Mediator between God and men, so there can eventually be only one Church, in which every distinction and division shall fall away. This is the "Una Sancta" of which the Nicene Creed speaks when it says: "We believe in One Holy Catholic and Apostolic Church."

There can be no question that this New Jerusalem symbolizes the church, but may it not at the same time be an actual city, some time to exist as described? We found reason to look upon the city of Rome as standing for the lust of the flesh, and the lust of the eyes and the pride of life, in other words, of "the world," the enemy of the church; but this did not hinder its being also an actual city, and its actual ruin being described in the very prophecy in which it is used as a symbol. So this heavenly city may also be, not merely a symbol of the church, but also a future tangible reality. Whether this is so or not, must be decided by an examination of what is said about it. Does the description correspond to any possible actuality?

As St. John saw the city coming nearer and nearer, he saw that the whole was like a transparent jewel, a diamond, or like a diamond. "Like unto a stone most precious, as it were a jasper stone, clear as crystal"; and this transparent city, like one great diamond, had "the glory of God." The same thing is said in verse 23: "The glory of God did lighten it." No one acquainted with the Old Testament can fail to recognize that phrase: "the glory of God." It is the standard expression for that outward and glorious theophany, or appearance of the divine majesty, that was given to the people of Israel on supreme occasions, and appears in the most exalted visions of the great prophets.

It was a reflection of that glory that shone in the face of Moses as he came down from the mount, after communing with God. When the tabernacle was set up, "the glory of the Lord filled the tabernacle." (Ex 40.34; Lev 9.23) When the people had sinned, once and again they were awed by the sudden appearance of "the glory of the Lord" (Ex 16.10; Num 14.10). Moses prayed that he might see it undimmed, but he was denied the privilege, for no man could see it unveiled and live; Isaiah saw it in the great vision of chapter six, when he received his call to be a prophet. Ezekiel has much to say of it. In 11.23, with sorrow he saw "the glory of the Lord" leaving the sinful and polluted city of Jerusalem; but in the concluding chapters of his prophecy, by the eye of faith, he saw that glory coming back. (43.2–5) This "glory of the Lord" is called, in later Jewish and Christian theology, although not in the Bible itself, the "Shekinah," the glorious manifestation of the presence of God. This is the glory that St. John saw from his mountain top, now coming finally to dwell with men.

The city "has a wall, great and high" (v 12). Of course it did: you could not have a city, in St. John's day, without a wall: it would have been no city at all, but defenseless open country. How high was the wall? It is not clear. We know the height of the city, for the angel measured it—there is no guesswork about it—and he found it to be twelve thousand furlongs each way—that is fifteen hundred miles long, broad, and high!

And he measured the city with the reed, 12,000 furlongs, the length, and the breadth, and the height thereof are equal.

This has been taken by some, who can not bear the thought of a city of fifteen hundred miles high, to be the total circumference, but the language of the text seems to make it fifteen hundred miles each way, and so it is taken by most interpreters.

But in what sense was the city so high? Was that the height of the outer wall? Perhaps, and yet, it doesn't say that: it says the city itself was that high. Then the account goes on to tell us that the wall measured 144 cubits, or about 216 feet, but whether this was the height or the thickness, is not stated. If we take it as the height, it is no more than a little marker around a city fifteen hundred miles high. In that sense, then, was that the height of the city? Was it the average height of its palaces? If we take it that the wall was fifteen hundred miles high and two hundred sixteen feet thick, we are puzzled at such inconceivable proportions, for this is as if a wall more than three thousand feet high should be but one inch thick!

The city had three gates on each side, surely not too many, seeing they are, at this rate, three hundred and seventy-five miles apart. It had also twelve foundations, understood by some to be twelve foundation stones, each section, between gates, being laid upon one great stone. Others, it seems to me better, consider these twelve foundations to rise, one above another, like tiers, all showing to the eye. The materials of the city are costly and splendid, but, if regarded as real materials, not less puzzling than the proportions. The streets are of gold, "like transparent glass." What kind of gold is that? Granted that it is within the power of God's omnipotence to create a material having the various qualities of gold, and also clear as crystal, the question would remain: by what right is such stuff as this called "gold"? So with pearls large enough to form city gates not only, but suitable gates for a city of this kind. What, also, of the river flowing down the golden streets, with trees on each side of it, rooted and growing in such soil? How can we form any comprehension of such things? Perhaps you think it tiresome for me to analyze the statements of this wonderful vision in this prosaic manner. I agree with you most heartily; but tiresome as it is, it will not be altogether useless if it causes us to see clearly—what I think it is of the utmost importance that we should see clearly—that this description of a symbolic city, *symbolic only,* not in any way to be thought of as actually existing, whether in heaven or upon earth, either now or at any time to come. It is like the sheet and the animals of St. Peter's vision on the housetop, present there in the vision, but not anywhere else. This is no more an actual city than the other symbols of this book are real things, the sword from the mouth of Christ, the Lamb that took the book and opened the seals thereof, the four horsemen, the star that was handed a key, the woman clothed with the sun, the dragon whose tail drew down the stars, the beast with seven heads and ten horns, the harlot riding the beast, etc., etc. All these are symbols and symbols only. So with this heavenly city, the New Jerusalem. It is a symbol of the church of God, in her final and eternal glory. It is a symbol, and so far as objective reality is concerned it never has existed, nor ever will exist; but what it symbolizes is real, the grandest and most enduring reality God ever made.

Before we leave this part of the subject, to clinch what has been said, let us see to what absurdities literalism will lead a commentator. Dr. J. A. Seiss says:[3]

> That a real city, as well as a perfected moral system, is here to be understood, I see not how we can otherwise conclude. ...Its location.—This is not specifically told, but the record is not without some hints. John sees it coming down out of heaven. The idea is that it comes close to the earth, but it is nowhere said that it ever alights upon the earth...The probabilities are that it will stand high above Palestine, and perhaps stationary, as the earth revolves under it.

How this is to be reconciled with the law of gravitation, I do not know, but that doesn't seem to trouble Dr. Seiss. What he should at least have stopped to explain to us, is how this city can stand over Palestine, stationary, while the earth revolves under it. Is Palestine also to remain stationary, while the rest of the world goes on revolving?

The structure of the city itself Dr. Seiss conceives of as similar to that of a great apartment house, for he says:[4]

> Here would be streets over streets, and stories over stories, up, up, up, to the height of 1,500 miles, and each street 1,500 miles long. ...How long, then, would it take a man to explore the city of gold, where every street is one-fifth the length of the diameter of the earth, and the number of

[3] Vol. III, p. 401.

[4] Vol. III, p. 409.

whose main avenues, though a mile above each other and a mile apart, would not be less than eight millions.[5]

I can not too earnestly impress upon the reader my conviction that this kind of thing is utterly out of place in our thoughts of this great closing vision. The measurements of the city have nothing to do with length, breadth and thickness, they are symbolic of perfection. The heavenly city is twelve times one thousand measures, long, broad and high. Twelve is the number of the church, for there were twelve tribes, and twelve apostles; and one thousand is the number of utmost fullness. The church of Christ is thus set before us in the utmost amplitude of her being. This also is the meaning of the measure of the wall, whether height or thickness does not matter, and should not even be inquired into. The dimension given is the cube of the number of the people of God—one hundred and forty-four, being twelve times twelve; the wall is therefore thick enough, high enough, and strong enough for perfect protection. The foundations bear the names of the twelve apostles and the gates the names of the twelve tribes, to teach us once again the unity of Israel and the church. The city is a perfect cube, to remind us of the Holy of Holies in the tabernacle and the temple; and to make this clearer still, the prophet sees no temple therein—of course not, for the entire city itself is the inmost sanctuary, and all its inhabitants are "ever with the Lord."

Perhaps some one will say, not without a feeling of disappointment: "I thought this was a vision of heaven, and now you tell me that it is only an imaginary city, a symbol of the church." Did you think that this was a description of heaven? You thought quite rightly about it; that is exactly what it is. Read it with this thought in mind, and you will be making the right use of it; but this is not really different from saying that it is a symbolical description of the church of God in her perfected and eternal glory; for what is heaven? Is it not the place and state where all our hopes are realized, where our redemption is at last complete? And what is the church, in her final and perfected glory? Is it not the company of the redeemed, "without spot or wrinkle, or any such thing?" You cannot separate these two things. What symbolizes the one includes the other. Heaven is where we shall always be with the Savior, where there shall be no more crying or tears or

---

[5] Thus Dr. Seiss, but according to my calculation there would be only about four and a half millions. On each floor of such a city, there could be no more than 1,501 streets running in one direction. Doubling this for others at right angles with them, and we have 3,022 on each floor, multiplied by 1,500 stories, or 4,503,000.

pain or death, no more danger or struggle, no more sin or sorrow; where everything God has promised us is to be fulfilled. Is not that heaven? Well, that is also the eternal and perfected state of the Christian church.

That the New Jerusalem stands for the fulfillment of all the promises of God to the redeemed People of God, the ultimate Israel, becomes very evident if we take our concordances or reference Bibles and trace the elements of which this description is compounded. I recommend the study most heartily to the reader. It will be found that the Holy Spirit, speaking through the apostle, has combed the Holy Scriptures from Genesis on for promises to name in these grand consummation chapters. Here we find again the Tree of Life, that stood in the Paradise of God. Lest man should stretch forth his sinful hands and eat of the fruit of it, he was expelled from the garden, but here it grows, yielding its fruit for the inhabitants of the city, not once a year, but every month. In Ezekiel we see a wondrous river, flowing from under the altar, where man is reconciled to God through sacrifice. Here is the same river, flowing down the golden streets. To Abraham God gave, as the climax of all His covenant promises with respect to his seed: "I will be their God, and they shall be my people." This is another promise the reader will do well to follow through the Bible, from beginning to end, for it appears again and again, in the law and the prophets, lest it should be forgotten. Here it is at last in perfect realization:

> Behold the tabernacle of God is with men, and he shall dwell with them, and they shall be his peoples, and God himself shall be with them, and be their God.

Notice, please, the plural, "peoples." No longer one nation, as of old: God now has all the peoples of the earth for His own, and so is fulfilled in its final and perfect form the word of the Lord to Abraham: "The father of a multitude of nations have I made thee." (Gen 17.5)

So it goes on. This vision is simply a gathering up of all the precious promises of God to Israel down the centuries, and an assurance that they will all be fulfilled. There shall not anything fail, of all the good things the Lord has promised. Now, as the fulfillment of every promise is precisely what constitutes the heavenly life, so nothing can be more appropriate than to call this a vision of heaven, and to use it as such. That is what it is intended to be, and all the time, just because it is a vision of heaven, it is also a vision of the eternal and perfected glory and blessedness of the Christian church.

Another may say to me: "What, then, are these nations, in verse 24, that walk in the light of the city, and these kings that bring their glory into it? Are not these distinct from the church?" Not at all. These that walk in the glory and light of the church, these are the members of the church. In symbolism this offers no difficulty. The Radiant Woman was the church, and her seed are at the same time the individual members of the church. She is the bride at the marriage feast of the Lamb, but the members of the church are the invited guests. So you can easily have a cartoon of Uncle Sam speaking to the people of America, although he himself is America. Such a separation is not possible in actual life, but it may take place in symbols.

Another question: "Why does the tree bear leaves for the healing of the nations, whereas there is no more sickness to be healed?" I reply, that the city did not then begin to exist when St. John saw it come down from heaven. It is in heaven before it comes down to earth, and there is no sickness in the perfected state, simply because, by these healing leaves, all sickness has been overcome. The nations are now being healed by the leaves from the heavenly tree.

Finally let us notice the pure spirituality of the delight reserved for those who are privileged to be citizens of this golden city. One blemish of the early Christian literature is the carnal pleasure expected in the millennium, by even some of the church fathers: pleasures of eating and drinking, of marrying and being given in marriage. How different it is here, in the Revelation of St. John. Here is the great delight promised to the children of God:

> His servants shall serve him, and they shall see his face, and his name shall be in their foreheads.

Each one of God's redeemed children shall be as the High Priest, who went into the Most Holy Place, into the very presence of God, bearing upon his forehead a golden plate, with the words: "Holiness unto the Lord." It remains for us, having caught a glimpse of the glory, to pray together daily that we may be among those found worthy to bear the name upon our foreheads, and to enter through the gates into the city.

BIBLIOGRAPHY

I. General Remarks

The number of books written on the Apocalypse of St. John is very great, and of these many books, probably a greater proportion, are worthless than of those written on any other topic. At any rate, this must be the judgment of one who chooses any of the three chief systems of interpretation, to the exclusion of the other two: for he must judge that those who write on the basis of the systems he rejects not only will be in error here and there, but must infallibly go further and further wrong in direct proportion to the earnestness and diligence with which they apply their fundamental principles of interpretation.

Since I myself reject, absolutely, the Futurist and Historicist systems, I cannot conscientiously recommend to the reader any commentary that adopts either one of them. They have value, in my judgment, only for him who must make himself acquainted with what has been said on the subject. The man whose object is to gain knowledge of the meaning of the Revelation will, it seems to me, do better to avoid them.

As the reader will not be long in discovering, the two commentaries which I have myself used with the greatest profit are Alford: *Greek Testament,* (with its equivalent, the *New Testament for English Readers*) and Swete: *The Apocalypse of St. John.*

These two are outstanding examples of that happy combination of profound scholarship and evangelical Christian faith so often found in the great scholars of the Church of England. The world is much indebted to them. For ministers and others who have the necessary preparation in a knowledge of Latin and Greek, there is nothing better than these two books. Also very excellent are the more recent commentaries of Isbon T. Beckwith and R. C. H. Lenski.

For the general Christian reader, those which seem to me most useful are Mauro: *The Things Which Must Shortly Come to Pass* (in spite of too much leaning to the "Historicist" system); Morris: *The Drama of Christianity* (a very fine little book); Russell: *Preaching the Apocalypse*, and Wishart: *The Book of Day*. For those who can use the Dutch language, Greijdanus: *De Openbaring des Heeren aan Johannes* is excellent. Naturally, this approval of the books named does not extend to every point of interpretation. It means that he who carefully reads them will get, on the whole, a sane and helpful approach to the meaning of the Revelation of St. John.

II. List of the Principal Works Consulted in the Preparation of this Discussion

Alford, Henry: *The Greek Testament.*
By Henry Alford, D.D., Dean of Canterbury. Four volumes, the fourth volume bound in two parts. London, Rivingtons, Waterloo Place. Based upon a critical study of the Greek text. Premillennial, but not dispensationalist. "Philosophy of History" school. 1862.

Alford, Henry: *The New Testament for English Readers.*
Essentially the same as the "Greek Testament," but arranged for those who know only the English language. Contains some remarks not found in the Greek edition. Two volumes, each volume bound in two parts. Lee & Shepard, Boston & New York. 1875.

Ante-Nicene Fathers.
Translations from the writings of the Fathers, down to AD 325. Edited by the Rev. Alexander Roberts, D.D., and James Donaldson, LL.D., American edition, chronologically arranged, with brief notes and prefaces, by A. Cleveland Coxe, D.D. Nine volumes, besides Bibliography and General Index. Christian Literature Publishing Company, Buffalo, New York. 1885.

Auberlen, Carl A.: *The Prophecies of Daniel and the Revelation of St. John, Viewed in Their Mutual Relation.*
By Carl August Auberlen, Doctor of Philosophy, Licentiate, and Professor Extraordinarius of Theology in Basle. Translation by the Rev. Adolph Saphir. W. F. Draper, Andover, 1857. "Philosophy of History" school.

Barnes, A.: *Notes Explanatory and Practical on the Book of Revelation.*
By Albert Barnes, Pastor of First Presbyterian Church, Philadelphia, Pa. Harper & Bros., New York. 1852. Postmillennial. "Historicist."

Bavinck, H.: *Gereformeerde Dogmatiek.*
By Dr. Herman Bavinck, Professor of Dogmatic Theology in the Free University, Amsterdam, the Netherlands. Four volumes. J. H. Kok, Kampen. 1885.

Beckwith, I. T.: *The Apocalypse of St. John.*
By Dr. Isbon T. Beckwith, formerly Professor of the Interpretation of the New Testament in the General Theological Seminary, New York City, and of Greek in Trinity College, Hartford. Macmillan Company, 1919. "Preterist."

Benson, E. W.: *The Apocalypse, an Introductory Study of the Revelation of St. John the Divine.*
By Edward White Benson, sometime Archbishop of Canterbury. Macmillan Company, 1900. "Philosophy of History" school. Not a commentary, but presents a new translation of the Apocalypse, with new arrangement and valuable discussion of certain important points.

Bleek, F.: *Lectures on the Apocalypse.*
By Friedrich Bleek, Professor Extraordinarius at the University of Bonn. English translation edited by Dr. Samuel Davidson. Williams & Norgate, London, 1875.

Bousset, W.: *Der Antichrist.*
By Johann Franz Wilhelm Bousset, Associate Professor of New Testament Exegesis at the University of Göttingen. English translation with prologue, by A. H. Keane, F.R.G.S., under title: "The Antichrist Legend." London, Hutchinson and Co., 1896.

Bultema, H.: *Verklaring van de Openbaring.*
By H. Bultema, Minister of the Word of God at Muskegon, Mich. Bereer Publishing Committee, Muskegon, Mich. 1921. "Futurist." Premillennial and dispensationalist.

Butler, C. M.: *Lectures on the Book of Revelation.*
By C. M. Butler, D.D., Rector of Trinity Church, Washington, D. C. Robert Carter & Bros., New York, 1860.

Carpenter, W. B.: *The Revelation of St. John the Divine.*
By the Rev. W. Boyd Carpenter, M.A., Vicar of St. James', Holloway; Being the exposition of the Apocalypse in "A New Testament Com-

mentary for English Readers," in three volumes, edited by Charles John Ellicott, D.D., Bishop of Gloucester and Bristol. E. P. Dutton & Co., New York, 1882.

Carroll, B. H.: *The Book of Revelation.*

By B. H. Carroll, D.D., President, Southwestern Baptist Theological Seminary, Seminary Hill, Texas. "Historicist." Postmillennial. Fleming H. Revell Co., New York and Chicago, 1913.

Charles, R. H.: *A Critical and Exegetical Commentary on the Revelation of St. John.*

By R. H. Charles, D.Litt., D.D., Archdeacon of Westminster, Fellow of the British Academy. Two volumes; being the commentary on the Apocalypse in the International Critical Commentary series. "Preterist," Left Wing, and the chief commentary of that school. This is an extraordinarily learned work. Much is made, in it, of the relation of the Apocalypse to the so-called "Apocalyptic Literature" and of other "sources" of the images and ideas of the Revelation. Charles Scribner's Son, New York, 1920.

Crafer, T. W.: *The Revelation of St. John the Divine.*

By Thomas Wilfred Crafer, D.D., Professor of Theology at Queen's College, London. "Preterist," Right Wing. This is the exposition of the Apocalypse in Bishop Gore's "New Commentary," a one-volume commentary on the entire Bible, including the Apocrypha. Macmillan Co., New York, 1928.

Dean, J. T.: *The Book of Revelation.*

This is the volume on Revelation in the series entitled, "Handbooks for Bible Classes and Private Students," edited by Principal Alexander Whyte, D.D., and the Rev. John Kelman, D.D. "Preterist," very brief. T. and T. Clark, Edinburgh, 1915.

De Hartog, A. H.: *Openbaring van Johannes.*

By Prof. A. H. De Hartog. Uitgeversmaatschappij, Amsterdam, The Netherlands, 1935. This book carries the principles and methods of the "Philosophy of History" school to an extreme, with the result that the whole book of Revelation, in the hands of the author, evaporates into generalities.

De Moor, J. C.: *De Hemel Geopend.*

By Dr. J. C. De Moor, Minister of the Word of God, of the Reformed (Gereformeerde) Church at The Hague, The Netherlands. J. H. Kok, Kampen, 1913. This is a series of sermons on the Revelation. Three volumes.

De Wette, Wm. L.: *Kurze Erklarung der Offenbarung Johannis.*
By Wilhelm Martin Leberecht De Wette, Professor at the University of Basle; being the exposition of the Revelation in his three-volume work: "Kurzgefasstes Exegetisches Handbuch zum Neuen Testament." Leipsig, Weidmannsche Buchhandlung, 1848.

Duesterdiek, F.: *Critical and Exegetical Handbook to the Revelation of St. John.*
By Friedrich Duesterdiek, D.D., Oberconsistorialrath, Hanover. Translated from the third edition of the German, and edited, with notes, by Henry E. Jacobs, D.D. Funk & Wagnalls, New York, 1887. "Preterist." This is the exposition of Revelation in "Meyer's Commentary."

Ellicott's Commentary.
See Carpenter, W. Boyd.

Elliott, E. B.: *Horae Apocalyticae.*
By the Rev. E. B. Elliott, A.M., late Vicar of Tuxford, and Fellow of Trinity College, Cambridge. Seeley, Burnside & Seeley, London, 1844. Four volumes. "Historicist." Premillennial, but not dispensationalist. This is the foremost representative of the "Continuous Church History" school of interpretation.

Erdman, W. J.: *Notes on the Revelation.*
Written by the father of Prof. Chas. A. Erdman, of Princeton, and edited by his son. "Futurist." Premillennial. Fleming H. Revell Co., New York & Chicago, 1930.

Fysh, F.: *The Divine History of the Church.*
By Rev. Frederick Fysh, M.A., Philadelphia, Pa., George and Wayne, 1845. "Historicist." This is a condensation of the work of Elliott. "There is here presented, in a concise and lucid manner, the results of Mr. Elliott's profound and learned investigations."

Frost, Henry W.: *The Second Coming of Christ.*
By Rev. Henry W. Frost, D.D., Emeritus Home Director for North America of the China Inland Mission. William B. Eerdmans Publishing Co., Grand Rapids, Mich. 1934. Premillennial and dispensationalist.

Gordon, S. D.: *Quiet Talks About the Crowned Christ.*
Fleming H. Revell Co., New York and Chicago, 1914. "Futurist." Premillennial and dispensationalist.

252 | The Lamb, The Woman, and The Dragon

Greijdanus, S.: *De Openbaring des Heeren aan Johannes.*
By Dr. S. Greijdanus, Professor of Theology at Kampen, The Netherlands. J. H. Kok, Kampen, 1930. "Preterist."

This is the volume on Revelation in the series entitled: "Korte Verklaring der Heilige Schrift," covering all the books of the Bible. To be distinguished from the commentary on Revelation issued independently by the same author in 1908, when pastor of the Reformed (Gereformeerde) Church at Rozenburg. That work was published by J. C. Van Schenck Brill, Doesburg.

Guinness, H. Grattan: *The Approaching End of the Age.* **A. C. Armstrong & Son, New York, 1881.**

Guinness, H. Grattan: *Light for the Last Days.* **A. C. Armstrong & Sons, New York, 1893.**

Guinness, H. Grattan: *History Unveiling Prophecy.* **Fleming H. Revell Co., New York and Chicago, 1905.**
The above three books are by Dr. H. Grattan Guinness, a distinguished advocate of Foreign Missions, Fellow of the Royal Astronomical Society. "Historicist." Premillennial, but not dispensationalist. The system that regards the Pope as Antichrist, and reckons prophecy by the "year-day" system, may be seen in these books at its best.

Hendriksen, William: *More Than Conquerors.*
By the Rev. William Hendriksen, Th.M., Professor of Exegetical Theology, New Testament, Calvin College and Seminary, Grand Rapids, Mich. Baker's Book Store, 1019 Wealthy Street, S.E., Grand Rapids, Mich. Recapitulationist, 1939.

Hengstenberg, E. W.: *The Revelation of St. John.*
By Ernst Wilhelm Hengstenberg, Professor at the University of Berlin. Translated by Dr. Patrick Fairbairn. Two volumes. Robert Carter & Bros., New York, 1852. "Preterist."

Hepp, V.: *De Antichrist.*
By Dr. Valentinus Hepp, Professor of Theology at the Free University of Amsterdam. J. H. Kok, Kampen, 1920.

Hitchcock and Brown: *The Teaching of the Twelve Apostles.*
By Roswell D. Hitchcock and Francis Brown, Professors in Union Theological Seminary, New York City. Charles Scribner's Sons, 1885.

Kuyper, Abraham: *Dictaten Dogmatiek.*
By Abraham Kuyper, Professor of Dogmatic Theology in the Free University of Amsterdam, of which he was also the founder. This work consists of notes taken by the students in his classes in dogmatics. Five volumes. J. H. Kok, Kampen, The Netherlands, 1910.

Kuyper, Abraham: *The Revelation of St. John.*
Consists of articles originally prepared for popular reading in a periodical, in The Netherlands. Published after the death of the author, in book form. Translated from the Dutch by John Hendrik De Vries, D.D. William B. Eerdmans Publishing Company, Grand Rapids, Mich., 1935. To those who know the high and well-deserved reputation of the author as a theologian and an exegete, this volume is a disappointment. "Futurist" and amillennial.

Lange, J. P.: *The Revelation of St. John.*
By John Peter Lange, D.D., Professor of Theology in the University of Bonn. Translated from the German by Evelina Moore, enlarged and edited by E. R. Craven, D.D., pastor of the Third Presbyterian Church at Newark, New Jersey. Charles Scribner's Sons, 1874.

Lenski, R. C. H.: *The Interpretation of St. John's Revelation.*
By the Rev. Richard Charles Henry Lenski, D.D., Professor of Systematic Theology in the Evangelical Theological Seminary of the Lutheran Joint Synod of Ohio, at Columbus, Ohio, 1935. Lutheran Book Concern, Columbus, Ohio. "Philosophy of History" school.

Lord, D. N.: *Exposition of the Apocalypse.*
Harper Brothers, New York, 1847. "Continuous Church History" school of interpretation. Premillennial.

Masselink, William: *Why Thousand Years?*
A discussion of the millennial problem in general. Exegesis of Revelation 20 in Chapter XIV. William B. Eerdmans Pub. Co., Grand Rapids, Mich., 1930.

Mauro, Philip: *The Things Which Must Shortly Come to Pass.*
William B. Eerdmans Pub. Co., Grand Rapids, Mich., 1933. This is a revised edition of the same author's book entitled: "Patmos Visions," issued by Hamilton Bros., Boston, Mass., 1925. The changes made are chiefly in the interpretation of the twentieth chapter.

Mede, Joseph: (Also written Mead) *The Key to the Revelation.*
By Joseph Mede, B.D., Fellow of Christ's College, Cambridge. Originally written in Latin, under the title: "Clavis Apocalyptica." Translated by Richard More, 1650. New translation was made by R. B. Cooper, London, 1833. "Historicist," and premillennial. Introduction by Dr. William Twisse, Moderator of the Westminster Assembly.

Milligan, William: *The Book of Revelation.*
By William Milligan, D.D., Professor of Divinity and Biblical Criticism in the University of Aberdeen. This is the exposition of the Apocalypse in the "Expositor's Bible." Issued separately by A. C. Armstrong & Son, New York, 1893. "Philosophy of History" school, and the outstanding commentary in this class. Very valuable.

Milligan, William: *Discussions on the Apocalypse.*
Contains discussions of some of the great problems connected with the book. Macmillan Company, London & New York, 1893.

Milligan, E. M.: *Is the Kingdom Age at Hand?*
This book is mentioned here chiefly to call attention to it, that the reader may avoid confusing it with the commentary of Dr. William Milligan, above. Premillennial and dispensationalist. George H. Doran Company, New York, 1924. The value of this work as a study of the Apocalypse may be fairly estimated from a remark in the introductory chapter (p. 20), to the effect that the writer used, in preparing it, no helps but a concordance and the Scofield Bible, with notes!

Moffat, James: *An Introduction to the Literature of the New Testament,* Charles Scribner's Sons, New York, 1927.

Moffat, James: *The Revelation of St. John the Divine.*
By James Moffat, Litt.D., D.D., LL.D., Washburn Professor of Church History, Union Theological Seminary, New York. This is the exposition of Revelation in the "Expositor's Greek Testament." (Not to be confused with the "Expositor's Bible"), Hodder & Stoughton, London and New York. The first three volumes of this set were issued by Dodd, Mead and Co., New York, 1897, 1900, and 1903 respectively. The last two volumes are undated. "Preterist."

Morris, S. L.: *The Drama of Christianity.*
By S. L. Morris, D.D., LL.D., Executive Secretary of Home Missions,

Presbyterian Church in the United States. Presbyterian Committee of Publication, Richmond, Virginia, 1928. "Philosophy of History" school.

Murray, Alexander A.: *Expositions of the Book of Revelation.*
A series of radio talks, in two parts, paper. By Alexander A. Murray, D.D. Westminster Presbyterian Church, Sydney, New South Wales, Australia—published by the author, 1939. Here may be found the "reductio ad absurdum" of the Futurist system.

Ottman, Ford C.: *The Unfolding of the Ages.*
Publication Office, "Our Hope," 456 Fourth Ave., New York City, 1905. Premillennial and dispensationalist. "Futurist."

Peake, A. S.: *The Revelation of John.*
By Arthur S. Peake, M.A., D.D., Rylands Professor of Biblical Exegesis in the University of Manchester, Tutor to Hartley Primitive Methodist College; sometime Fellow of Merton College, Oxford. Holborn Press, London, 1920. "Preterist."

Preusz, Hans: *Der Antichrist.*
By Dr. Hans Preusz, Gymnasialoberlehler in Leipsig. One of the pamphlets in the series: "Biblischen Zeit und Streit Fragen," 1909. Edwin Lunge, Lichterfelde, Berlin. "Preterist."

Russell, D.: *Preaching the Apocalypse.*
By Daniel Russell, minister in Rutgers Presbyterian church, New York City. The Abingdon Press, New York, Cincinnati, and Chicago, 1935. "Preterist." Excellent model for homiletical use of the Apocalypse.

Ramsay, William: *The Letter to the Seven Churches of Asia.*
By Sir William Ramsay, D.C.L., Litt.D., LL.D., Professor of Humanity in the University of Aberdeen. George H. Doran Co., New York City. Undated, but subsequent to 1902.

Sadler, M. F.: *The Revelation of St. John the Divine.*
By the Rev. M. F. Sadler, Rector of Honiton and Prebendary of Wells. George Bell & Sons, London and New York, 1893.

Schouten, A.: *Naar de Voleinding.*
By the Rev. A. Schouten, minister at Aalten, The Netherlands. Published by N. V. D. Graafschap, Aalten, 1928. Prevailingly, though not consistently,

of the "Philosophy of History" school. Amillennial. This is a set of sermons, and not infrequently the homiletical interest wins over the exegetical.

Scofield, C. I.: *Holy Bible: Scofield Reference Edition.*

This is the text of the King James, or Authorized Version of the Bible, with divisions into paragraphs, paragraph and chapter headings, references, and notes by the Rev. C. I. Scofield, D.D., Oxford University Press, New York, 1917. The "Notes" are largely directed towards inculcating as Scriptural teaching the "dispensationalist" form of premillennialism that took its rise from John Nelson Darby. It is regarded by all who wish to understand this system.

Scott, C. A.: *Revelation.*

By C. Anderson Scott, M.A., B.D. (Cambridge) Oxford University Press. This is the exposition of the Apocalypse in the series entitled: "The New Century Bible." "Preterist." Undated.

Seiss, J. A.: *The Apocalypse.*

Lectures on the Book of Revelation, in three volumes. 1865. Premillennial and dispensationalist. Here is premillennial literalism in full flower. "Futurist." Philadelphia School of the Bible.

Stevens, W. C.: *Revelation, the Crown Jewel of Biblical Prophecy.*

Two volumes. Christian Alliance Publishing Company, Harrisburg, Pa., and New York City, 1928. "Futurist." Premillennial and dispensationalist.

Stonehouse, N. B.: *The Apocalypse in the Ancient Church.*

By Ned Bernard Stonehouse, Th.D., being a thesis submitted to the faculty of the Free University of Amsterdam, in partial fulfillment of the requirements for the degree of Doctor of Theology. Oosterbaan & Le Cointre, Goes, Holland, 1929.

Stuart, Moses: *Commentary on the Apocalypse.*

By Moses Stuart, Professor of Sacred Literature in the Theological Seminary at Andover, Mass. Two volumes. Allen, Marrett and Wardell, Andover, 1845. "Preterist."

Swete, H. B.: *The Apocalypse of St. John.*

By Henry Barclay Swete, D.D., Litt.D., Regius Professor of Divinity, Gonville and Caius College, Cambridge. The Macmillan Co., New York City. "Preterist." 1906.

Timbrel, John Hamilton: *The Last Message of Jesus Christ.* Eaton & Mains, New York, 1905.

Trench, R. C.: *Commentary on the Epistles to the Seven Churches in Asia.* By Richard Chevenix Trench, D.D., Dean of Westminster. Charles Scribner's Sons, New York, 1862.

Warfield, B. B.: *Biblical Doctrines.* By Benjamin Breckinridge Warfield, D.D., late Professor of Dogmatic and Polemic Theology in the Theological Seminary of Princeton, New Jersey. This is a collection of essays on theological subjects, assembled and published in book form after the death of the author. Chapters XV, "The Prophecies of St. Paul," and XVI, "The Millennium and the Apocalypse," bear upon the problems of eschatology. Westminster Press, New York, 1929.

Weiss, B.: *Commentary on the New Testament.* By Professor Bernhard Weiss, D.D., of the University of Berlin. Translated from the German by Prof. George H. Schodde, Ph.D., and Prof. Epiphanius Wilson, M.A. Four volumes. Funk & Wagnalls Co., New York, 1906.

Wishart, C. F.: *The Book of Day.* By Dr. Charles Frederick Wishart, President of the College of Wooster, Ohio. Oxford University Press, New York, 1935. "Preterist."

Zahn, Theodor: *Die Offenbarung des Johannis.* By Dr. Theodor Zahn, Professor of Pedagogics and New Testament Exegesis at the University of Eelangen, 1924. "Futurist." Dr. Zahn is the foremost conservative scholar in Germany, in the field of New Testament Literature and Exegesis.

ACKNOWLEDGMENTS

Grateful acknowledgment is hereby made to the following publishers for permission to use selections from their copyrighted publications:

Arno C. Gabelein, Inc., New York, for permission to quote from *The Unfolding of the Ages*; Ford C. Ottman;

Rev. H. Bultema, Muskegon, Mich., for permission to quote five passages from his commentary on "The Apocalypse," (published in Dutch), entitled: *Verklaring van de Openbaring*;

E. P. Dutton and Co., New York, for permission to use a selection from the commentary on "The Apocalypse" by W. Boyd Carpenter, in *Ellicott's Bible Commentary*, published by Cassell and Co., Ltd., in Great Britain, and E. P. Dutton and Co., in the United States;

William B. Eerdmans Publishing Company, Grand Rapids, Michigan, for permission to make two quotations from *The Second Coming of Christ*; Henry W. Frost;

Funk and Wagnalls Company, New York, for permission to make use of selections from the following: Duesterdieck's Commentary on "Revelation," in *Meyer's Commentary on the New Testament; The Jewish Encyclopedia; A Commentary on the New Testament*, by Bernard Weiss. Translated by George H. Schodde; (Vol. IV);

Harper and Brothers, New York, for permission to quote from *The Letters to the Seven Churches*; Sir William Ramsay;

Howard Severance Company, Chicago, Ill., for permission to use an extract from Art. on "The Revelation of John," by James Orr, in *The International Bible Encyclopedia*, (Vol. IV);

Loizeaux Brothers, Bible Truth Depot, New York, for permission to use a sentence from *The Mysteries of God*; H. A. Ironside;

Lutheran Book Concern, Columbus, Ohio, for permission to use two selections from *The Interpretation of St. John's Revelation*; R. C. H. Lenski;

Macmillan Company, New York, for permission to use numerous selected passages from the following: *The Book of Enoch*; R. H. Charles; T. W. Crafer's Commentary on "The Apocalypse," in *Gore's New Commentary; The Apocalypse of St. John*; H. B. Swete;

Philip Mauro, Washington, D.C., for permission to quote freely from *Of Things Which Soon Must Come To Pass*;

Oxford University Press, London and New York, for permission to use a passage from *Biblical Doctrines*; Benj. B. Warfield;

Presbyterian Committee of Publication, Richmond, Virginia, for permission to quote the Table of Contents of *The Drama of Christianity*; S. L. Morris;

Fleming H. Revell Co., New York, for permission to use three passages from *The Book of Revelation*; B. H. Carroll;

Chas. Scribner's Sons, New York, for permission to quote from the following: *New Commentary on Genesis*; Franz Delitzsch; *Commentary on Revelation*; John T. Dean; *The Didache, or Teaching of the Twelve Apostles*; Hitchcock and Brown; *Books Which Influenced Our Lord and His Disciples*; J. H. Thompson.

The Methodist Book Concern, N. Y., for permission to quote from *The Last Message of Jesus Christ, or the Apocalypse in a New Light* by John Hamilton Timbrel.

DeWard Publishing Company would like to thank Dr. Pieters' family for their kind permission to publish this edition and Michelle Mitchell, David McClister, and John Keohane for their help in producing it.

AFTERWORD
Reflections from a Grandson

I am grateful to know that these words of Albertus Pieters are still considered valuable to read. I am glad that people more expert than I appreciate what he wrote. Having known Dr. Pieters, I think he would appreciate it too.

It is for those more expert on the Bible and theology to comment on his words, but I had a special relationship with Albertus Pieters, and savor my knowledge of the man. He was my grandfather. I didn't call him "Albertus," "Dr. Pieters," or what his Emma called him, which was "Bert." I called him "Grandpa," and I loved him very much.

Albertus and Emma had six children all of whom were born in Japan. The first five, all daughters, grew to adulthood. The youngest, Henry, died as a toddler. They had two granddaughters and four grandsons, and my guess is that I was the grandson closest to Grandpa, even though Bill is older.

My mother, Mary Pieters Keohane, was his and Emma's youngest daughter. By the time I was born, Grandpa was 71 years old, and he and Grandma lived in two-story, white, Cape Cod-house in Holland, Michigan, which had been built using an inheritance to her. They didn't have a lot of money and never owned a car or a TV, but they were so strong in things of the spirit that I, for one, never noticed.

By the time I arrived, Grandpa was probably officially retired. He certainly was "retired" a couple years later, when his book *Psalms In Human Experience* was published and copyrighted by the Board of Publication of the Reformed Church in America. Underneath the name Albertus Pieters are these words:

Minister of the Word of God and Emeritus Dosker-Hulswit Professor of English Bible and Missions in the Western Theological Seminary of the Reformed Church in America.

To say that he was really retired, would be to diminish this man. The book on the Psalms was only the first of four written when he was in his 70s. At least two more came in his 80s. If he were living today, I think he'd still be writing, and probably would have upgraded from that manual typewriter to a personal computer.

Through him I learned to love church. Oh, I went to Sunday school at home in Chicago and to church with my parents, but going to church with Grandpa and Grandma was always an event to remember. As I recall he had a special hearing aid provided, and Dr. and Mrs. Pieters were always honored special guests, with a pew saved, close to the front, for all of us. His advice was sought. I was always honored to be introduced as his grandson.

Grandpa taught me to play chess, and would not just play to win, but to instruct. "Well, if you do this, I'll be able to checkmate you this way. Perhaps you'd like to take it back." I'd be allowed to do so. When I was too young to shave, but pushed to learn, he taught me to shave. He used shaving cream, and mug and brush, and a Gillette razor, on which one changed the blades. I did this, for the longest time, after instant shaving cream came, and after disposable razors were in.

I loved meals in Holland, except for the toast. Meals were at fixed times. They always started with Grandpa saying grace, but that toast at breakfast was frustrating. Grandpa toasted without regard for market, making it all the time. For me, this brought on tough choices. The older toast seemed more deserving, but newer was better, and on top of the pile. I know, from speaking with Cousin Bill, that he found this frustrating too.

All in all, Grandpa was a wonderful man. He'd appreciate it, that this book is being republished. I do, too, and I'm so enriched from having known the author.

John Keohane
Austin, Texas

HERITAGE
OF FAITH LIBRARY

The **DeWard Publishing Company Heritage of Faith Library** is a growing collection of classic Christian reprints. DeWard has already published or has plans to publish the following authors:

- A. B. Bruce
- Atticus G. Haygood
- H. C. Leupold
- J. W. McGarvey
- William Paley
- Albertus Pieters
- B. F. Westcott

Future authors and titles added to this series will be announced on our website.

www.deward.com

DEWARD
PUBLISHING COMPANY

ALSO FROM DeWARD PUBLISHING:

Beneath the Cross: Essays and Relfections on the Lord's Supper
Jady S. Copeland and Nathan Ward (editors)

The Bible has much to say about the Lord's Supper. Almost every component of this memorial is rich with meaning—meaning supplied by Old Testament foreshadowing and New Testament teaching. The Lord's death itself is meaningful and significant in ways we rarely point out. In sixty-nine essays by forty different authors, Beneath the Cross explores the depths of symbolism and meaning to be found in the last hours of the Lord's life and offers a helpful look at the memorial feast that commemorates it. 329 pages. $14.99 (PB); $23.99 (HB).

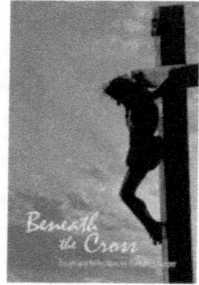

Invitation to a Spiritual Revolution
Paul Earnhart

Few preachers have studied the Sermon on the Mount as intensively or spoken on its contents so frequently and effectively as the author of this work. His excellent and very readable written analysis appeared first as a series of articles in Christianity Magazine. By popular demand it is here offered in one volume so that it can be more easily preserved, circulated, read, reread and made available to those who would not otherwise have access to it. Foreword by Sewell Hall. 173 pages. $10.99 (PB).

Boot Camp
Jason Hardin

According to best-selling author Stephen Arterburn, "This is a great book to help us men live opposite of this world's model of a man." Boot Camp: Equipping Men with Integrity for Spiritual Warfare is the first volume in the new IMAGE series of books for men by Jason Hardin. It serves as a Basic Training manual in the spiritual war for honor, integrity and a God-glorifying life. 237 pages. $13.99 (PB); $24.99 (HB).

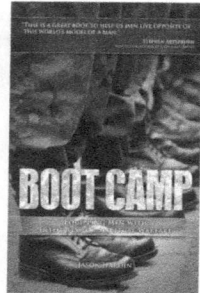

Prepared to Answer: A Guide to Christian Evidences
Rob van de Weghe

Follow the personal odyssey of a man of science as he journeys from skepticism to faith. Logic, science, and history become bridges instead of barriers, as doubt is transformed into confidence. Scrutinize the evidence that compels the verdict that Christian faith rests upon truth and fact, not legend and myth. 450 pages. $18.99 (PB).

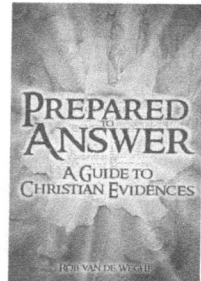

Thinking Through Jeremiah
L.A. Mott

When Jesus came, some of his contemporaries thought that he was Jeremiah reincarnated. Yet many Bible students today know less about him than about a host of other Old Testament heroes. One who turns to commentaries for help will find that many of them are filled with complex discussions of strange Hebrew words and consideration of technical, critical questions with which most of us are totally unconcerned. A serious Bible student wishing to know Jeremiah and to understand his character, his preaching and his times will be grateful for L.A. Mott's Thinking Through Jeremiah. Foreword by Sewell Hall. 214 pages. $12.99 (PB).

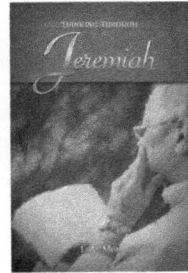

The Growth of the Seed: Notes on the Book of Genesis
Nathan Ward

A study of the book of Genesis that emphasizes two primary themes: the development of the Messianic line and the growing enmity between the righteous and the wicked. In addition, it provides detailed comments on the text and short essays on several subjects that are suggested in, yet peripheral to, Genesis. 537 pages. $19.99 (PB).

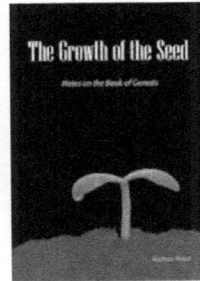

Churches of the New Testament
Ethan R. Longhenry

Have you ever wondered what it would be like to be a Christian in the first century, to meet with the church in Philippi or Ephesus? Churches of the New Testament explores the world of first century Christianity by examining what Scripture reveals about the local churches of God's people. It examines background information about the geography and history of each city, as well as whatever is known about the founding of the church there. Centuries may separate us from the churches of the New Testament, but their examples, instruction, commendation, and rebukes can teach us today. 150 pages. $9.99 (PB).

For a full listing of DeWard Publishing Company books, visit our website:

www.deward.com